Money in the Great Recession

BUCKINGHAM STUDIES IN MONEY, BANKING AND CENTRAL BANKING

Series Editor: Tim Congdon CBE, *Chairman, Institute of International Monetary Research and Professor, University of Buckingham, United Kingdom*

The Institute of International Monetary Research promotes research into how developments in banking and finance affect the wider economy. Particular attention is paid to the effect of changes in the quantity of money, on inflation and deflation, and on boom and bust. The Institute's wider aims are to enhance economic knowledge and understanding, and to seek price stability, steady economic growth and high employment. The Institute is located at the University of Buckingham and helps with the university's educational role.

Buckingham Studies in Money, Banking and Central Banking presents some of the Institute's most important work. Contributions from scholars at other universities and research bodies, and practitioners in finance and banking, are also welcome. For more on the Institute, see the website at www.mv-pt.org.

Money in the Great Recession

Did a Crash in Money Growth Cause the Global Slump?

Edited by

Tim Congdon CBE

Chairman, Institute of International Monetary Research and Professor, University of Buckingham, United Kingdom

BUCKINGHAM STUDIES IN MONEY, BANKING AND CENTRAL BANKING
IN ASSOCIATION WITH THE INSTITUTE OF ECONOMIC AFFAIRS

Edward Elgar
PUBLISHING

Cheltenham, UK • Northampton, MA, USA

Published by
Edward Elgar Publishing Limited
The Lypiatts
15 Lansdown Road
Cheltenham
Glos GL50 2JA
UK

Edward Elgar Publishing, Inc.
William Pratt House
9 Dewey Court
Northampton
Massachusetts 01060
USA

A catalogue record for this book
is available from the British Library

Library of Congress Control Number: 2016962567

This book is available electronically in the **Elgar**online
Economics subject collection
DOI 10.4337/9781784717834

ISBN 978 1 78471 782 7 (cased)
ISBN 978 1 78471 783 4 (eBook)

Typeset by Servis Filmsetting Ltd, Stockport, Cheshire
Printed and bound by CPI Group (UK) Ltd, Croydon, CR0 4YY

Contents

Contributors

Philip Booth is Professor of Finance, Public Policy and Ethics at St Mary's University, Twickenham, United Kingdom. From 2002 to 2016 he was Academic and Research Director (previously, Editorial and Programme Director) at the Institute of Economic Affairs. Previously he was Professor of Insurance and Risk Management at Cass Business School, City University, and also worked for the Bank of England as an adviser on financial stability. He is both an economist and a qualified actuary.

Juan E. Castañeda is the Director of the Institute of International Monetary Research at the University of Buckingham, United Kingdom. He was awarded his PhD by the University Autónoma of Madrid, Spain in 2003 and has been a lecturer in Economics at the University of Buckingham since 2012. Dr Castañeda has worked with and prepared reports for the European Parliament's Committee of Economic and Monetary Affairs.

Tim Congdon is the Chairman of the Institute of International Monetary Research, which he founded in 2014. He was a member of the Treasury Panel of Independent Forecasters (the so-called "wise men") between 1992 and 1997, which advised the Chancellor of the Exchequer on economic policy. Although most of his career has been spent as an economist in the City of London, he has been a visiting professor at the Cardiff Business School and the City University Business School (now the Cass Business School), and he is currently a Professor of Economics at the University of Buckingham. Professor Congdon is often regarded as the UK's leading representative of "monetarist" economic thinking.

Charles Goodhart is one of the world's leading authorities on the theory and practice of central banking. He served as a member of the Bank of England's Monetary Policy Committee from June 1997 to May 2000. He was Norman Sosnow Professor of Banking and Finance at the London School of Economics, United Kingdom from 1985 to 2002, and is now Emeritus Professor.

Steve Hanke is a Professor of Applied Economics at the Johns Hopkins University in Baltimore, Maryland, USA. Well known for his work as a currency reformer in emerging economies and one of the world's authorities on currency boards and dollarization, he is the Director of the Troubled Currencies Project at the Cato Institute in Washington, DC. He was a senior economist with President Reagan's Council of Economic Advisers from 1981 to 1982, and has served as an adviser to heads of state in countries throughout Asia, South America, Europe and the Middle East.

David Laidler is one of the world's leading figures in the monetarist tradition of analysing the role of money in determining inflation and short-run economic fluctuations. The theme of David Laidler's research is summed up by the title of his 1988 presidential address to the Canadian Economic Association, "Taking money seriously". He was a research assistant for Milton Friedman and Anna Schwartz's *Monetary History of the United States, 1867–1960*. He joined the economics faculty at the University of Western Ontario, Canada in 1975 and was Bank of Montreal Professor there from 2000 to 2005. He is now Professor Emeritus.

Adam Ridley is a British economist, civil servant and banker. He was a Special Adviser to the Chancellors of the Exchequer between 1979 and 1984, and later a Director of Hambros Bank and Morgan Stanley, Europe. In the 1990s he played a critical role in devising a settlement for the litigation then afflicting the Lloyd's of London insurance market. The settlement was followed by Lloyd's recovery and renewal. He was Director-General of the London Investment Banking Association from 2000 to 2005.

Robert Skidelsky is Emeritus Professor of Political Economy at Warwick University, United Kingdom. His three-volume biography of John Maynard Keynes (1983, 1992, 2000) won five prizes and his book on the financial crisis – *Keynes: The Return of the Master* – was published in September 2010. He was made a member of the House of Lords in 1991 (he sits on the cross-benches) and elected a fellow of the British Academy in 1994. *How Much is Enough? The Love of Money and the Case for the Good Life*, co-written with his son Edward, was published in July 2012. His most recent publications were as author of *Britain in the 20th Century: A Success?* (2014) and as editor of *The Essential Keynes* (2015).

Ryland Thomas is a Senior Economist at the Bank of England, where he has worked since 1994. He is attached to the Monetary Assessment and Strategy Division, where his work has focused on the role of money and credit in the economy. Currently he looks after the Bank of England's historical macroeconomic database and data on the Bank of England's historical balance sheet.

Foreword

Have we learned all the lessons of the recent recession, which hit so many countries at different times after the banking crisis began in 2007? And were all the policy reactions to it correct? Even in 2017 it would be a bold man who answered those questions with a confident "yes". This volume of essays focuses largely on the role of monetary policy. That is hardly surprising since it has been brought together by Tim Congdon, one of the leading monetary economists in the UK. When I was Chancellor, and in 1992 set up a panel of economists to advise me, of course Tim was one of the automatic choices precisely because of his longstanding expertise in monetary economics. The book has many other distinguished contributors and the fact that they do not agree on all points adds to the importance of the collection.

One of the key questions discussed is how far the collapse of money in the period leading up to and during the recession was similar to what happened in the USA in the Great Depression from 1929. Further, was it, as Friedman believed of the earlier episode, a failure of official policy, particularly by the Federal Reserve? Tim Congdon argues that parallels do exist between the two episodes. In the recent recession, too, while bankers and financial institutions were far from blameless in their greed and recklessness, nevertheless equal blame belongs to policy-makers, particularly central banks. Tim argues that the global recession of 2008–09 was caused by the collapse in the rate of growth of the quantity of money; he analyses the data in the three jurisdictions of the USA, the Eurozone and the UK to make his point.

Another section of the book touches on different definitions of money, a controversy I remember well from the debates about government policy in the early 1980s. Several of the contributions also concentrate on what Adam Ridley calls "the New Regulatory Wisdom", the calls for ever more bank capital and increases in regulatory capital asset ratios to make the banks "safe". It does seem extraordinary that policy-makers seemed so insouciant about the apparent contradiction in pursuing policies that must inevitably shrink banks' balance sheets, while at the same time calling on and expecting the banks to lend more. It seems clear that regulators' policies of this kind were instrumental in collapsing the growth of money and exacerbating the recession at a crucial point. The impact on output was severe. Inevitably the names of Milton Friedman and Maynard Keynes are much invoked in these arguments, particularly in speculation about how Keynes might have interpreted the 2008–09 recession. This is a theme on which I have read Tim Congdon before. He has frequently emphasized the importance that money had in Keynes's work, where he made clear that Keynes was a strong supporter of stimulatory monetary policy in recession conditions. Keynes advocated central bank purchases of assets to draw down interest rates in a manner very similar to today's QE. In that respect Friedman was closer to Keynes than some so-called modern Keynesians.

Not everyone will agree with the views expressed in this volume. Nor, as Tim says, will the book settle every problem in quantity theory analysis. However, in its rigour and questioning it is an invaluable contribution to our attempts to understand what has happened.

Norman Lamont
The Right Honourable Lord Lamont of Lerwick

Introduction: the quantity theory of money – why another restatement is needed, and why it matters to the debates on the Great Recession

Tim Congdon

Were bankers the only culprits for the Great Recession of late 2008 and 2009? Were governments and politicians responsible to some extent? And did central banks and regulators make mistakes? Was the Great Recession, which had many echoes back to the Great Depression of 1929–33, attributable to the faults of free-market capitalism or blunders in public policy? Indeed, do economies with a privately owned, profit-motivated financial system have a systemic weakness? Do they suffer – intrinsically and inevitably – from extreme and unnecessary cyclical instability in demand, output and employment? Or were both the Great Depression and the Great Recession due to faulty public policies and misguided action by the state?

These questions are some of the most contentious in contemporary economic debate. The purpose of the collection of essays in the current volume is to throw light on them both by identifying and analysing possible causes of the relatively recent Great Recession, and by comparing the intellectual response to the Great Recession with that to the Great Depression roughly 80 years earlier. The exercise is inherently problematic. A range of causal influences might be probed, at different levels of remoteness from the key events. For example, a valid and interesting approach would be to survey the macroeconomic ideas held by the principal decision-takers, and the development of their beliefs from the start of their careers. Such books as Ben Bernanke's *The Courage to Act*, Mervyn King's *The End of Alchemy* and Hank Paulson's *On the Brink* do indeed give insights into the aetiology of the Great Recession.[1] But they have not settled the issue of why so much, so quickly, went wrong in the main Western economies in late 2008.

Inescapably, any approach has to be selective to some degree. The focus here is on what is termed "the monetary interpretation of the Great Recession". In this interpretation movements in demand (and hence in output and employment) are seen as reflecting prior or coincident movements in the quantity of money. The quantity of money is understood to play a major causal role in cyclical instability. The monetary interpretation of the Great Recession pivots on the proposition that the collapses in economic activity seen in the worst quarters of 2008 and 2009 were due to falls in – or at any rate sharp declines in the growth rate of – the quantity of money. Moreover, as the Great Recession was international in scope, this claim needs to be credible in several countries. When the evidence is assembled, all of the badly affected countries ought to have reported marked weakness in money growth at some stage in the Great Recession.

I

Discussion of the Great Recession needs to be set in the context of previous thinking about macroeconomic instability and, in particular, thinking about the Great Depression. For most of the 1930s and 1940s the Great Depression was regarded as a failure of free-market capitalism, and so as justifying some sort of government intervention to boost output and to create jobs. The performance of the American economy, where real national output fell by a quarter from autumn 1929 to the start of 1933, was contrasted unfavourably with the apparent triumph of Stalin's first five-year plan (1928–32) in the communist Soviet Union. According to no doubt exaggerated official Russian statistics, the plan more than tripled the output of heavy industry.

Many thoughtful and well-intentioned people, around the world, concluded that in future economic progress would be promoted by centralized planning. Moreover, a plausible view was that centralized planning would be easier to implement in a society with extensive public ownership of property. The Soviet Union's victory in the Second World War further boosted the prestige of socialist doctrine, and heartened European and American critics of the free-market system. Even in the 1950s and early 1960s belief in the efficiency and success of the Soviet economy was widely held in Western countries, notably among many top academics and civil servants.[2] So widespread was the admiration for the communist economic model that a 1961 book questioning Soviet propaganda was given the sarcastic title *Are the Russians Ten Feet Tall?*[3] While Western economies achieved far better macroeconomic stability in the first two decades after the Second World War than in the 1930s, the improvement was not attributed to their underlying characteristics and certainly not to capitalist patterns of property ownership. Instead the accolade was usually given to the so-called "Keynesian revolution". This revolution, inspired by John Maynard Keynes's 1936 classic work *The General Theory of Money, Interest and Employment*, was often understood – or even defined – as the expansion of the state's control over the economy.

An important corrective came in 1963 with the publication of *A Monetary History of the United States 1867–1960* by Milton Friedman and Anna Schwartz. Its authors knew that the Great Depression was viewed as a black mark against capitalism, and particularly against the Wall Street financial institutions that were alleged to have ramped up share prices to unsustainable levels in 1929. The heart of the Friedman and Schwartz counter-argument relied on the quantity theory of money, which asserted that a long-run relationship held between changes in the quantity of money and nominal national income. To test the hypothesis they put together monetary data for the USA over many past decades. They identified a big drop in the quantity of money, of almost 40 per cent between October 1929 and April 1933, as a distinctive feature of the period.[4] They further proposed that monetary policy was the main causal driver behind the crash in the money supply, and hence the slump in demand and output. Controversially, they denounced the American central bank, the Federal Reserve, for the plunge in the quantity of money.

The larger message was that free enterprise did not produce the Great Depression. On the contrary, blame should fall on the incompetence of a state-sponsored institution. To quote, "A governmentally established agency – the Federal Reserve System – had been assigned responsibility for monetary policy. In 1930 and 1931 it exercised this responsibility so ineptly as to convert what would otherwise have been a moderate contraction into a major catastrophe."[5] The analysis carried a powerful implication. As long as those in charge of monetary policy were able to maintain stable growth of money from year to year, a capitalist economy would grow smoothly. Cyclical wobbles might persist, but they would be minor and manageable. According to Friedman and Schwartz, free-market capitalism was a benign and efficient method of organizing an economy, and it did not suffer – because of its inherent characteristics – from serious instability.

Their thesis has been much challenged. In his 1973 book on *The World in Depression 1929–39*, Charles Kindleberger, often regarded as the doyen of American mid-twentieth-century economic historians, set the American slump in an international context and preferred a multi-causal explanation of events. There can be little doubt that a majority of academic economists distrusted the mono-causality of the Friedman and Schwartz view. Robert Solow, a colleague of Kindleberger's at the Massachusetts Institute of Technology, mocked that, "Everything reminds Milton of the money supply. Well, everything reminds me of sex, but I keep it out of my papers".[6] Even so the significance of the argument in *A Monetary History of the United States* was quickly and widely recognized.

In the 1940s and 1950s the USA's political debate seemed to be moving ever further away from the individualism and aversion to state action that had characterized its first 150 years as an independent nation. But from the 1960s a conservative reaction gathered momentum. According to George Nash in his 1976 *The Conservative Intellectual Movement in America since 1945*, the thesis of *A Monetary History* represented a "liberating revisionism" that "rapidly became part of the conservative scholarly arsenal".[7] *A Monetary History* was highly empirical, but Friedman expanded the discussion with both theoretical contributions to professional journals and readable newspaper articles. Such was his effectiveness in espousing his views that he is often said to have pioneered "the monetarist counter-revolution" against "the Keynesian revolution".[8] As David Laidler remarks at the end of Chapter 10 below, "Most economists continue to accord deep respect to the *Monetary History*." If today its main issues are very much back on the agenda, that testifies to "the enduring importance of this great book".[9]

For over 25 years Friedman was the leading figure in the University of Chicago's economic faculty. From some date in the 1940s the term "Chicago School" began to circulate. It referred to both the enthusiasm for the free market expressed by Friedman and his colleagues, and to the importance that Chicago economists placed on good monetary management to the success of capitalist economies. Friedman's influence extended far beyond Chicago. As a student at the MIT in the 1970s, Bernanke read *A Monetary History* and found it "fascinating". In his words, "After reading Friedman and Schwartz, I knew what I wanted to do. Throughout my academic career, I would focus on macroeconomic and monetary issues."[10]

The Friedman and Schwartz position may not be universally accepted, but even its antagonists concede that it has analytical force and integrity. What, then, is to be said about the Great Recession? If an almost 40 per cent drop in the quantity of money can be condemned as the villain of the piece in the Great Depression, what is to be said about the behaviour of the quantity of money in the Great Recession? One problem for Friedman and Schwartz was that the indispensable money numbers required rearrangement as well as interpretation when they started their research.[11] Since official economic statistics were rudimentary in the late nineteenth and early twentieth centuries, they had to compile monetary data using a range of disparate sources. Nowadays all central banks publish comprehensive money supply numbers after only a short lag. Indeed, the USA has weekly

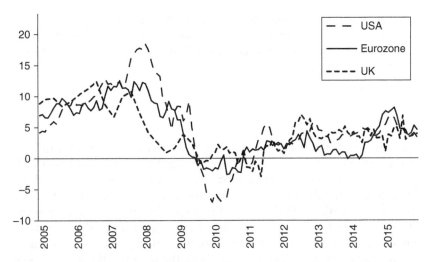

Figure I.1   Growth rates of money in the USA, the Eurozone and the UK, 2005–15 (% annualized growth rate of the quantity of money in the last six months)

figures for the money supply which are available in a matter of days from the date to which they relate.

What happened to the quantity of money, in the USA and elsewhere, in the critical period from 2007 to 2010? Did the change in the quantity of money slow markedly in these years? If so, what does that imply for causality? Can it be proposed, along the lines of the Friedman and Schwartz thesis about the Great Depression, that the Great Recession was the result of a collapse in money growth? Was the Great Recession then due to crass decisions by officialdom, and not to the follies and inadequacies of the capitalist financial system? Figure I.1 shows the behaviour, in terms of the annual rates of change over six-month periods, of (one measure of) the quantity of money in three major advanced monetary jurisdictions, the USA, the Eurozone and the United Kingdom, in the decade from 2005.[12] (The identity of this measure will soon be disclosed.) Along with Japan, the nations in this group have accounted for over 60 per cent of world output for most of the last 50 years and their impact on global demand growth remains profound. It is immediately clear that a decline in rate of change in the quantity of money must have had a role in the Great Recession, just as it did in the Great Depression. Between late 2008 and 2010 – the period in which the Great Recession hit – money growth fell sharply in all three of the jurisdictions. The fall was particularly severe in the USA, where the change was from almost plus 20 per cent at the peak to minus 7 per cent at the trough. Although more research and analysis are needed before strong statements about causality can be ventured, the graph does establish the case for conducting that research and analysis, and so provides the rationale for the current volume.

II

Because Friedman was crucial to the monetarist counter-revolution, it makes sense to review his ideas and beliefs in this area of economics. He never claimed that his thinking was particularly original, acknowledging intellectual indebtedness to forerunners at the University of Chicago and Irving Fisher (1867–1947), the first champion of the quantity theory of money. In fact, when asked to define his position Friedman preferred the phrase "the quantity theory of money" to the new-fangled word "monetarism". Unfortunately, both the quantity theory of money and monetarism are elusive schools of thought. Supposedly authoritative statements are beset by looseness of definition and conceptual inconsistency.[13] This lack of clarity was part of the motivation for one of Friedman's most celebrated papers, 'The quantity theory of money: a restatement', which appeared in 1956 and is generally regarded as the theoretical launching-pad for the monetary counter-revolution. It highlighted how the demand to hold money balances needed to be set within a rigorous microeconomic framework, as one asset in portfolios with many non-monetary assets. In Friedman's words, "the theory of the demand for money is a special topic in the theory of capital".[14] The technical sophistication of the 1956 paper buttressed the quantity theory's core empirical tenet, that the quantity of money and national income move at similar rates over the long run.

But the critics were not satisfied. Paul Samuelson, a leading Keynesian economist and an articulate opponent of Friedman's analyses, judged that *A Monetary History* had too much history and narrative, and was light on theory. In a 1969 comment on US stabilization policies, he decried "garden-variety monetarism" as "a black-box theory", with "mechanistic regularities" that were unreliable because they could not be "spelled out by a plausible economic theory".[15] He sneered at the monetarists, making the charge that they had not elucidated in detail the channels by which money balances affected wealth and expenditure. The black-box allegation has stuck, with the phrase appearing in the title of a widely quoted 1995 paper, 'Inside the black box: the credit channel of monetary policy transmission', by Bernanke and Mark Gertler.[16] The 1995 paper helped to establish Bernanke's academic reputation and so to put him on the path to becoming chairman of the Federal Reserve in February 2006, a mere two years before the start of the Great Recession.

Friedman and other monetarists rejected the black-box allegation. Even a casual glance at his publications shows that Friedman repeatedly applied price-theoretic tools to monetary analysis. He shared Keynes's belief, stated in *The General Theory*, that national income and wealth were determined only when the demand to hold money balances was equal to the quantity of money created by the banking system.[17] In the same year that their highly readable *Monetary History* was published, Friedman and Schwartz placed a more technical paper on 'Money and business cycles' in *The Review of Economics and Statistics.*[18] Here they went to considerable lengths to specify and explain the process of connection between money and macroeconomic outcomes, although they did not use Samuelson's word "channel". Their "tentative sketch of the mechanism transmitting monetary changes" detailed numerous links from a change in the rate of monetary growth to interest rates and asset prices, and thence to the demand for capital goods, including houses and consumer durables, and on to macroeconomic activity as a whole, including ultimately to wages and prices.[19]

However, in two important respects Friedman's critics drew blood, and the wounds were deep and lasting, and still have not properly healed. First, as several definitions of the "quantity of money" have been proposed, the concept is bedevilled by ambiguity. Money is usually understood to consist of assets that are valid for use in transactions and constant in nominal-value terms when they are so used.[20] One definition (of so-called "broad money", denoted by M2, M3 or M4, depending on the nation under consideration) encompasses every asset that might conceivably be money. Typically broad money is equal to notes and coin in circulation with the public, and all of banks' deposit liabilities to genuine non-bank private sector agents.[21] By contrast, "narrow money" (M1) includes notes and coin in circulation with the public and only bank deposits that are available for spending without notice. (Such deposits are called "demand deposits" or "sight deposits" in American parlance and "current accounts" in British.)

A tricky question arises, "to which concept of money – narrow or broad – do the key monetarist propositions relate?". The question is much deeper and more troublesome than it seems. In 2008, as the Great Recession was unfolding, M1 in the USA was about $1400 billion, which was under 10 per cent of nominal gross domestic product, whereas M3 was heading towards $14000 billion and was roughly the same size as GDP.[22] There are monetarist economists who ground their macroeconomic analyses in M1, and downplay or ignore broad money. These are exemplified by Allan Meltzer in his history of the Federal Reserve, which defined the stock of money as "currency and demand deposits".[23] But the channels of interaction between money and the economy must be radically different for M1 and M3. It is difficult to believe that changes in M1 could impact on portfolio decisions and expenditure commitments in the same way, or to the same extent, as changes in M3.

Friedman made numerous comments on the "which aggregate?" debate in his career, but they varied over the decades. The argument in *A Monetary History* about the causes of the Great Recession relied on the behaviour of broad money. This feature of the book was noted by, for example, Robert Lucas, the leader of the so-called New Classical School and a Nobel laureate who developed elements of monetarist thinking in his own work.[24] On the whole Friedman's preference was indeed for broad money and, more specifically, for the M2 aggregate where the Federal Reserve's own series starts in 1959.[25] But in the early 1980s he shifted towards the narrow money measure, M1, the growth of which was targeted for a few years by the Federal Reserve in the big anti-inflation drive during Paul Volcker's chairmanship. The shift to M1 proved to be a serious error. It caused Friedman to predict an upturn in inflation in the mid-1980s, which simply did not happen. The forecasting mistake undermined his credibility in both academic and policy-making circles.[26] Later he renewed his allegiance to broad money, particularly to M2.

Friedman was far from being alone in failing to stick loyally to one money measure. The chopping and changing alienated many observers who might otherwise have been interested in quantity-theory ideas. At about the same time as Friedman's flirtation with M1, in the UK the Labour politician, Peter Shore, scorned the money supply as "a wayward mistress" for policy-makers. The "which aggregate?" debate continues to reverberate, as the Great Recession was accompanied by sharp divergences in the growth rates of different money aggregates in the leading nations. But – as will emerge in this volume – the experience of the Great Recession has gone far to confirm the correctness of the emphasis on broad money in *A Monetary History*. (To end the suspense, the money measure in the graph in Figure I.1 was broadly defined.)

III

The squabbles about the aggregates were bad for monetarism's public image. But the second conceptual wound inflicted by the anti-monetarists was perhaps even more fundamental. Most macroeconomists – including undoubted Keynesians such as Paul Samuelson – accepted that the equality of the demand to hold money with the actual quantity of money in the economy is a condition of macroeconomic equilibrium. In other words, they agreed with Friedman that large changes in national income are likely to be associated with large changes in the quantity of money.[27] However, that raised the question of how the quantity of money is determined. Since most of broad money consists of bank deposits, their creation must in some sense be the work of the banking system. But how exactly does money come into being? By what process or processes do banks introduce new money into the economy?

In one of his theoretical papers Friedman ducked the issue by appealing to "helicopter money", conjuring up a vision of bank notes falling from the sky.[28] This was obviously an imaginative conceit intended only to aid exposition. Even so, it caused widespread amusement and even derision.[29] Friedman may have wanted to recall the era when gold or silver were the principal monetary assets, and the quantity of money increased adventitiously – as if out of the sky – when new mines were discovered. Nowadays money has ceased to be a commodity like a precious metal. Instead all money is a liability of banks, whether it takes the form of legal-tender notes issued by the central bank or of deposits issued by commercial banks. In one sense the creation of new money in this sort of world, the world of so-called "fiat money", is straightforward. Because the central bank's notes are legal tender and must be taken in payment, they can be increased by the simultaneous addition of identical sums to both sides of its balance sheet. Shockingly (or so it seems), new money comes out of "thin air". As Galbraith remarked in his 1975 *Money: Whence it Came, Where it Went*, "The process by which money is created is so simple that the mind is repelled."[30]

At first glance commercial banks are in a similar position. People believe that payments can be made from bank deposits, as long experience has established that this is the case. It seems to follow that deposits can be increased by the simultaneous addition of identical sums to both sides of a bank's balance sheet. The expansion of its balance sheet occurs if a bank sees a profitable opportunity to buy a security (when it credits a sum to the account of the person who sells the security and the security becomes part of its assets) or to make a new loan (when it credits a sum to the borrower's deposit, which is its liability, and registers the same sum on the assets side of the balance sheet as a loan). It is certainly the case that in modern circumstances much money creation does take place in this way, so that deposits have been described as "fountain-pen money", "cheque-book money" or "keyboard money" to reflect the ever-evolving technology of writing.[31]

But there is a catch. Commercial banks do not have the power to issue legal-tender cash. Since they must at all times be able to convert customers' deposits back into central bank notes, they must keep a cash reserve (partly in their vaults and tills, and partly in a deposit at the central bank) to meet deposit withdrawals. If an individual bank expands its balance sheet too quickly relative to other banks, it may find its deposits have become so large that cash withdrawals exceed cash inflows. Potentially it could run out of cash. The expansion of deposits by commercial banks is therefore constrained by the imperative to maintain a positive cash reserve. Indeed, over multi-decadal periods in many nations commercial banks have kept a relatively stable ratio of cash to their deposit liabilities.

The discussion in the last few paragraphs has suggested two approaches to conceptualizing the creation of money in a fiat-money economy. The creation of money can be seen, first, as the result of the extension of credit by the banking system, where it is consolidated and embraces both the central bank and the commercial banks. The "credit counterparts" on the assets side of the consolidated banking system's balance sheet must equal the liabilities on the other, and can be categorized in several ways. For example, assets could be viewed as the sum of loans, securities and cash. However, to split them into claims on the domestic private and public sectors, and the overseas sector, is more interesting, as private borrowers and the government have different motives when they seek bank finance. It is of course the deposit liabilities which are monetary in nature and so are of most significance to the subject in hand. Non-monetary liabilities include banks' equity capital plus their bond issues plus an assortment of odds and ends, such as deferred tax. Clearly, an identity can be stated:

> Change in the quantity of money (i.e., in bank deposits, and notes and coin in circulation) = Change in banking system assets − Change in its non-monetary liabilities;

and in more detail

> Change in the quantity of money = Change in banks' net claims on the public sector + Change in net claims on the private sector + Change in banks' net claims on the overseas sector − Change in their non-monetary liabilities.

Central banks and the International Monetary Fund have large data-bases on the credit counterparts to money growth, and the information is regarded as basic to monetary analysis.[32]

The other approach to money creation takes its cue from banks' need to maintain cash reserves to honour obligations to customers (that is, obligations to repay deposits and to fulfil payment instructions). As has been noted, in some historical periods banks have maintained stable ratios of cash to deposit liabilities. In their transactions members of the non-bank public can use either cash or bank deposits, depending on their relative convenience and cost. If transactions technology is fairly stable, the ratio of the non-bank public's cash to its deposits ought also to change little over time. It follows that deposits held by the non-bank public can be viewed as a multiple of their cash holdings. Indeed, the quantity of money as a whole can be understood as a multiple of the total amount of cash issued by the central bank.[33] The total amount of cash issued by the central bank is sometimes known as the monetary base or "high-powered money". The quantity of money is then equal to the "money multiplier" (or "base multiplier") times the monetary base.

The credit counterparts arithmetic and the base multiplier approach add value to thinking about the monetary situation, and no one can dispute that both are legitimate as accounting frameworks. However, some researchers have gone further and argued that the base multiplier has causal significance. They believe that, because of the assumedly well-attested stability of both non-banks' and banks' ratios of cash to deposits, an increase in the monetary base will lead to a proportionally similar increase in the quantity of money. The phrase "high-powered money" reflects this purported ability of a change in base money to engineer an expansion of the quantity of money that is a multiple of itself. Indeed, in the late 1950s and 1960s many influential economists were so impressed by the reliability of the past relationship between the base and the quantity of money that they advocated an arrangement known as "monetary base control". Since the monetary base is comprised almost entirely of its liabilities, the central bank was thought to be able to determine the amount of base in the economy. Further, with the ratios of cash to deposits taken to be more or less constant, deliberate management of the base ought – in their view – to enable the state to control the quantity of money.

Throughout his career Friedman believed in this approach to monetary control.[34] A fair generalization is that Friedman did not persuade the majority of his profession that monetary base control was worthwhile or even practicable.[35] Many opponents of the idea have pointed out that banks want to minimize their cash holdings, because cash is an unremunerative asset. Banks' practice is therefore to arrange credit lines with the central bank, so that they can borrow cash when withdrawals by customers are unduly and erratically large. In consequence, banks do not vary the size of their balance sheets in response to changes in the monetary base. Instead the size of the monetary base varies in response to changes in banks' borrowing needs. (The policy issues that arise when banks suffer severe cash runs, and have to borrow from the central bank as "lender of last resort", are not discussed in any detail now. However, when last-resort loans are extended, the central bank is concerned less with the size of the monetary base than with ensuring the convertibility of deposits into cash. An argument can be made that monetary base control is incompatible with the central bank's function of helping banks with their cash management, particularly when it has to act as lender of last resort in emergencies.)[36]

Moreover, experience showed that in periods of financial stress the two key ratios – that is, of non-banks' and banks' cash to bank deposits – were not stable. Notably, the Great Depression was one such period, with Friedman and Schwartz's *Monetary History* quantifying some of the anomalous numbers. The trauma of thousands of banks being forced to close in 1932 and 1933, in the worst phase of the downturn, caused the remaining banks to conduct their affairs with extreme caution. In particular, they operated with much higher ratios of cash reserves to deposit liabilities than in the 1920s. People and companies were also so chastened by losses on their bank deposits that sometimes they decided to hold more of their wealth in legal-tender notes and less in bank deposits. The statistical appendices at the back of *A Monetary History* reported that broad money fell by nearly 40 per cent between October 1929 and April 1933, but in the same period the monetary base increased by 10 per cent.[37] At first glance the monetary base was weak-powered as an instrument of monetary policy in this particular episode. Even admirers of Friedman and Schwartz's scholarship objected to their account of money supply determination on the grounds that it was too schematic.[38] (For a counter-argument, see pp. 237–42 in David Laidler's Chapter 10. Like old soldiers, some economic controversies never die.)

IV

Although it had its points of vulnerability, the Friedman and Schwartz interpretation of the Great Depression was cogent and persuasive overall. It was so influential that it ought already to have stimulated an attempt to interpret the Great Recession in similar terms. Perhaps surprisingly, at the time of writing (September 2016), hardly any such attempt has appeared in the academic literature or indeed anywhere else. The oversight is the more remarkable, in that an initial review of the evidence – such as that in the graph above – gives support to a money-based view. But the omission of money from contemporary macroeconomic discourse has become extreme. As I point out in my first contribution to this volume, a review article in the 2012 *Journal of Economic Literature* of 21 books on the Great Recession contained not a single reference to any money aggregate.[39]

While the discussion in this Introduction has applauded the work done by Friedman and Schwartz over 50 years ago, it has also called attention to potential flaws in it that are still problematic. These flaws weakened the case for a monetary interpretation of the Great Depression. But also, and perhaps more fundamentally, they harmed the reception of Friedman's monetary economics, and "monetarism" at large. The fault-lines in monetarist thinking have persisted in the decades since the publication of *A Monetary History*. In summary, monetarist economists could not (and cannot) agree on the money aggregate that was (and is) most relevant to their key propositions and of greatest potency in the determination of macroeconomic outcomes, and they could not (and cannot) formulate an account of the determination of the favoured money measure which convinced (and convinces) non-monetarists.

While the contributions to this volume may not settle every problem in quantity-theory analyses, they would not have been written if all were well with policy-making before and during the Great Recession. Let it be accepted that the collapse in money growth between 2007 and 2010 indicated a policy failure of some sort. Two questions arise. Why did money growth fall so precipitously? And what were policy-makers' attitudes towards the fall in money growth, if indeed they had any organized thinking on the subject at all? Of course, the answer to the second question is crucial to understanding the attitudes and beliefs – indeed, the economic theories – that motivated policy decisions.

Readers must look at the individual chapters, as the authors here have their own views. Even so a reasonable generalization is that most contributors believe that analysis of the credit counterparts, not the monetary base, is the best way to explain the fall in money growth. (In his Chapter 10 Laidler is an exception. See p. 233 and pp. 237–41 below). In my two chapters (Chapters 1 and 2), and also in Thomas's (Chapter 3) and Hanke's (Chapter 7), the behaviour of bank lending to the private sector is seen as vital in explaining the money slowdown. Hanke, Ridley (Chapter 5) and I proceed to attack the abrupt tightening of bank regulation – particularly the demands for extra bank capital and the raising of capital/asset ratios from October 2008 – as badly mistimed and inappropriate, and as the principal influence on the crash in lending. This line is disputed by Goodhart (Chapter 6) and Thomas. They accept that the virtual cessation of new bank lending to the private sector was responsible, in an accounting sense, for the money slowdown. But they believe that in late 2008 the banking system was in danger of implosion because of the perceived insufficiency of capital in the banking system and the undoubted illiquidity of a high proportion of banks' assets. On that basis, extra bank capital was needed.

The motivation for the official emphasis on bank capital in late 2008, and the persistence of this emphasis in the following years, become all-important in analysis of the Great Recession. In Chapter 2 I suggest that the G20 meetings at that time, which determined much of the policy response, were "piloted" by Ben Bernanke and Mervyn King. No doubt many other individuals were involved, but it seems that these were the two principal players. (High-level international meetings are conducted in English, and the American and British representatives set the tone. They do so, even though the UK is not now a particularly important country in terms of economic weight.) Bernanke and King are directly criticized in this volume by Hanke and myself, although not by other contributors. It is very much my view that – if the theme of policy action in autumn 2008 had been to boost the quantity of money and not to impose capital demands on the banks – the Great Recession would not have happened.[40] (Why were European voices not more vociferous in protesting against the assault on the banks? In Chapter 4 on the evolution of the European Central Bank's organization of monetary policy from 1999, Juan Castañeda and I show that the ECB's interest in a monetary "pillar" of analysis had been downgraded from 2003 onwards.)

The radical shift in UK policy in early 2009, towards deliberate measures to boost the quantity of money in so-called "quantitative easing", and subsequent changes in the same direction in other countries, prevented further slides in demand, output and employment. (As Skidelsky remarks in Chapter 9, Keynes was an advocate of what he termed "monetary policy *à outrance*" to combat slump conditions. An interesting question is, "do QE and monetary policy *à outrance* come to much the same thing?" See note 7 on pp. 71–2 for one reply.) But the tardiness and equivocation in the move towards a quantity-of-money answer reflected muddles in academic and official thinking. As I have discussed elsewhere, leading figures in central banks, finance ministries and regulatory agencies were bemused by inconsistent and sometimes incoherent advice from economists who lacked a serviceable, well-integrated theory of the determination of national income and wealth. Any observer could see that banks and bankers were in the thick of the traumatic events in late 2008 that foreshadowed the Great Recession. But three of the four main bodies of fashionable theoretical reasoning – Old Keynesianism (income-expenditure modelling, plus an enthusiasm for fiscal policy), New Keynesianism (focused on a mere three equations, and the determination of inflation in product and labour markets with no reference to the quantity of money) and the New Classical School (concerned with expectations formation, while dismissing the banking industry as irrelevant to the business cycle) – had no room for banking and money at all.[41] (Booth's analysis of asset price formation in Chapter 8 reviews New Keynesianism and the New Classical School, and compares them with quantity-theory thinking.)

The fourth fashionable body of theory – "creditism", pioneered by Bernanke in academic articles – did pay attention to the banking industry, but in my view it looked at the wrong side of the balance sheet. According to the creditists, aggregate spending depends on bank lending *by itself*.[42] In the hurly-burly of the crisis period Bernanke, King and many others hurried to a superficially plausible conclusion. This was that another Great Recession/Depression could be stopped if banks had so much spare capital that they could continue lending even after suffering big losses. Here was an important element in the rationale for the late 2008 upheaval in bank regulation and the exaltation of high bank capital/asset ratios in subsequent official policy. Was that the best approach? Surely it needs to be reviewed and questioned. As banking is a risky business, it needs stable regulation. Large, arbitrary and unforeseen changes in capital/asset ratios can do – and in this case have done – immense damage. The equilibrium levels of national income and wealth are to be viewed as functions of the quantity of money, on the broad definitions, not of bank lending *by itself*.[43] Further, the creation of money by the state is a straightforward matter. Crucially, no extra bank capital at all is needed, as in normal jurisdictions claims on the state are free from default risk.

Sir Charles Bean, chief economist at the Bank of England from 2000 to 2008, once remarked that the Great Recession had so many guilty parties that it was like Agatha Christie's *Murder on the Orient Express*.[44] This is fair enough, in that many people – including the senior executives of international banking groups – did silly things in the run-up to the crisis. For example, the board of Lehman Brothers took on unhedged equity risk (with heavy investment in real estate) in a business with banking-style leverage.[45] But – as I note in Chapter 1 – the blunders of one management and the insolvency of one business (even quite a big business) should not cause an economy-wide slump in activity. Economic policy in liberal capitalist economies needs to be structured so that extensive insolvencies in a particular area of the economy, including the banking industry, can occur without causing a general downturn. The key prescription here – as Milton Friedman and many others have explained since the start of modern industrialism in the late eighteenth century – is to maintain stability in the rate of growth of the quantity of money. Ignorance about the quantity theory of money was widespread in the years leading up the Great Recession, despite Friedman's restatement over 50 years earlier.[46] This volume is intended to restore interest in quantity-theory principles and analysis, so that such disasters as the 1929–33 Great Depression in the USA and the 2008–09 global Great Recession are not repeated. Perhaps it is time for another restatement of the quantity theory of money.

* * *

The chapters in this volume reflect writings at different dates for different purposes, although they share common themes. They were not prepared for an academic conference and the book is not a collection of conference papers. Nevertheless, the themes of the following chapters were discussed at a meeting organized by the Institute of Economic Affairs and International Monetary Research Ltd in November 2013, and held at the IEA's office in London. I organized the meeting, with help from the IEA's staff, in particular Philip Booth, Christiana Hambro and Diego Zuluaga, to whom I wish to express many thanks. The chapters were not all complete when the meeting was held, and I have felt free to publish material finished many months after November 2013, and to revise contents with new facts, statistics and publications. The text of this volume was submitted to the publisher in September 2016.

I am grateful to the other participants in the IEA/International Monetary Research Ltd meeting and, above all, to those who wrote the essays that form chapters in the current volume. Each chapter stands on its own. It was no one's intention – it was certainly not mine – to impose a collegial view, even if that were possible. Perhaps all the contributors to the book agree that a monetary interpretation of the Great Recession is worth examining. But I don't want to suggest that they favour a monetary interpretation above others or that only one version of the monetary interpretation is valid.

I want to mention two further matters. First, I dislike using the first person ("in my view", "in our judgement", and so on), as it is all too often a sign that someone is losing the argument. Logic and the facts should carry the day. But I use the first person in this Introduction and the introductions to each part, simply because the result would otherwise be very stilted. In my chapters I revert to "the author". My apologies if the result seems inconsistent. Secondly, both Keynes and Friedman are abiding presences in most chapters, and references to Keynes's *Collected Writings* are scattered throughout the notes. Rather than write out the full title of every volume, with publisher and editorial details, I generally follow the convention of specifying the volume number next to *CW*. The only exception is the first time a reference is made to the *CW* in each chapter's notes, when I have ensured that a full reference is given. Again, my apologies if the result seems inconsistent.

NOTES

1. Ben Bernanke *The Courage to Act* (New York and London: W.W. Norton & Company, 2015); Mervyn King *The End of Alchemy* (London: Little, Brown, 2016); and Hank Paulson *On the Brink* (New York: Hachette Book Group, and London: Headline Publishing Group, 2010).
2. This may seem overstated, but memories are short. According to George Orwell, writing in 1945, "Among the intelligentsia, it hardly needs saying that the dominant form of nationalism is Communism . . . A Communist . . . is one who looks upon the USSR as his Fatherland and feels it his duty to justify Russian policy and advance Russian interests at all costs. Obviously such people abound in England today, and their direct and indirect influence is very great." Sonia Orwell and Ian Angus (eds) *The Collected Essays, Journalism and Letters of George Orwell*, vol. III (Harmondsworth: Penguin Books in association with Secker & Warburg, 1971, paperback reprint of 1968 original), p.414. For another somewhat later example, see C.P. Snow's *The Two Cultures* (Cambridge: Cambridge University Press, 9th printing of book with part II added, 2006, original publication 1959, based on the Rede Lecture). According to Snow, "Among the rich are the US, the white Commonwealth countries, Great Britain, most of Europe, and the USSR" (p. 41). Further, "Russia is catching up with the US in major industry . . ." (p. 44).
3. Werner Keller *Are the Russians Ten Feet Tall?* (London: Thames and Hudson, 1961).
4. In October 1929 the US quantity of money – understood as the sum of currency held by the public, and demand and time deposits at commercial banks – was $48 155 m. In April 1933 it was $29 747 m, over 38 per cent lower. See Milton Friedman and Anna Schwartz *A Monetary History of the United States, 1867–1960* (Princeton: Princeton University Press, 1963), pp.712–14. See also p.238 in Chapter 10 below.
5. The quotation is from p.169 of Milton Friedman *Capitalism and Freedom* (Chicago: University of Chicago, 1962).
6. The quote appeared in Paul Krugman's essay 'Who was Milton Friedman?' in the 15 February 2007 issue of *The New York Review of Books*.
7. George Nash *The Conservative Intellectual Movement in America since 1945* (New York: Basic Books, 1976), p.287.
8. In 1970 the Institute of Economic Affairs published a pamphlet by Friedman on *The Counter-Revolution in Monetary Theory* (London: IEA, 1970, IEA Occasional Paper no. 33). Harry Johnson wrote a paper on 'The Keynesian Revolution and the Monetarist Counter-Revolution', which appeared the following year in the *American Economic Review*. (See *American Economic Review*, vol. 61, no. 2, *Papers and Proceedings of the Eighty-Third Annual Meeting of the American Economic Association* [May, 1971], pp.1–14.) The word "monetarism" had been coined by Karl Brunner in a 1968 article ('The role of money and monetary policy') in the July 1968 issue of the Federal Reserve Bank of St Louis' *Review*.
9. See below, p.252.
10. Bernanke *The Courage to Act*, p.30.
11. Lauchlin Currie *The Supply and Control of Money in the United States* (Cambridge, USA: Harvard University Press, 1934), originally a doctoral thesis at Harvard, may have been the first book-length analysis of monetary data. Currie used data prepared by the US Treasury and Federal Reserve, as did Friedman and Schwartz later. I am grateful to David Laidler and Roger Sandilands for bringing my attention to Currie, who in many ways anticipated the Friedman and Schwartz work.
12. The graph, which is of monthly data, shows the six-month annualized rate of change in a broadly defined measure of money. In other words, the value for June 2009 is the actual increase in money in the six months from December 2008 to June 2009, but scaled up on the assumption that the rate of change in this six-month period continued for a full year. It was decided to express the change in a six-month annualized rate because of the weaknesses of alternatives. The annual rate misleads as it includes the experience

of nine to twelve months earlier, while the three-month annualized rate can be erratic. The aggregate chosen was M3 in the USA, that is, the measure for which data were prepared by the Federal Reserve from 1959 to February 2006, but for which estimates by the private research company, Shadow Government Statistics, are needed subsequently. In the Eurozone the aggregate was M3, as prepared by the European Central Bank. In the UK the aggregate was M4x and the data are from the Bank of England. The M4x series was prepared by the Bank on a quarterly basis before 2009. To make the UK data monthly before 2009, interpolation has been used. The justification for adopting M4x is that the more traditional measure, M4, includes money held by so-called "intermediate other financial corporations", which are similar to banks. Like inter-bank deposits, such money balances have no obvious bearing on macroeconomic outcomes and so can properly be excluded from a money concept.

13.   Mark Blaug, in a discussion published in 1985 that was sympathetic towards monetarism and the quantity theory of money, noted in the fourth edition of his much-admired *Economic Theory in Retrospect* that monetarism was being split into a "left wing" (emphasizing lags and other difficulties in the transmission mechanism) and a "right wing" (focusing on the purity of the comparative-static results). See Blaug *Economic Theory in Retrospect* (Cambridge: Cambridge University Press, 1985), p. 692.

14.   Milton Friedman (ed.) *The Optimum Quantity of Money* (London and Basingstoke: Macmillan, 1969), p. 52.

15.   Paul Samuelson *The Collected Scientific Papers of Paul Samuelson* (Cambridge, MA: MIT Press, 1972), vol. 3, p. 755.

16.   Ben Bernanke and Mark Gertler 'Inside the black box: the credit channel of monetary policy transmission', *Journal of Economic Perspectives* (Nashville, TN: American Economic Association), Fall 1995 issue, vol. 9, no. 4, pp. 27–48.

17.   Elizabeth Johnson and Donald Moggridge (eds) *The Collected Writings of John Maynard Keynes*, vol. VII: *The General Theory of Employment, Interest and Money* (London and Basingstoke: Macmillan for the Royal Economic Society, 1973), pp. 84–5.

18.   The paper was republished as Milton Friedman and Anna Schwartz 'Money and business cycles', in Milton Friedman (ed.) *The Optimum Quantity of Money*, pp. 189–235.

19.   Friedman (ed.) *The Optimum Quantity of Money*, pp. 229–34.

20.   Friedman (ed.) *The Optimum Quantity of Money*, footnote 2 at the bottom of p. 172.

21.   Inter-bank deposits are excluded from money, which creates a problem for the deposits of organizations which are quasi-banks. Hence the word "genuine", to define the relevant non-banks, is used in the text. Definitional issues also arise with deposits held by non-residents and with foreign currency deposits held by residents.

22.   The Federal Reserve stopped preparing M3 data in February 2006. The M3 figure given in the text is taken from data prepared by the research company, Shadow Government Statistics, which guesstimates the M3 total from publicly available information about M3's components. For further discussion, see Tim Congdon *Money in a Free Society* (New York: Encounter Books, 2011), pp. 346–50.

23.   Allan Meltzer *A History of the Federal Reserve*, vol. 1, 1913–51 (Chicago, USA and London, UK: University of Chicago Press, 2003), p. 372.

24.   Robert Lucas *Collected Papers on Monetary Theory* (Cambridge, MA and London, UK: Harvard University Press, 2013), 'Review of Milton Friedman and Anna Schwartz *A Monetary History of the United States, 1867–1960*', pp. 361–74. The paper originally appeared in the first issue of the 1994 *Journal of Monetary Economics*. For more on the New Classical School, see p. 196 in Philip Booth's Chapter 8 below.

25.   The evolution of monetary data preparation in the USA is surprisingly complex. See Richard Anderson and Kenneth Kavajecz 'A historical perspective on the Federal Reserve's monetary aggregates: definition, construction and targeting', *Federal Reserve Bank of St. Louis Review*, vol. 76, no. 2, March/April 1994, pp. 1–31.

26.   Edward Nelson 'Milton Friedman and US monetary history: 1961–2006', *Federal Reserve Bank of St Louis Review*, vol. 89, no. 3, 2007, pp. 153–82. See, particularly, p. 163.

27. Samuelson's 1948 textbook – by far the best-selling economics textbook of all time – included a section on Hicks' IS–LM model, originally proposed in Hicks' 1937 review article on *The General Theory*. The LM function represented those points where both the interest rate and national income were consistent with the equivalence of money demand with money supply. So Samuelson's textbook did include money. But Samuelson and the Keynesians differed from the monetarists over a wide front. Quite apart from the matters discussed in the main text here, the Keynesians and the monetarists disagreed on the relative importance of money and other economic drivers in the determination of national income, and on the direction of causation. The Keynesians were inclined to regard money as being determined by the economy; they did not see macroeconomic variables as being determined by the banking system and the quantity of money.

28. Friedman (ed.) *The Optimum Quantity of Money*, pp. 4–5.

29. In November 2002 Bernanke gave a speech in which he mentioned "helicopter money" as a weapon to defeat entrenched deflation. He was advised by the Fed's media relations officer to drop it, as it was too recondite for financial markets to appreciate. Bernanke *The Courage to Act*, p. 64.

30. John Kenneth Galbraith *Money: Whence it Came, Where it Went* (Boston: Houghton Mifflin, 1975), p. 29.

31. See p. 58 of Gordon Pepper and Michael Oliver *The Liquidity Theory of Asset Prices* (Chichester: John Wiley & Sons, 2006) for fountain-pen money; see pp. 43–7 of William Barber *The Works of Irving Fisher*, vol. 11: *100% Money* (London: Pickering & Chatto, 1997, originally published 1935) for cheque-book money, or "check-book money" in Fisher's American spelling; the phrase "keyboard money" has appeared in newspapers in recent years, to express the typing of scriptural money amounts on computer keyboards.

32. Perhaps the most important of the papers crucial to the development of credit counterparts analysis was written in the mid-1950s by the International Monetary Fund's second head of research, Jacques Polak. See Jacques Polak 'Monetary analysis of income formation and payments problems', *IMF Staff Papers* (Washington: IMF, 1957), vol. 6, issue 1, pp. 1–50. See also Gerald Steel 'The credit counterparts of broad money: a structural base for macroeconomic policy', *Lancaster University Management School Economic Working Paper Series*, 2014, no. 4.

33. The derivation of the banking system multiplier is a textbook commonplace. But see, for example, Friedman and Schwartz *A Monetary History of the United States*, pp. 776–808 for a rigorous treatment and pp. 238–9 in David Laidler's Chapter 10 below.

34. Friedman *A Program for Monetary Stability* (New York: Fordham University Press, 1959, based on the Millar Lectures) was Friedman's earliest extended discussion of the topic.

35. For an example of a measured critique of monetary base control, see Chapter VII (pp. 202–18) in Charles Goodhart *Monetary Theory and Practice* (London: Macmillan, 1984).

36. I made this argument in Tim Congdon 'First principles of central banking', *The Banker*, April 1981 issue. It is also one theme of Tim Congdon *Central Banking in a Free Society* (London: Institute of Economic Affairs, 2009).

37. See note 4 above and Friedman and Schwartz *A Monetary History of the United States, 1867–1960*, pp. 803–4.

38. James Tobin 'A monetary interpretation of history', Chapter 23, in *Essays in Economics: vol. 1 Macroeconomics* (Amsterdam: North Holland, 1971), pp. 471–96. See, especially, pp. 476–81. The chapter originally appeared as a review article in the 1965 *American Economic Review*.

39. See p. 48 below.

40. I accept that a cyclical reverse after the excessive money growth of 2005–07 was unavoidable, but in my view it ought to have been mild. In early 2007 I warned of trouble ahead in evidence to the House of Commons' Treasury Committee, but I had

no inkling of the severity of the setback that was to happen. I did not anticipate – and could not have anticipated – the folly of international officialdom (as I see the matter) in late 2008. Drastic changes in bank regulation of the kind seen in late 2008 had never occurred before.

41. Tim Congdon *Money in a Free Society* (New York: Encounter Books, 2011), pp. xii–xix.
42. See note 20 to Chapter 2 on p. 74 for more discussion of creditism.
43. Of course new bank lending to the private sector creates new money balances, and money matters in the usually understood fashion. National income is a function of the quantity of money, not of the loans that banks extend.
44. Every passenger in the train compartment was involved in the murder of a villain.
45. Lawrence McDonald and Patrick Robinson *A Colossal Failure of Common Sense: The Inside Story of the Collapse of Lehman Brothers* (New York: Three Rivers Press, 2009).
46. Friedman *The Optimum Quantity of Money*, pp. 51–68, reprinted from Milton Friedman (ed.) *Studies in the Quantity Theory of Money* (Chicago: University of Chicago Press, 1956).

PART I

What Were the Causes of the Great
Recession?

Introduction to Part I

Tim Congdon

The first part of the current volume is concerned most directly with money's role in the causation of macroeconomic instability. The main contention of three of its chapters is that the Great Recession of late 2008 and 2009, like the USA's Great Depression in the four years to 1933, was caused by a collapse in the rate of growth of the quantity of money, where the quantity of money is defined to include all (or nearly all) bank deposits.

The first chapter, which I wrote in early 2014, contrasts what I term the "mainstream" approach to understanding the Great Recession with the monetary interpretation. The mainstream approach is criticized for not appealing to a recognized and well-developed theory of national income determination. Its line of argument seems to be that something went wrong in the financial system, particularly in the banks, resulting in "an increase in financial fragility", "a loss of confidence", "a shock to animal spirits" or whatever, which caused a fall in asset prices and a downturn in spending. I regard the mainstream approach as woolly and imprecise, and as journalistic rather than scientific in spirit.

The proponents of the mainstream view come from many and varied perspectives. They nevertheless all manage to agree on appropriate reme-dial measures, which – in essence – are about "tidying up banks' balance sheets". Since the mainstream approach regards the financial system as guilty for the Great Recession, the implied criticism of the market economy is similar to that which was prevalent in the 1930s following the Great Depression. Richard Posner, a pioneer of the economics of law who is often seen as pro-market and even as a representative of the Chicago free-market tradition, wrote a 2009 book with the title *A Failure of Capitalism: The Crisis of '08 and the Descent into Depression.*[1] A year later he judged that, "The inherent instability of capitalism is a fact, not a criticism".[2]

I propose that, on the contrary, the Great Recession should be seen as just another illustration of the power of large fluctuations in money growth to cause macroeconomic instability, in line with long-established

theory and vast bodies of evidence. I further argue that the large fluctuations in money growth seen in the major economies between 2005 and 2010
were due to mistakes by officialdom.

By far the worst of these was the tightening of bank regulation from
October 2008. An abrupt, drastic and hurried "tidying-up of bank balance
sheets" was wholly inappropriate. The attempt to punish the banks for their
sins had the effect of checking the expansion of their balance sheets and
causing a collapse in money growth. The impacts on demand and output
were viciously deflationary at just the wrong moment. The banking industry was singled out for chastisement, but – because banks issue money in
the form of deposits and everyone uses bank deposits to make payments –
the effects were pervasive as well as damaging. Indeed, because of the link
between financial regulation and banks' decisions on asset size and quality,
and then the link between such decisions and money growth, actions by
governments and central banks quickly led to stock market declines and
falling house prices. Sharp rises in corporate bankruptcies and unemployment followed in short order. To recall Friedman's comment on the Fed in
the Great Depression, officialdom exercised its responsibilities "so ineptly
as to convert what would otherwise have been a minor contraction into a
major catastrophe".

At the start of the third millennium economists sometimes pretend to
be practising a "science" or at least an intellectual discipline with scientific
pretensions. (Joseph Stiglitz, awarded the Nobel prize in economics in
2001, says in the preface to the first volume of his projected six-volume
Selected Works, that the aim will be "to bring together my major scientific papers in economics".[3]) But has science been at work in economists'
discussion of the Great Recession? Any interpretation of an episode as
important as the Great Recession ought, in my view, to be compatible with
a theory of national income determination, while (as I say below) that
theory ought "to be applicable in the same way with the same variables on
a large number of occasions". The monetary interpretation of the Great
Recession fits the bill. It can and must be tested against statistical data,
and the data to conduct the tests must be prepared by the relevant official
agencies (and for the most part the data are indeed so prepared). By contrast, much of the pseudo-theory, conjecture, rhetoric and journalism that
constitute the mainstream view of the Great Recession is untestable, and
deserves to be condemned as unscientific and shoddy.

My first chapter is mostly about the USA, but policy responses to
the crisis were similar in Europe, including the UK. My second chapter
expands a note for my research consultancy (International Monetary
Research Ltd) on the UK economic situation prepared in July 2013.
(The note was circulated to clients, but has not otherwise been pub-

lished. Its conclusions were the same as in a letter to the *Financial Times* ['Quantitative easing in the US was both desirable and necessary'] of 22 July 2013.) The chapter gives a brief statement of the monetary theory of national income determination, as a prelude to explaining how "quantitative easing" (that is, large central bank asset purchases) could combat the deflationary forces behind the Great Recession. It is taken for granted, first, that a broadly defined measure of money is the correct one to deploy in macroeconomic analysis, and, second, that changes in broad money are best analysed by examining the credit counterparts. I say nothing about the monetary base. (Implicitly, I agree that Friedman and Schwartz were right in their 1963 *Monetary History* to favour broad money as the aggregate that mattered in the Great Depression. But I disagree with them that the changes in quantity of money should be understood as a variable determined by the monetary base and the "base money multiplier". See pp. 8–12 of the Introduction for more on this debate.)

The third chapter is by Ryland Thomas, an economist at the Bank of England since 1994, who has published important research under its imprimatur. In particular, he has carried out pioneering analyses on the money demand functions of the UK's various sectors, exploiting data series for money held by households, companies and financial institutions since 1963.[4] He has also co-authored papers in the *Bank of England Quarterly Bulletin* that explore the relationship between the quantity of money and national income.[5] The favoured money aggregate in his contribution to this volume – which is exclusively about the UK's Great Recession – is broadly defined. Further, he considers that the most useful approach to the determination of the quantity of money is to review the credit counterparts on the assets side of banks' balance sheet. Like my second chapter, Thomas's contains no references to the monetary base at all.

However, Thomas's conclusions are very different from mine. In a meticulous discussion of the velocity of circulation, he says that the downturn in demand in 2008 and 2009 reflected changes in velocity as well as the fall in money growth. He also emphasizes the often neglected point that the credit counterparts to money growth are not independent. (For example, a squeeze on money balances due to restrictions on new bank lending to the private sector is likely to lead to a depressed economy, which improves a nation's external payments and pulls in money from abroad.) He considers a "counter-factual" scenario in which bank regulation was not tightened in late 2008. He suggests that, without all the extra capital and liquidity mandated by the regulatory authorities, bank credit to the private sector would have been even weaker in 2009 and 2010 than it actually was.

The fourth chapter, jointly authored by Juan Castañeda and myself, looks at money trends in the Eurozone since the introduction of the single currency in 1999. Rates of money growth are examined, both for the Eurozone as a whole and in its individual member states. Of course, the concept of a national "quantity of money" in a multi-government monetary union is awkward. Nevertheless, totals of bank notes and deposits continue to be held by the residents of particular countries. So comparisons can be made of national money growth rates and national changes in nominal GDP, among other standard exercises. The expected relationships prevailed before, during and after the Great Recession. A plunge in money growth for the Eurozone as a whole from late 2008 preceded, and arguably precipitated, the worst of the slide in economic activity. Those nations with the sharpest decline in money growth had the most severe cyclical retreats in demand and output. An alarming finding is that the volatility in money growth in Greece and Ireland in the six years 2008 to 2013 inclusive was higher than in the USA in the six years 1928 to 1933 inclusive, which included both the tail end of the stock market bubble of the Roaring Twenties and the appalling Great Depression.

NOTES

1. Richard A. Posner *A Failure of Capitalism* (Cambridge, MA: Harvard University Press, 2009).
2. Richard A. Posner *The Crisis of Capitalist Democracy* (Cambridge, MA: Harvard University Press, 2010), p. 2.
3. Joseph Stiglitz *Selected Works of Joseph E. Stiglitz*, vol. 1, *Information and Economic Analysis* (Oxford: Oxford University Press, 2009), p. ix.
4. Ryland Thomas 'The demand for M4: a sectoral analysis, part 1, the personal sector' and 'The demand for M4: a sectoral analysis, part 2, the corporate sector', *Bank of England Working Papers*, Nos 61 and 62, 1997.
5. See Michael McLeay, Amar Radia and Ryland Thomas 'Money creation in the modern economy' and Michael McLeay, Amar Radia and Ryland Thomas 'Money in the modern economy: an introduction' in *Bank of England Quarterly Bulletin* (London: Bank of England), Q1 2014 issue.

1. What were the causes of the Great Recession? The mainstream approach vs. the monetary interpretation*

Tim Congdon

What were the causes of the Great Recession of late 2008 and 2009? The current chapter distinguishes and contrasts two ways of thinking about this question. The first, which has dominated official discussion and media coverage, can be seen as "the mainstream approach"; the second, which has had less attention, may be called "the monetary interpretation".[1] The main claim here is that the mainstream approach is inadequate and unconvincing, while the evidence is consistent with an analysis in which the quantity of money plays a central causal role. As the Great Recession was international in scope, one difficulty is to specify the particular jurisdiction to which the discussion relates. An Appendix will review the monetary experience of the key nations, but the analysis in the main text will appeal mostly to statistics from the USA. An advantage of the monetary interpretation is that during the crucial period it fits data for all the key nations, with the exception of Japan. The first section describes and interrogates the mainstream approach. It tries to do so fairly, although the author's views are hardly disguised. The second section expounds the monetary interpretation. It applies the monetary theory of the determination of national income *and wealth* to both a narrative of events and key statistical series. A short conclusion contends that policy-makers and their economic advisers, as well as the economics profession at large, ought to pay more attention to the work that the quantity of money plays in motivating the business cycle, including such extreme events as the Great Recession.

I

Explanations of the Great Recession have been diverse. Andrew Lo's review article of 21 volumes on the crisis in the 2012 *Journal of Economic Literature* opined that, "no single account of this vast and complicated calamity is sufficient to describe it". It separated the books into the academic and the journalistic, and said that the academic were the more interested "in identifying underlying causes", but then remarked that the academic contributions "seem to exhibit the most heterogeneity".[2] A problem with such heterogeneity was that it risked failing to provide a single cut-and-dried set of policy prescriptions. Nevertheless, in the aftermath of the crisis policy-makers seemed to share enough of a consensus about causation that they could agree on an agenda of remediation.[3] In that agenda banks were in future to operate with higher capital-to-asset ratios, more substantial buffers of liquid assets to total assets and less wholesale funding, and they were to be subjected to tighter regulatory scrutiny. The near unanimity on the correct policy response argues that officialdom had a widely agreed interpretation of the crisis, even if this interpretation might have been better elucidated.

The sequence of events may have prompted the thinking behind one element in the mainstream discussion. By common consent, the crisis began with the freezing of the international inter-bank market in August 2007. Financial organizations that had been reliant on inter-bank funding of their assets in earlier years suddenly found themselves unable to access new lines and often had trouble rolling over existing facilities. A plausible view was that the interruption of inter-bank credit was due to mutual distrust within the banking industry, as the better-placed institutions worried about weaker counterparties' asset quality and capital adequacy. The crisis was therefore about banks' lack of solvency and indeed, if the worst came to the worst, about outright insolvency.

The emphasis on solvency seemed to make sense in autumn 2008. On 15 September 2008 Lehman Brothers defaulted in the world's largest ever bankruptcy, with losses to its creditors that might theoretically reach $600 billion. By implication, policy-makers were right to demand that in future banks operate with higher capital ratios, stronger liquidity buffers and so on. Also by implication, the severe global downturn in late 2008 and early 2009 was due to lack of confidence in a broken financial system. More generally, the Great Recession was caused by the follies of free market capitalism. The tightening of regulations from 2008 was therefore viewed as necessary to bring capitalism under control and to force banks to shrink their businesses.

Mainstream thinking has appeared in many places, if with a variety of emphases. In his massively influential column in the *New York Times*, Paul Krugman has been a leading expositor, and he is cited below in the present chapter and several times elsewhere in this book. A salient strand has been that financial market practitioners took excessive risk relative to capital, with their actions motivated by inordinate "animal spirits". This strand has been highlighted in the work of Robert Shiller, one of the Nobel economics laureates in 2013 and a well-known spokesman for "behavioural finance". Shiller co-authored with George Akerlof, another Nobel prize-winner, a 2009 book actually entitled *Animal Spirits*, which drew on "an emerging field called behaviour economics" and averred that their investigation "describes how the economy really works".[4] Similar emphases were found in Alan Greenspan's 2013 book *The Map and the Territory*. The first chapter was called 'Animal Spirits' and had a section on "behavioural economics". In the next two chapters Greenspan focused on the crisis period and at one point mentioned "herd behaviour" in the context of asset price bubbles. The reference clearly invited the interpretation that fluctuations in asset prices were (and always are) to be attributed to the changing moods of investors. Later, Greenspan posited that, "market liquidity is largely a function of the degree of risk aversion of investors, clearly the dominant animal spirit that drives financial markets".[5]

The buoyant asset prices of the 2005–07 mini-boom period immediately ahead of the crisis are seen in the mainstream approach as the result of contagious euphoria, in line with the animal spirits thesis. Asset price movements become a function of changing human psychology instead of being related to other macroeconomic variables. Akerlof and Shiller did in fact offer sceptical words in their 2009 book about any substantive theory of asset price determination. To quote, "No one has ever made rational sense of the wild gyrations in financial prices, such as stock prices."[6] However, mainstream authors often argue that the big declines in spending in late 2008 and 2009 were explicable in balance-sheet terms.[7] As Figure 1.1 shows, in the USA the decline in net worth was concentrated in the six quarters to the first quarter of 2009 and amounted to over one year of personal disposable income (PDI). The slide in the stock market in 2008 and, above all, the crash in residential real estate from 2006 to 2009 tend to be emphasized in mainstream analyses, while the fall in asset prices is contrasted with the heavy burden of debt incurred in the good years before 2007.

Informal comments on the growth of debt often have a moral tinge.[8] Worries about debt may be stated more rigorously in terms of the concept of "leverage", with the sustainability of debt assessed relative to servicing ability or collateral. Greenspan, like other observers, was particularly exercised in *The Map and the Territory* about the allegedly "extraordinary leverage . . .

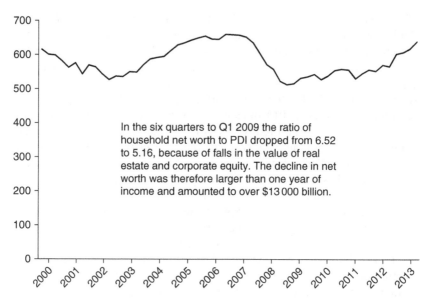

In the six quarters to Q1 2009 the ratio of
household net worth to PDI dropped from 6.52
to 5.16, because of falls in the value of real
estate and corporate equity. The decline in net
worth was therefore larger than one year of
income and amounted to over $13 000 billion.

Source: Data are quarterly and are from the Federal Reserve.

*Figure 1.1   Household net worth as a percentage of personal disposable
income in the USA*

taken on by US investment banks", citing balance sheet totals that might be
"twenty-five to thirty times tangible capital".[9] But excessive leverage is also
said to have been a characteristic of the entire American banking system,
including the commercial banks, ahead of the crisis period.[10]

Excessive debt and risk-taking could of course be found in both the
banking sector and among non-bank private sector agents. However, much
mainstream commentary on the Great Recession regards banks' balance-
sheet patterns as having particular macroeconomic significance, in line
with the emphasis placed on the special nature of bank credit in influential
articles on "the credit channel" by Robert Bernanke, Alan Blinder and
Mark Gertler.[11] The mainstream interpretation of the Great Recession
does give banks a starring role in the drama, even if they are its anti-heroes.
This is an important merit in view of the unrealistic neglect of banks in,
for example, the three-equation New Keynesianism that was fashionable
among central bank economists in the years preceding the crisis.[12] The
emphasis in the mainstream discussions is on the assets side of banks'
balance sheets as having the vital macroeconomic effects. Little or no reference is made to the deposits on the liabilities side, which are the principal
component of the quantity of money as usually defined.

Proponents of the mainstream analysis, with their belief in the special-ness of banks' assets, concluded in late 2008 and 2009 that a resumed flow of bank credit was a precondition of recovery. This thought remained influential throughout the crisis period and afterwards. According to the Federal Reserve website as updated on 19 July 2013, the Federal Reserve Board had decided that month to implement the Basel III package of bank regulation. The package was justified, in its view, on the grounds that, "banks [must] maintain strong capital positions that will enable them to continue lending to creditworthy households and businesses even after unforeseen losses and during economic downturns".

Of course the extension of credit involves risks, against which banks must in the ordinary course of business maintain a protective layer of capital. So, again to quote from the Fed website, the adoption of Basel III would increase "both the quantity and the quality of capital held by US banking organizations". The supposed beneficence of high bank capital levels appears to be agreed by the overwhelming majority of experts and commen-tators on the crisis. In late 2008 Paul Krugman praised UK policy-makers, notably the Prime Minister Gordon Brown, in his *New York Times* column because their bank-recapitalization plan was judged to be superior to the US Treasury's scheme to purchase so-called "toxic securities" from the banks.[13] In his 2013 book *After the Music Stopped*, Alan Blinder – one of Bernanke's co-authors and a former vice-chairman of the Federal Reserve Board – opined, "The crisis exposed numerous flaws in the nation's regula-tory system. One painfully obvious one was that banks and other financial institutions had been allowed to operate with too much leverage, that is, with too little capital."[14] To summarize, the mainstream interpretation

- sees bank insolvency, actual or potential, as the main symptom of an unsatisfactory financial system and an important cause of the wider crisis;
- it indicts the bankers, understood to be greedy and driven by animal spirits, as particularly to blame for the macroeconomic setbacks of the Great Recession;
- it praises the tightening of bank regulation and bank recapitaliza-tions of autumn 2008 as the key feature of an appropriate policy response; and
- it upbraids the financial system in Western liberal democracies as inherently unstable and dysfunctional, and as an entrenched weak-ness of modern capitalism.[15]

But is the mainstream interpretation persuasive? One problem is the thinness of its conceptual basis, since an appeal to "lack of confidence" (or "animal spirits") as a determinant of aggregate demand is difficult to fit in a robust theory of national expenditure and output. How is the notion of "confidence" to be quantified and then tested with data? If an account of events invokes a theory of some sort in order to have at least a semblance of scientific status, it needs to be applicable in the same way with the same variables on a large number of occasions. In their *Animal Spirits* book Akerlof and Shiller recalled the multiplier theory of national income determination in Keynes' *General Theory*, but downplayed Hicks' classic statement of that theory and advanced claims for their own notion of "a confidence multiplier".[16] It may well be true that people increased their spending in 2007 because they were "more confident" and spent less in 2009 because they were "more worried". But does that take us very far?

Further, with the passage of time the focus on banks' solvency, and on their leverage and capital positions, has become questionable. A common refrain was that confidence collapsed because banks were "bust". But how many banks were bust, meaning that they had exhausted all their equity capital, and so were unable to meet obligations to bondholders, depositors and other creditors? In the American context a key distinction is between *commercial* and *investment* banks. According to the usual understandings, commercial banks extend loans, take deposits, and provide depositors with money transmission and cash settlement services. By contrast, investment banks are in the very different business of trading securities with customers and underwriting securities issues by corporate customers; they are not usually involved in money transmission or cheque clearing, and fund their securities holdings not from retail depositors but from wholesale sources, including inter-bank lines. In the USA commercial banks have long been supervised by the Federal Reserve, whereas investment banks were traditionally regulated by the Securities and Exchange Commission. Admittedly, some overlap exists between the two kinds of bank, partly because over the last 20 years the emergence of bank holding companies (with both commercial and investment banking businesses answering to the same group of shareholders) has muddied the picture.

The Federal Reserve has long compiled data on the condition of the commercial banks that come under its wing. The two main issues raised by the mainstream interpretation are:

1. the level of banks' capital/asset ratios at different times, particularly the level today and in the recent past compared with historical norms;
2. the vulnerability of banks' capital to actual or expected losses, and more specifically the extent to which banks' capital at the start of the Great Recession was eliminated by losses during it.

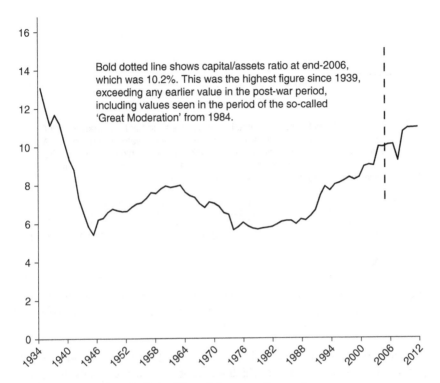

Bold dotted line shows capital/assets ratio at end-2006, which was 10.2%. This was the highest figure since 1939, exceeding any earlier value in the post-war period, including values seen in the period of the so-called 'Great Moderation' from 1984.

Source: Data are from the Federal Deposit Insurance Corporation.

Figure 1.2 Equity capital to total assets ratio of US commercial banks, 1934–2012 (showing ratio, %, at year-end)

The relevant numbers are readily available from well-known sources. On the first issue, two graphs present the most important information. The first (Figure 1.2) covers the period from the foundation of the Federal Deposit Insurance Corporation to 2012 and uses the FDIC data for year-ends; the second (Figure 1.3) relates to the Great Recession itself, taken for these purposes to begin in 2007, with the data being quarterly and sourced from the Federal Reserve. The first graph shows that US banks' equity/capital ratio just before the Great Recession, at end-2006, was the highest it had been since 1939. The average value of the ratio in the 61 post-war years (that is, 1946 to 2006 inclusive) had been 7.2 per cent. The end-2006 value was over 40 per cent higher than this, at 10.2 per cent. The second graph shows that US banks' capital was resilient during the crisis period. A dip in the capital/asset ratio did occur during 2008, with the figure for the fourth quarter of 2008 at 9.4 per cent being 0.8 per cent of assets lower

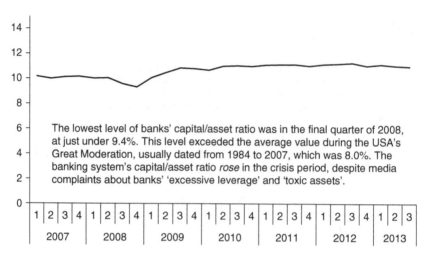

The lowest level of banks' capital/asset ratio was in the final quarter of 2008, at just under 9.4%. This level exceeded the average value during the USA's Great Moderation, usually dated from 1984 to 2007, which was 8.0%. The banking system's capital/asset ratio *rose* in the crisis period, despite media complaints about banks' 'excessive leverage' and 'toxic assets'.

Source: Data are from Federal Reserve.

Figure 1.3   *Equity capital to total assets ratio of US commercial banks in the Great Recession and after (showing ratio, %, quarterly)*

than a year earlier. However, this left the end-2008 value still at over 90 per cent of that a year earlier, which – to repeat – was the highest for more than 65 years.

What about the second issue, the vulnerability of banks' capital to loss? The last paragraph has demonstrated that during the Great Recession the American commercial banking system was at no point near to insolvency. However, this apparent robustness may have been due to massive capital-raising after heavy losses, which would hardly be reassuring. Data are needed also for the loss experience of the US banks during these years. Again the Federal Reserve compiles the necessary data. A key metric, the per cent return on equity, is shown in Figure 1.4, with the values being both as actually reported for each quarter and as a four-quarter moving average of these reported numbers.

The main point here is that the US commercial banking system, taken in the aggregate, had only one quarter of loss in the Great Recession. This was in the final quarter of 2009 and amounted to a trivial 1.0 per cent of equity. As Figure 1.4 shows, the fourth-quarter 2009 loss was less than that in the second quarter of 1987 (6.0 per cent of equity), when the New York money centre banks wrote off much of their Third World debt. However, the quarterly values may be misleading, in that the Third World debt write-offs were concentrated in a few quarters of 1987 and the sharpness

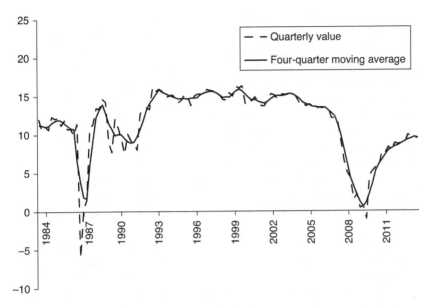

Source: Federal Reserve data.

Figure 1.4 *Return on equity in US commercial banking, 1984–2013 (%, quarterly)*

of the dip indicated by the line in the chart is deceptive. The line for the four-quarter moving average suggests that American banks had a rougher time in the Great Recession than in the 1980s, with a longer period of low profitability, which is in accordance with the media stereotype. However, outright losses would need to have been recorded before being able to accuse the banks that they might "go bust" and hence imperil the safety of deposits. It is evident that this was not so. On this basis, American banks did not in the aggregate incur a dangerous level of losses during the Great Recession.[17]

The USA, frequently identified as the epicentre of the problems, had a banking system that was solvent at the start of the crisis, remained solvent during the worst of the turmoil and still is solvent today. Indeed, the much-repeated assertion that "leverage" was exceptional in the pre-crisis period is false, at least as far as the American *commercial* banking industry is concerned. (Note that the Lo article in the 2012 *Journal of Economic Literature* argued that even the investment banks had similar leverage in 1998 and 2006.[18]) As widely noted at the time, in the early 1980s the equity capital to asset ratios at the New York money centre banks were mostly under 5 per cent.[19] In the decade to end-1997 the ratio of US commercial banks' equity to assets averaged 7.3 per cent and in the following decade it averaged 9.3 per cent. Both these figures were therefore well above the level maintained during the Third World debt problems 30 years earlier.

Just before the Lehman debacle itself the ratio was 10.1 per cent, and nowadays, because of the regulatory pressure from officialdom, the ratio is higher still. (See Chapters 5 to 7 for more on the changes in banks' capital to assets ratios since 2008.) Roughly speaking, the average American bank now has an equity capital to assets buffer which is three times thicker than that at the New York money centre banks 30 years ago. If the American people cut their spending in 2009 because they thought their banks were bust, why did they raise their expenditure in 1983 and 1984 at the start of the Reagan boom when the data show that their banks had a higher risk of failure?

No doubt, more discussion is needed before the current attempt to refute the mainstream interpretation is altogether convincing. Although the American banking system in the aggregate was robust during the Great Recession, some individual institutions did have large losses and either "went bust" or were on the borderline between insolvency and solvency.[20] However, these losses were never sizeable relative to the capital of the banking system as a whole and no new government money was needed to shore up the Federal Deposit Insurance Corporation. In her book *Bull by the Horns*, Sheila Bair, chairman of the FDIC, noted Warren Buffett's view that in early 2009 the American banking system was essentially sound. In her words, reporting a conversation between them, "Most of the banking institutions [then being subject to stress tests] were relatively healthy, he said, and in any event, fourteen of the nineteen banks being stress tested, could easily be resolved under the FDIC's normal processes if they got into trouble."

Remarkably, she then acknowledged that "Buffett was right".[21] Bair also said that the various financial interventions (that is, guarantees and loans, as well as capital subscriptions) by the US government and its agencies during the Great Recession had ultimately proved profitable, although expressing dismay at a system which envisages picking "winners and losers with taxpayer money".[22] (But the FDIC has received no grants or capital injections from the US government since its creation in 1933 and in that sense the reference to "taxpayer money" is not correct. The FDIC's solvency is protected by insurance premiums received from shareholder-owned commercial banks. To quote from a note 'Who is the FDIC?', published in 2008 on its 75th anniversary and still available [September 2016] on its website, "The FDIC receives no Congressional appropriations."[23])

The financial outcome of the government interventions is crucial. In the 1980s and 1990s the US taxpayer lost substantial sums, usually estimated at about $150 billion, from government involvement in the savings and loans crisis. (Macroeconomic trends in the early 1980s undermined the financial viability of hundreds of savings and loans associations. The "S&L's" had long-term mortgage assets which returned interest income on fixed-rate terms. They could not cover their funding costs, given the surge in interest rates.)[24] But the resolution of the savings and loans crisis had been accompanied by far less trauma than seen in the 2008–10 period. Indeed, the losses to the American taxpayer from the resolution of the savings and loans associations coincided with the benign years of the Great Moderation. The compatibility of such losses with macroeconomic stability again casts doubt on the claim that potential *commercial* bank insolvency, due to excessive leverage and inadequate capital, was the central problem for the American economy in the Great Recession.

Let it be admitted that the American *investment* banks had far more trouble in the crisis years than the much larger commercial banking system, particularly in the egregious case of Lehman Brothers Holdings Inc. Lehman did indeed have a large deficiency in its North American operations when it was wound up. But an obvious puzzle is to explain how losses of $150 billion or so from one business were capable of subverting the entire American economy, with an annual output in the relevant period of about $15 000 billion and a capital stock worth over $80 000 billion.[25] Relative to fluctuations in the value of the USA's net wealth, because of changes in the general level of asset prices, the Lehman deficiency was miniscule. Nevertheless, in a curious comment in a 2014 book on *What Have We Learned? Macroeconomic Policy after the Crisis*, Akerlof implied that the Lehman deficiency was indeed of great importance, as policy-makers had astutely put "a finger in the dyke" to stop the dam of insolvency bursting.[26] (Space constraints prohibit detailed discussion of the Lehman case, as also of such places as Cyprus, Iceland and Ireland. Banking systems in these small nations lost substantial sums relative to national output and became insolvent, but the figures were minor in an international context. Chapter 4 discusses Ireland's problems in more detail, on pp. 121–3.)

II

The time has come to set out the monetary interpretation of the Great Recession. A virtue of this interpretation is that it appeals to a recognized theory of national income determination. This theory has both a well understood equilibrium condition and a clear account of how equilibrium is restored when it has been disturbed. The equilibrium condition has been stated in several ways in the textbooks, but the core idea is that the demand to hold money balances is equal to the actual quantity of money created by the banking system at one and only one value of national income. In that sense the equilibrium value of national income is determined by the quantity of money. Keynes in *The General Theory* was among many authorities who endorsed this idea.[27]

The process of re-equilibrating an economy subject to a monetary shock (such as a sudden and unexpected change in the quantity of money or in the rate of money growth) has also been discussed many times in a large body of literature. The main themes of all such statements are that

- agents have a well-defined money demand function in which national income and a handful of other variables are the key arguments; and
- the money demand function has the property that, for any given set of values of the "other variables", agents have a constant desired ratio of money to income.[28]

If the rate of money growth shifts abruptly in a short period from an established equilibrium, agents have "too much" or "too little" money relative to the level implied by this desired ratio. If money growth has risen and agents have too much money, each agent seeks to pass on part of his or her money holding to another agent by spending above income. But attempted transactions on these lines cannot change the aggregate quantity of money. The money once held by buyers does not disappear from the economy, but must end up in the hands of the sellers. In a well-known statement from Milton Friedman, "If individuals as a whole were to try to reduce the number of dollars they held, they could not all do so ... [T]hey would simply be playing a game of musical chairs." The excess supply of money is extinguished not by a change in the quantity of money, but by a rise in sales or prices, that is, by higher national income. To quote Friedman again, while individuals in the aggregate may be "[f]rustrated in their attempt to reduce the number of dollars they hold [if they all have an excess supply of money], they succeed in achieving an equivalent change in their position, for the rise in money incomes and prices reduces the ratio of these balances to their income ... This process will continue until this ratio ... [is] in accord with their desires".[29]

The chain of events described by Friedman is sometimes known as "the hot potato argument". It evokes the circulation of unwanted money between agents, like that of a disagreeably hot potato, until a new equilibrium with higher prices has emerged and everyone can cool down. The hot potato argument is usually applied to markets in goods and services. It has the purpose of demonstrating how, after an unexpected acceleration in money growth, people and companies react when "too much is chasing too few goods". However, the idea is equally applicable to asset markets.[30] Wealth-holders must at all times balance their money holdings against non-money assets. Given certain characteristics of money and non-money assets (notably their relative rates of return), wealth-holders have a desired ratio of money to non-money assets, including such assets as corporate equity and real estate. Logically, a monetary theory of the determination of national wealth determination must be an associate of the monetary theory of national income determination, since all assets can be viewed as the capitalizations of income streams. Excess money can drive asset price surges, as investors try to rid themselves of the unwanted hot potato of superfluous cash. A situation can arise in which "too much money is chasing too few assets".

How is the notion of a monetary theory of wealth determination to be harnessed in an analysis of the Great Recession? Money balances are held by a range of agents for different motives. Much of the household sector's money is used for immediate transactions needs, and relatively few individuals are balancing money against substantial portfolios of non-money assets in their own names.[31] Nowadays a high proportion of a society's risk assets are managed by specialist intermediaries, such as mutual funds, pension funds and life insurance companies. Virtually all of these intermediaries' money holdings are run as the most liquid component of larger portfolios dominated by equities, real estate and bonds. Valuable insights into asset price determination might come from monitoring their money balances.[32]

In 2006 the author carried out a data collecting exercise with the USA's flow-of-funds data in order to consider the relationship between savings institutions' money holdings and their total assets. The exercise covered five types of institution (private pension funds, state and local government's employee retirement funds, life-insurance companies, property-and-casualty insurance companies, and mutual funds) and used data going back to the first quarter of 1952 and ending in the fourth quarter of 2005. The money holdings and total assets of the five types of institution were added together on a quarterly basis, and then compared. In the 54-year period the total assets of the USA's five main kinds of long-term savings institution increased by 187.1 times at a compound annual rate of 10.2 per cent, while their money holdings rose by 214.2 times at a compound annual rate of 10.5 per cent. Alternatively put, both total assets and money balances increased over this period of more than half a century by about 200 times, but the ratio between the two variables (which is akin to the notion

Table 1.1   *Money and asset holdings of large US savings institutions,*
2000–2013 (comparing % changes in year to fourth quarter)

	Value of:		
	Total assets held by large US savings institutions	Money holdings of large US savings institutions	Quantity of money, as measured by M3 aggregate
2000	1.1	0.6	8.6
2001	−0.9	−10.4	12.9
2002	−1.9	8.5	6.6
2003	16.1	8.2	3.6
2004	12.3	3.9	6.3
2005	8.2	1.9	7.6
2006	10.4	15.7	10.6
2007	7.0	7.2	14.9
2008	−15.0	3.8	8.9
2009	13.7	−3.8	0.4
2010	10.4	−4.5	−3.1
2011	1.6	−0.9	3.2
2012	9.6	30.1	4.4
2013	10.5	7.0	4.0
– 2000 Q1 to 2013 Q3			
Average % annual change	5.9	4.8	6.4
Compound % annual change	5.4	4.7	6.3
– 2007 Q1 to 2013 Q3			
Average % annual change	5.4	5.6	4.7
Compound % annual change	4.8	5.6	4.5

Source: Federal Reserve flow-of-funds data and M3 until 2006, Shadow Government Statistics for M3 numbers after 2006.

of a "velocity of circulation") changed by just under 15 per cent (that is, at a compound annual rate of about a quarter of a per cent).[33]

The citing of numbers does not establish a definite causal link or prove a rigorous theory beyond contradiction.[34] But the data are surely suggestive. They argue that a better understanding of the Great Recession may be achieved if the figures are updated to the end of 2013. Table 1.1 shows the changes in the year to the fourth quarter in the quantity of money (as measured by M3), and the long-term savings institutions' total assets and money holdings, going back to 2000. On a year-by-year basis, these variables can diverge widely. However, over the medium term they are similar. The numbers could be construed as supporting two hypotheses, that:

- first, confidence (or "animal spirits") may be relevant to asset price determination over short-run periods of a few quarters, associated with noticeable changes in the ratio of savings institutions' money to total assets; but
- second, money dominates the determination of nominal asset prices in the medium and long runs, since over periods of several years or more, changes in the ratio of savings institutions' money to total assets are small compared to changes in the level of either institutions' total assets or their money holdings.

The wider implication of the evidence is that large fluctuations in the growth rate of aggregate money are likely to be accompanied by similarly large fluctuations in the growth rate of money held by the specialist fund management sector. With the fund management industry keeping the ratio of money to total assets fairly stable over the medium term, transactions between different institutional investors (as well as transactions by other investors) cause swings in the rate of money growth to be matched by comparable movements in asset prices.

While the USA's long-term savings institutions are key participants in the markets for quoted corporate equity and bonds, they are far less important as investors in residential real estate. A notorious feature of the years before and during the Great Recession was a pronounced boom and bust in house prices. Is it not a drawback of the present emphasis on the specialist fund management sector that it says little or nothing about the US housing market? The answer is that a capitalist economy has a range of mechanisms by which arbitrage between different asset markets prevents prices and yields in one asset class moving out of line with prices and yields in another. A rich individual can deploy his wealth in rented housing or in his own portfolio of common stocks or in a mutual fund or in a private equity vehicle, and he has constantly to compare their prospects. If an acceleration in aggregate money growth is accompanied in the first instance by massive inflows into the fund management industry and consequent buoyancy in quoted stocks, wealthholders notice the risk of an over-valued stock market. They may divert funds to the purchase of houses for rent or to a fund concentrating on foreign assets or to another vehicle involved in an entirely different asset class.

Milton Friedman and Anna Schwartz co-authored an article on 'Money and business cycles' in the *Review of Economics and Statistics* in 1963, at about the same time that their classic *A Monetary History of the United States* was published. After a survey of the facts about the cyclical behaviour of money from 1867 to 1960, they offered a "tentative sketch of the mechanism transmitting monetary changes" to the economy as a whole. In this sketch an unexpected rise in the rate of growth of the quantity of money was conjectured to disturb "an Elysian state of moving equilibrium, in which real income per capita, the stock of money and the price level" were "changing at the same constant annual rates". In the first round "holders of redundant balances" were seen as acquiring "fixed-interest coupon, low-risk obligations", bidding up their prices. Later money holders would "look further afield" to "higher-risk fixed-coupon obligations, equities, real property, and so forth". Over time the "initially redundant money balances" would "spread throughout the economy".

In understanding the actual pattern of events, Friedman and Schwartz noted that, "it is necessary to take a . . . broader view, to regard the relevant portfolios as containing a much wider range of assets, including not only government and private fixed-interest and equity securities, . . . but also a host of other assets, even going so far as to include consumer durable goods, consumer inventories of clothing and the like".[35] So the hot potato of excess money circulates from one asset market to another, and from asset markets to markets in goods and services. In short, arbitrage between apparently remote asset classes was a basic feature of Friedman and Schwartz's vision of "how the economy really works". In this vision – clearly different from that of Akerlof and Shiller in their 2009 book – asset markets were not an undignified playground for animal spirits. Instead asset prices were recognized as being potentially volatile both upwards and downwards, but still as being determined by explicit economic forces. Highly variable asset prices were seen as being subject to heavy influence from the quantity of that asset which is defined by the fixity of its nominal value, that is, from the quantity of money. (In Chapter 10 Laidler mentions the "tentative sketch" as an important intellectual associate of Friedman and Schwartz's *Monetary History*, and they were indeed published in the same year, 1963. See p. 23. In Chapter 8 Booth also discusses the role of money in asset price determination on pp. 190–94.)

In early 2006 the Federal Reserve stopped publishing data for the M3 aggregate, on the grounds that the costs of collecting the data for this concept of money were excessive relative to its usefulness in analysing the economy. In 2006 and early 2007 the rate of M3 growth accelerated markedly, so that by early 2008 the annual rate of increase had climbed to

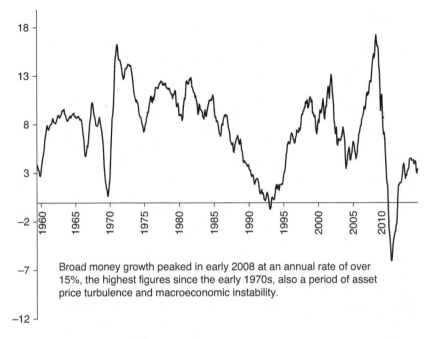

Broad money growth peaked in early 2008 at an annual rate of over 15%, the highest figures since the early 1970s, also a period of asset price turbulence and macroeconomic instability.

Source: For data sources, see text.

Figure 1.5   Money growth in the USA, 1960–2014 (% annual rate of change, in M3 aggregate, monthly data)

over 15 per cent. (See Figure 1.5. The M3 aggregate is chosen because the above account of the role of money in the economy emphasizes the need to rationalize the holding of money in portfolios. It is difficult to see how any aggregate smaller than an all-inclusive one could make sense in this setting. The author discussed the relative merits of different money aggregates in his 2011 book *Money in a Free Society.*[36] After the Federal Reserve ended the publication of M3, the research company, Shadow Government Statistics, began estimating M3 from publicly available information on its components. The series prepared by Shadow Government Statistics is used in this chapter. It can be cross-checked against the M3 numbers for the USA published by the International Monetary Fund, on data that are still supplied to the IMF by official US sources.)

The broad money growth rates of the 18 months to early 2008 were the highest since the early 1970s, as shown in Figure 1.5. The surge in money growth was accompanied by a proliferation of intermediation via financial organizations, which were quasi-banks or subsidiaries of bank holding companies. These were often highly leveraged in the fashion deplored by Greenspan and others, and relied on wholesale funding rather than retail deposits to finance their assets.[37] A similar efflorescence of financial inter-mediation was also found in the Eurozone and the UK, and again it was associated with fast growth of broad money and financial market excesses. On this view, the asset price excesses and demand buoyancy of 2006 and 2007 were due to too rapid growth of the quantity of money.[38]

Central banks, including the Federal Reserve in the USA, could and should have restrained that boom. They had this responsibility, even if private-sector financiers took many unwise decisions. Of course some banks were foolish to pursue expansionist strategies while the boom gathered pace. As later events showed, the collateral on their loans proved vulnerable in the downturn and a proportion of their loan portfolios became non-performing or worse. But the commercial banking system as a whole was robust. Sure enough, in 2008 and 2009 the hodgepodge of shadow banks and much of the investment banking industry were embarrassed by the collapse in US house prices and the losses in mortgage-backed securities. But only part of their liabilities was of a monetary nature.[39] If their operations are viewed as important because of feedbacks to the commercial banks as such and because commercial banks' deposits are part of the quantity of money, the troubles of the investment banks and the shadow banks do indeed need to be integrated in the story. However, a valid argument for not overplaying their role in the Great Recession is that their losses were for the most part visited on shareholders and bondhold-ers, not on the banks which had lent to them or (in the important case of the money market mutual funds) on the holders of the funds.

From a monetary perspective the banking industry received two major shocks in the key period of about 18 months from August 2007. The first shock was, as already noted, the freezing of inter-bank credit in August 2007. For some years many banks and quasi-banks, and in the USA the investment banks and shadow banks, had used the inter-bank market to fund asset expansion. The closure of the inter-bank market meant that these organizations would be unable to grow as rapidly as before, and that in turn implied a slowdown in money growth from the rates seen in the previous two years. Nevertheless, even in spring 2008 the slowdown in money growth was not exceptional by past standards in most countries and did not signal severe macroeconomic breakdown. (The UK was an exception and did experience a marked money deceleration, following the Northern Rock imbroglio. See pp. 170–73, in Chapter 7 below, for more on Northern Rock's problems.) The freezing of the global inter-bank market may have been due to mutual distrust within the banking industry, but central banks and regulators in the main economies ought to have known enough about banks' assets to recognize that the industry was solvent. The crisis arose because some banks (and investment banks and shadow banks) had difficulty in funding their assets; it was principally a crisis of illiquidity.

The second shock came in September and October 2008, in the weeks following the Lehman default. Arguably, the key event was on 10 October, when G7 finance ministers and central bank governors met in Washington. According to Bernanke in lectures on *The Federal Reserve and the Financial Crisis*, most such meetings are "a terrible bore because much of the work is done in advance by the staff". But on this occasion, the people present "tore up the agenda" and agreed "a statement of principles written from scratch, based on some Fed proposals". The aim was "to make sure that banks and other financial institutions had access to funding from central banks and capital from governments", and to organize international cooperation "to normalize credit markets".[40] Other meetings followed in the next few weeks, notably that of G20 heads of state on 14 November in Washington, with the key items on the agenda being mandatory increases in banks' capital and in their capital/asset ratios, and requirements that banks hold a higher proportion of liquid assets to total assets and reduce their dependence on wholesale funding. The emergency conditions were seen by many as justifying an exceptional response, with policy-makers entitled to override convention, precedent and the interests of banks' shareholders. On 21 November President Obama's chief of state, Rahm Emanuel, proclaimed at a *Wall Street Journal* press conference that, "You never let a serious crisis go to waste. And what I mean by that it's an opportunity to do things you think you could not do before." By early 2009 the Bank for International Settlements in Basel was well advanced in developing a new and drastically more stringent capital regime for the banking industry.

The accepted narrative is unequivocal. Officialdom and academe agreed, with hardly any exceptions, that extra bank capital was the answer to the crisis the banking industry had been facing since August 2007. However, from a monetary control standpoint, the demands for higher capital/asset ratios were disastrous. Bernanke's notion of capital coming "from governments" raised issues about shareholder property rights, contributing to marked weakness in bank share prices. Further, to the extent that banks were recapitalized from private sources, the result was to destroy bank deposits.[41] (An investor purchases new stock only by making a payment from a deposit. The claim on the banking system takes the non-monetary form of equity or bonds, instead of the monetary form of a deposit.) The increases in capital/asset ratios were also catastrophic in their immediate effects on both credit availability and the quantity of money. The collapse in banks' share prices reduced their access to capital markets. They were therefore unable to obtain the extra capital needed to sustain balance-sheet expansion. At best banks had to stop growing their assets. In many cases they took active steps to shrink balance sheets. They sold off securities and loan portfolios, and sometimes even called in loans. (If securities are sold to non-banks, non-banks must pay for them from deposits, which disappear from the economy. When a loan is repaid by cancelling a deposit, the effect is again to destroy money.)

In most of the leading advanced economies the rate of money growth, which had run at a double-digit annual rate in 2006 and 2007, crashed to negligible levels. In both the USA and the Eurozone the annual rates of change were for some months at zero or less. (See the Appendix for more detail.) The zero rate of money growth was bad enough, but money could have contracted – for the first time since the 1930s – if central banks had not engaged in expansionary asset purchase operations, including the "quantitative easing" schemes of the USA and the UK. Households were reluctant to cut back on their money holdings, perhaps for precautionary reasons.[42] The zero rate of aggregate money growth therefore led to severe cash strains for economies' other money holders, including many companies and financial institutions.[43] This squeeze on money balances was accompanied by drops in asset prices and by consequent adverse "wealth effects" on expenditure, as already remarked in the discussion of the relationship between money and asset prices. The processes at work recalled the "tentative sketch" advanced by Friedman and Schwartz in 1963, but they operated in reverse, as the quantity of money was being squeezed rather than expanded.

The narrative of events in the 2008–10 period was not identical to that in previous deep recessions, but obvious similarities suggested a common pattern of causation. For all their idiosyncrasies, data on the quantity of money go back decades and are amenable to rigorous statistical analysis. Indeed, a monetary interpretation of the Great Recession echoes in many of its features the monetary interpretation of the Great Depression advanced by Milton Friedman and Anna Schwartz in their celebrated 1963 volume *A Monetary History of the USA, 1867–1960*. For most of the 1920s the USA's money stock increased by about 5 per cent a year; between 1929 and 1933 it plummeted by almost 10 per cent a year and, over the whole four-year period, it fell by more than a third. The asset price tumbles in the Great Recession were less bad than in the Great Depression (when the US stock market dropped by over 90 per cent from peak to trough). Nevertheless, in both episodes a sharp change in the rate of increase in the quantity of money had damaging effects on the stock market and real estate. It should also be noted that the instability in money growth in the 2006–10 period was the most extreme since the early 1970s, which were also accompanied by macroeconomic upheaval, and large movements in asset prices and inflation rates.[44]

The monetary approach to the Great Recession not only interprets events from a theoretical standpoint at variance with the mainstream approach, but also allocates blame in different ways. In brief, the monetary interpretation

- sees bank illiquidity, not insolvency, as the main weakness of the financial system in the crisis period;
- it condemns officialdom for the drastic and hurried tightening of bank regulation from October 2008, as this tightening was the dominant influence on the collapse in money growth which in turn was responsible for the severity of the global downturn in the following two or three quarters; and
- it applauds central bank action to boost the quantity of money (usually termed "quantitative easing") from spring 2009, since without QE the regulatory tightening would have resulted in an even more vicious macroeconomic slump.

III

The standard and monetary interpretations of the Great Recession have the same cast of characters (central bankers, regulators, commercial bankers and so on) and same stage props (institutions like central banks and regulatory agencies). But the interpretations can be seen as rival whodunits, and they have different scripts and identify different culprits. In the standard interpretation the villains are bankers, because they ran – or are alleged to have run – their businesses irresponsibly in the run-up to the crisis, and so risked insolvency. In the monetary interpretation much of the blame instead attaches to central bankers and regulators, and in particular to those members of officialdom and the commentariat who urged rapid bank recapitalization in late 2008. According to the monetary school, the threat to the system then was illiquidity, not insolvency. Prompt, large-scale action both to fund the banking system (by means of central bank loans to commercial banks) and to boost the quantity of money was vital. Such action would have prevented the Great Recession. Banks should have been given time to recapitalize, so that money growth would decelerate only gradually from the highs of 2006 and 2007. Alternatively, bank recapitalization should have been accompanied immediately by QE-type operations to boost the quantity of money. It was the abrupt bank recapitalizations and step jumps in regulatory capital/asset ratios that caused the money growth collapse and macroeconomic trauma of early 2009.

The debate between the standard and monetary interpretations of the Great Recession is basic both to the future of the international financial system and to the proper definition of the state's role in a modern economy. So far the mainstream approach has been very much in the ascendant, with the Lo review article in the 2012 *Journal of Economic Literature* containing not a single reference to a monetary aggregate. More analysis and other reviews of the evidence will be needed before the debate is settled. This chapter, and those that follow, argue that the monetary interpretation has to be taken far more seriously than has been the case until now.

NOTES

*   This chapter is a modified version of the paper which first appeared in *World Economics* (June 2014) and is reproduced with permission.

1.   A book-length contribution from the monetary side of the debate is Robert Hetzel *The Great Recession: Market Failure or Policy Failure?* (Cambridge: Cambridge University Press, 2012).

2.   Andrew W. Lo 'Reading about the financial crisis: a twenty-one book review', *Journal of Economic Literature*, 2012, vol. 50, no. 1, pp. 151–78. The quotations are from p. 153 and p. 155.

3.   A virtually unanimous theme has been that the answer must include tighter financial regulation, as, for example, elaborated in Chapter 3 (pp. 57–120) of Joseph E. Stiglitz *The Stiglitz Report* (New York and London: The New Press, 2010).

4.   George A. Akerlof and Robert J. Shiller *Animal Spirits* (Princeton, NJ, USA and Oxford, UK: Princeton University Press, 2009), p. xi.

5.   Alan Greenspan *The Map and the Territory* (London: Allen Lane for Penguin Books, 2013), p. 53 and p. 71.

6.   Akerlof and Shiller *Animal Spirits*, p. 131.

7.   See, for example, pp. 120–27 of Johan Lybeck *A Global History of the Financial Crash of 2007–10* (Cambridge: Cambridge University Press, 2011) for a discussion of the effect of house prices and debt on overall household wealth.

8.   Debt, any kind of debt, is sometimes seen as morally repugnant. "Debt is a means of unfairly living high on the hog today only to pay a bigger bill tomorrow," while "When capitalism is unfair, we have financial crashes." The quotations are from p. 183 and p. 189 of Will Hutton 'The financial crisis and the end of the hunter-gatherer', pp. 182–9, in Rowan Williams and Larry Elliott (eds) *Crisis and Recovery: Ethics, Economics and Justice* (Basingstoke: Palgrave Macmillan, 2010).

9.   Greenspan *The Map and the Territory*, p. 115, on the investment banks.

10. See also Joseph E. Stiglitz *Freefall: Free Markets and the Sinking of the Global Economy* (London: Allen Lane for Penguin Books, 2010), p. 163, for his views on investment bank leverage. But Stiglitz often mentioned "excessive risk-taking" in the context of "banks" in general, inviting the interpretation that the commercial banks as well as the investment banks had over-geared their balance sheets.

11. Bernanke seems to have had second thoughts about the "special-ness" of banks in his speech on 'The financial accelerator and the credit channel' to a conference on the credit channel held by the Federal Reserve Bank of Atlanta on 15 June 2007, where he described the notion as "rather dated".

12. The key reference is R. Clarida, J. Gali and M. Gertler 'The science of monetary policy: a New Keynesian perspective', *Journal of Economic Literature*, 1999, vol. 37, no. 2,

pp. 1661–707. The neglect of banks in New Keynesianism has been widely noted and criticized. See, for example, Laidler's comments on pp. 247–8 below.

13. Paul Krugman 'Gordon Does Good', 12 October 2008, column in *New York Times*. According to Krugman, ". . . we do know . . . that Mr. Brown and Alistair Darling . . . have defined the character of the worldwide rescue effort, with other wealthy nations playing catch-up."

14. Alan S. Blinder *After the Music Stopped* (New York: The Penguin Press, 2013), p. 271.

15. Even authors usually regarded as supporters of free markets have attacked the financial system. See, for example, Kevin Down *Alchemists of Loss* (Chichester: John Wiley & Sons, 2010).

16. Akerlof and Shiller *Animal Spirits*, pp. 14–17.

17. Loan loss write-offs as a percentage of total assets were unusually adverse in the Great Recession, notably for residential mortgage loans, but they did not reach such high levels as to wipe out banks' operating profits. According to an analysis conducted by the Federal Reserve's research staff, the net interest income of the US commercial banking system in 2009 was 3.02 per cent of assets, and non-interest income 2.07 per cent of assets, both figures not that different from the immediately preceding years. Unhappily, loss provisions ran at 1.95 per cent of assets in 2009, up from only 0.27 per cent in 2006. But even in 2009, which was the worst year in the Great Recession, the US banking system as a whole had a positive return on equity. See 'Profits and balance sheet developments at US commercial banks in 2009', *Federal Reserve Bulletin* (Washington, DC: Federal Reserve), May 2010 issue, pp. A1–A37, and in particular p. A28 and p. A37 for the overall profitability of the system.

18. In 2009 and 2010 many banks had loan write-offs that were similar to operating profits, although their capital was intact or even rose because they raised new capital. See Lybeck *A Global History*, pp. 160–62.

19. "By the early 1980s many banks including the largest were recording capital ratios of 5 per cent or less." Brian Kettell and George Magnus *The International Debt Game* (London: Graham & Trotman, 1986), p. 9. The author discussed the debt crisis of the 1980s in a popular book, *The Debt Threat* (Oxford: Basil Blackwell, 1988). He noted the fragility of banks with a 3.6 per cent equity to assets ratio on p. 176 of *The Debt Threat*, as part of a wider review of "the leveraging of America".

20. A guide to the vulnerability of the whole system to losses in particular banks (i.e., because of a wide dispersion of profit and loss outcomes between industry players) is provided by the experience of the Federal Deposit Insurance Corporation. The FDIC did incur significant "losses", in the sense that it had to set out provisions for prospective shortfalls in banks' deposit liabilities, and these losses did cause the so-called "Fund Balance" (which is a notional figure, since reported losses may in the end not materialize) to be recorded as negative at the end of 2009 to the tune of almost $21 billion. However, in the three years to end-2012 over $10 billion of the provisions turned out to have been unnecessary, and the "Fund Balance" was back to a positive $33 billion by end-2012. (The information here is from FDIC annual reports reported on its website.) Note that the $21 billion negative figure in the end-2009 FDIC's Fund Balance was trivial compared with US commercial banks' total equity capital at the same time, which was over $1200 billion.

21. Sheila Bair *Bull by the Horns* (New York: Free Press, 2012), p. 159. The acknowledgement of the solvency of the system was followed by a complaint about the bias of top American policy-makers to protect the big banks rather than the small.

22. Bair *Bull by the Horns*, p. 358.

23. Note on 'Who is the FDIC?' updated on 18 January 2013 and available on FDIC website at 18 March 2014.

24. The Wikipedia entry on the savings and loans crisis is clear and sufficient. It mentions the 1996 General Accounting Office estimate that the total cost of the S&L clean-up was $160 billion, including $132.1 billion from taxpayers.

25. The Lehman losses did not fall on the US taxpayer, but on Lehman creditors. In April

2011 the FDIC published a report on 'The orderly liquidation of Lehman Brothers Holdings under the Dodd–Frank Act', claiming that powers granted to the FDIC by the Dodd–Frank Act would have led to a much higher recovery rate on Lehman liabilities than actually seen in practice. In the paper's view a more orderly procedure under FDIC oversight would have enabled "general unsecured creditors" to achieve 90 cents on every dollar of claims "compared with approximately 20 cents on claims estimated in the most recent bankruptcy plan". The report was available on the FDIC website under the 'Regulations & Examinations' button at end-March 2014.

26.   See George Akerlof 'The cat in the tree and further observations', pp. 317–20, in George Akerlof, Olivier Blanchard, David Romer and Joseph Stiglitz (eds) *What Have We Learned? Macroeconomic Policy after the Crisis* (Cambridge, MA, USA and London, UK: MIT Press, 2014). The quotation is from p. 319.

27.   John Maynard Keynes *The General Theory of Employment, Interest and Money*, vol. VII in Donald Moggridge and Elizabeth Johnson (eds) *Collected Writings of John Maynard Keynes* (London and Basingstoke: Macmillan, 1973, originally published 1936), pp. 84–5.

28.   This proposition is related to "the homogeneity postulate" that lies at the centre of monetary theory, as explained, for example, by Patinkin in *Money, Interest and Prices*. (See p. 175 of Don Patinkin *Money, Interest and Prices* (New York: Harper & Row, 2nd edition, 1965).)

29.   See Milton Friedman 'Statement on monetary theory and policy', given in Congressional hearings in 1959, reprinted in R.J. Ball and Peter Boyle (eds) *Inflation* (Harmondsworth: Penguin, 1969), pp. 136–45. The quotations are from p. 141.

30.   In the current policy literature the processes at work are frequently lumped under the "portfolio rebalancing channel". For an example in real-world policy-making, see Marvin Goodfriend 'Policy debates at the Federal Open Market Committee, 1993–2002', pp. 332–73, in Michael D. Bordo and William Roberds *The Origin, History, and Future of the Federal Reserve* (Cambridge: Cambridge University Press, 2013), particularly p. 364.

31.   In the UK the Bank of England has prepared data on the money holdings of the economy's main sectors (households, companies, financial institutions) since 1963. A clear research finding is that the household sector's money demand function is stable, according to the usual statistical tests. See, for example, Alec Chrystal and Leigh Drake 'Personal sector money demand in the UK', *Oxford Economic Papers* (Oxford: Oxford University Press), 1997, April issue, vol. 49, no. 2, pp. 188–206.

32.   An extreme case could be imagined in which equities are held only by specialist non-bank financial institutions, these institutions hold constant the ratio of money to total assets, and their money holdings grow at the same rate of the aggregate quantity of money. In this extreme case it is obvious that the rate of increase in share prices must be equal to the rate of increase in the aggregate quantity of money.

33.   Tim Congdon 'Broad money vs. narrow money: a discussion following the Federal Reserve's decision to discontinue publication of M3 data', London School of Economics' Financial Markets Group Special Paper Series, no. 166. An amended version of this paper appeared as essay 16, pp. 346–73, in Tim Congdon *Money in a Free Society* (New York: Encounter Books, 2011).

34.   Can the same kind of relationships as those discussed in the text also be found in other economies? The author considered the evidence for the UK in his 2005 study on *Money and Asset Prices in Boom and Bust* for the Institute of Economic Affairs. See Tim Congdon *Money and Asset Prices in Boom and Bust* (London: Institute of Economic Affairs, 2005) and also essay 15 in Congdon *Money in a Free Society*, which is a condensed version of the 2005 study.

35.   See Milton Friedman and Anna Schwartz 'Money and business cycles', pp. 189–235, in Milton Friedman *The Optimum Quantity of Money* (London and Basingstoke: Macmillan, 1969). The quotations are from pp. 229–31.

36.   See, particularly, essay 16 (pp. 346–73) in Tim Congdon *Money in a Free Society* (New York: Encounter Books, 2011).

37. One example of the over-leveraging was the Carlyle Capital Corporation, a highly geared bond fund conceived and marketed by the Carlyle Group, well-regarded specialists in private equity. Launched in November 2006, it borrowed more than 20 times its own equity in highly-rated mortgage paper. It went bust in March 2008. According to a story in the *Financial Times* of 30 November, 2009 (Henny Sender 'Leverage levels a fatal flaw in Carlyle fund'), "By the end of 2007, CCC had borrowed $21bn. At the end of the following February, in its annual letter to investors, John Stomber, CCC's chief investment officer referred to the fund's 'decisive action to reduce risk, enhance liquidity and preserve the value of shareholders' capital'. The fund's leverage, Mr Stomber noted, was 32 times greater than its equity."
38. Some sources mentioned the role of money in the cycle at an early stage. See Charles A.E. Goodhart *The Regulatory Response to the Financial Crisis* (Cheltenham, UK and Northampton, MA, USA: Edward Elgar Publishing, 2009), p. 10 and p. 52, drawing on papers written in 2008.
39. Money market mutual funds are part of M3. The fears in 2007 and 2008 that these products would "break the buck" (that is, fail to pay back 100 cents in the dollar) need to be mentioned in a monetary account of the crisis. In this respect it has to be conceded that the emphasis on the commercial banks in the present paper is incomplete.
40. Ben S. Bernanke *The Federal Reserve and the Financial Crisis* (Princeton, NJ: Princeton University Press, 2013), pp. 74–5.
41. See Jonathan Bridges, Neil Rossiter and Ryland Thomas 'Understanding the recent weakness in broad money growth', pp. 22–35, *Bank of England Quarterly Bulletin* (London: Bank of England), 2011 (Q1), vol. 51, no. 1. Note, particularly, the discussion on pp. 27–8.
42. If the money balances of one sector of the economy (such as the household sector) are stable, changes in the growth rate of aggregate money are necessarily accompanied by proportionately larger changes in growth rate of money held by other sectors (such as companies and financial institutions). The point was emphasized by the author in Chapter 2 of his study *Money and Asset Prices in Boom and Bust* (London: Institute of Economic Affairs, 2005), see particularly pp. 32–7.
43. As noted in note 31 above, UK data on the main sector's money holdings have been published since 1963. A recurrent feature of UK business cycles has been markedly higher volatility in the money holdings of financial institutions than of the household sector, as noted in the author's 2005 *Money and Asset Prices in Boom and Bust*. This was again seen in the Great Recession. In the 10 quarters to the final quarter of 2007 the average annual growth rate of money in the hands of financial institutions (excluding so-called "intermediate other financial corporations" or quasi-banks) was 16.6 per cent; in the 12 quarters to the final quarter of 2011 it was 0.5 per cent. (Data are from the Bank of England's interactive statistical database, using series mnemonic RPQB66Q, as at end-March 2014.)
44. The marked instability in money growth in both the early 1970s and the Great Recession was noted in Congdon *Money in a Free Society*, pp. 384–7.

APPENDIX: BROAD MONEY GROWTH TRENDS IN THE MAJOR ADVANCED COUNTRY JURISDICTIONS, 2000–2013

The purpose of this Appendix is to review the monetary experience of the major advanced country jurisdictions (the USA, the Eurozone, Japan and the UK) in the years before, during and after the Great Recession. The M3 broad money measure is used, except for the UK where the M4x measure is preferred. (The M4x measure excludes money held by so-called "intermediate other financial corporations", on the grounds that such balances are those of bank affiliates or semi-banks, and should be kept out of money estimates for the same reason that these exclude inter-bank deposits.)

The USA is covered first. The graph shows a fair degree of stability in money growth in the years before the financial excesses and boom of 2006 and 2007, and the subsequent macroeconomic trauma. In 2004 and 2005 the average annual growth of M3 was 5.5 per cent, with little variation. However, in 2006 a pronounced acceleration in money growth emerged. The 18 months to the first quarter of 2008 saw extremely fast expansion of bank deposits, although a proportion of the increase may have been due to re-intermediation of financial business from shadow banks and related institutions, particularly in late 2007. The peak in the three-month annualized growth rate of M3 was recorded in October 2007, coinciding with a stock market high. From early 2008 money growth collapsed, with the three-month annualized rate of change dropping to 3 per cent in November 2008 and going negative in late 2009. A fair comment is that US broad money did *not* lead the economy in the Great Recession period, since late 2009 was a period of stock market recovery and a strongly positive contribution to demand from the inventory cycle. However, the compound annual growth rate of M3 in the three years from September 2008 was only just positive, at 0.2 per cent, whereas in the three years to September 2008 it had been 12.6 per cent. The shrinkage of the American banking system was such that the quantity of money actually declined in the year to mid-2010, for the first time over a significant period since the 1930s. The USA was characterized by a boom–bust pattern in money growth in the Great Recession period, in association with the boom and bust in demand and output.

The message of the data for the Eurozone is clearer than that for the USA. M3 growth was again moderate in 2004, with an average annual growth rate of 5.8 per cent. The acceleration to double-digit annual growth rates started earlier than in the USA, with late 2005 and 2006 being characterized by extraordinarily high annual money growth rates (often into the twenties per cent) in some of the peripheral countries, such as Ireland. In

Sources: For sources, see text.

Figure 1A.1   *Growth of broad money (M3) in the USA 2000–2013 (monthly data, % changes)*

these nations very high money growth occurred in tandem with wild real estate booms. The three-month annualized rate of change of Eurozone M3 just touched the low teens in 2007, with a peak in November of 13.8 per cent. Figure 1A.2 shows the first marked deceleration from that rate, to a figure in the mid-single digits, by autumn 2008. The tightening of bank regulation was then announced in the closing months of 2008, bringing money growth to a halt. By late 2009 the annual rate of change went negative. The Eurozone therefore also underwent a marked and obvious boom–bust phenomenon in money growth, and it is relatively straightforward to relate that boom–bust phenomenon to other macroeconomic developments. The compound annual growth rate of M3 in the three years from September 2008 was a positive 0.3 per cent, whereas in the three years to September 2008 it had been 10.5 per cent.

The UK enjoyed monetary stability in a period of almost 15 years from its exit from the European exchange rate mechanism in 1992, with broad money growth typically somewhat above 5 per cent a year, which was consistent with steady growth in nominal GDP at about 5 per cent a year as agents were prepared to increase the ratio of their money holdings to income. However, in 2005 and particularly in 2006 money growth accelerated, with the three-month annualized growth rate topping out at 12.6 per cent in autumn 2006 (see Figure 1A.3). Strong gains in house prices and the stock market accompanied the high money growth. The Northern Rock affair from September 2007 led to a deceleration in money growth, earlier than in other countries. In the third quarter of 2008 the banking system had virtually stopped growing, with the three-month annualized rate of increase in M4x down to 2.6 per cent. The tightening of bank regulation in late 2008 was followed by a further slowdown and in early 2010

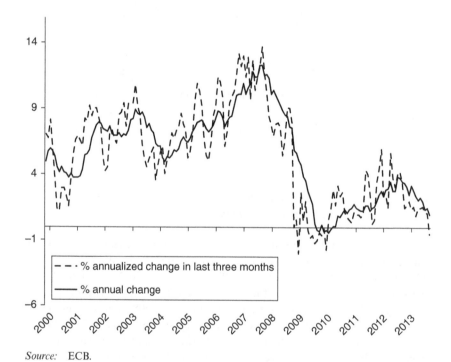

Source: ECB.

Figure 1A.2   Growth of broad money (M3) in the Eurozone 2000–2013 (monthly data, % changes)

the annual increase in M4x was a mere 1 per cent. The compound annual growth rate of M3 in the three years from the first quarter of 2008 was 1.1 per cent, whereas in the three preceding years it had been 9.1 per cent.

The USA, the Eurozone and the UK had different macroeconomic trajectories in the Great Recession, and in the years immediately before and afterwards. Nevertheless, in every case broad money growth was at or near double-digit annual rates in the three years before the banking system began to retrench, and close to zero in the following three years. As noted in the opening paragraph of the main text, Japan does not fit this pattern. It had very weak money growth in the years leading up to the Great Recession, with a trough in 2006 (see Figure 1A.4). Money growth recovered from 2009, to be typically about 2 or 3 per cent a year. Japan nevertheless suffered severely in the Great Recession, with a decline in GDP in 2009 of over 5 per cent. The main factor here was a slump of about a quarter in the volume of exports of goods and services (offset by a fall of 15 per cent

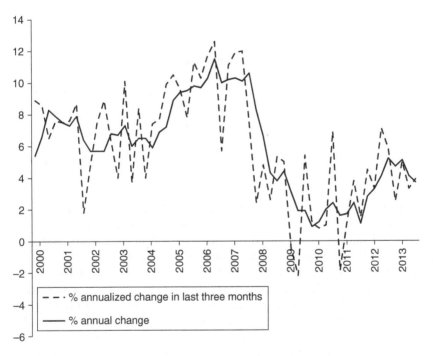

Source: Bank of England.

Figure 1A.3 Growth of broad money (M4x) in the UK 2000–2013 (quarterly data, % changes)

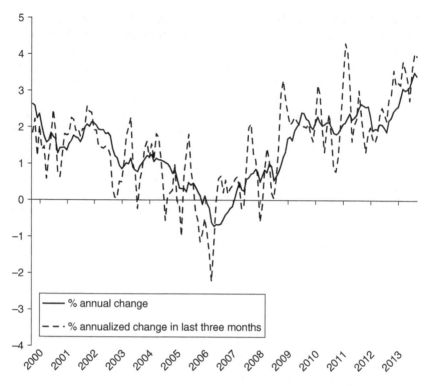

Source: Federal Reserve, using Bank of Japan data.

Figure 1A.4   *Growth of broad money (M3) in Japan 2000–2013 (monthly,
             % changes)*

in imports), which can be interpreted as partly caused by an abrupt real
exchange appreciation in late 2008 and early 2009. The rise in the yen
reflected the closing of so-called "carry trades" in the foreign exchange
markets. In the years up to late 2008 short-term interest rates in other
advanced countries had been well above those in Japan, enabling foreign
exchange market participants to capture a favourable interest rate differen-
tial by shorting the yen. The tightening of bank regulation from October
2008 was such a severe deflationary shock that it had to be countered by
interest rate reductions, to a virtually zero rate, in the USA, the Eurozone
and the UK. The carry trades were closed, the yen soared against other
currencies, and Japanese exports suffered from a lack of competitiveness
as well as a collapse in demand due to the Great Recession.

2. The debate over "quantitative easing" in the UK's Great Recession and afterwards

Tim Congdon

Commentary on monetary policy in the UK's Great Recession was more than usually confused. Views about "quantitative easing" in particular were jumbled and all over the place. At one extreme, Liam Halligan in his *Sunday Telegraph* column compared QE to "money printing in banana republics", "Zimbabwe-style economics" and "grotesque policy vandalism".[1] The reference to Zimbabwe implied that QE might lead to hyperinflation and hence that QE must be an extraordinarily powerful weapon in the monetary policy armoury. On the other hand, Martin Wolf, chief economics commentator of the *Financial Times*, repeatedly doubted the effectiveness of monetary policy in general and QE more specifically.[2] Wolf did not see his position as heretical, since a world-renowned monetary theoretician, Michael Woodford of Columbia University, had authored a 2011 op-ed piece in the *Financial Times* asserting that the economic rationale for QE "has always been flimsy".[3] Almost two years after Woodford's comment appeared, another contributor to the *Financial Times* still seemed perplexed. The journalist, Jonathan Davis, claimed that assessing the effects of ending QE "is ultimately a matter of subjective judgment, not a simple binary decision that can be derived from objective analysis of data".[4]

The author organized a joint letter to the *Financial Times* in 2011 to disagree with Woodford and wrote another one in his own name in July 2013 to rebut the Jonathan Davis article.[5] (He conducted an exchange with Halligan separately, in *The Sunday Telegraph* on 15 February 2014. By then it was obvious that QE, on the scale implemented, had not led – and would not lead – to hyperinflation.[6]) This chapter elucidates in more detail both the data relating to the UK's QE operations and the bearing of these operations on the UK's macroeconomic situation. Its main purpose is to establish more rigorously the counter-factual claim in the 2013 letter that, without the QE operations from March 2009, the UK's quantity of money would have been "hundreds of billions of pounds" lower than was in fact the case.

What about the wider macroeconomic significance of the QE exercises? As long as one accepts the standard account of the monetary determination of national income, the relationship between QE and nominal national income is straightforward in essentials. The long-run similarity of the rates of increase in the broadly defined quantity of money and nominal national income is clear in virtually all nations. Suppose the validity of the counter-factual claim is demonstrated in this chapter. Suppose, in other words, that without QE the quantity of money in the UK in mid-2013 would have been "hundreds of billions of pounds" – indeed about 20 to 25 per cent – lower than it was in reality. The point of the argument then becomes simple. With the quantity of money 20 to 25 per cent less, the equilibrium levels of national income and wealth in nominal terms would also have been 20 to 25 per cent less, roughly speaking. QE prevented the Great Recession becoming a second Great Depression.

I

How did QE work in practice? How indeed does it work in theory? The initial impact of *quantitative* easing, as understood in the UK public debate, is to increase the *quantity* of money.[7] So QE matters to macro-economic outcomes in the same way that any increase in the quantity of money would matter to them. The discussion of QE's effectiveness is therefore subordinate to the monetary theory of national income determination. According to standard theory, the equilibrium level of national income in nominal terms is determined by the interaction between the demand to hold money balances and the quantity of money created by the banking system. As noted elsewhere in this volume, the proposition was elaborated by Keynes at the end of Chapter 7 of *The General Theory* and is routine in macroeconomics textbooks.[8]

To expand the argument, some words are needed on the phrase "the demand for money", where its meaning is "the demand to hold money balances". (A recurrent confusion is that "the demand for money" con-notes "the demand for bank credit". Let it merely be stated in the main text here that the phrase connotes nothing of the sort. A discussion in the following note is more detailed.[9]) Non-bank private sector agents have a money demand function, with their demand to hold money depending on the level of income (and/or wealth), the attractiveness of money relative to other assets and other variables. (They have a money demand function, just as they have demand functions for Weetabix, red socks and holidays in

Spain, and – as with these demand functions – the variables that determine the quantity demanded are relative price, income and other variables.) With the quantity of money given, and with the non-income variables in the demand function also set at particular values, the money demand function implies that only one level of nominal national income is consistent with macroeconomic equilibrium. In that sense the quantity of money determines nominal national income.

Further, if (quite a big "if" in practice) the non-income variables in the money demand function are stable over time, theory says that changes in the quantity of money and *equilibrium* national income are equi-proportional. In the real world changes in the quantity of money usually differ from changes in nominal national income in short-run periods of a few quarters or even two or three years. The differences are largely due to agents' difficulties in matching the demand to hold money with the actual quantity of money in existence. In other words, over extended periods agents suffer from "monetary *disequilibrium*".[10] Nevertheless, in nearly all countries over the long run the differences between the annual rates of change of money and national income are small compared with the cumulative changes in both money and national income.

What is being claimed implicitly in the last paragraph? Suppose that, over a period of (say) ten years, policy-makers deliberately cause the quantity of money to rise by 100 per cent more than would otherwise have been the case. Then nominal national income will also rise – roughly – by 100 per cent more than would otherwise have been the case. That is the point of the quantity theory of money. It follows that policy actions influencing the quantity of money are hugely important to macroeconomic outcomes.

The discussion can return to QE. The state can always create money by borrowing from the banking system, and using the proceeds either to finance a budget deficit (that is, the purchase of goods and services from the non-bank private sector) or the purchase of assets from the non-bank private sector. Of course, the payment for the goods and services, or the assets, is in money. So the quantity of money held by the non-bank private sector rises pound for pound, dollar for dollar, euro for euro, or whatever, by the value of the goods purchased by or assets sold to the state. QE is to be understood as the purchase of assets, by the state (either the government or the central bank) from the non-bank private sector, to increase the quantity of money. Suppose that we are talking about the UK, and that QE amounts to £250 billion and the quantity of money at the start of the process is £1000 billion. Then – in a simplified account focusing only on the impact, first-round effect – QE by itself *causes* the quantity of money to rise by 25 per cent. Given the equi-proportionality of changes in the quantity of money and nominal national income just discussed, which admittedly holds only over the long run and "in equilibrium", the increase in the quantity of money also *causes* nominal national income to be 25 per cent higher than it would otherwise be.[11] In other words, in the situation discussed, QE of £250 billion has the result of boosting equilibrium nominal national income by 25 per cent.

II

QE – the large-scale creation of money by the state – is the equivalent in monetary policy of nuclear weaponry in national defence or foreign affairs. Despite its megaton capacity, academic discussion and public debate about QE – in the UK and elsewhere – have been plagued by misunderstandings. Two such misunderstandings received some comment in the Introduction, but need further mention here. The first is confusion about the relevant measure of "the quantity of money", and the second relates to a widespread inability to see exactly how changes in this relevant "quantity of money" affect expenditure and hence alter equilibrium national income.

On the first question, the relevant measure is taken to be one that is broadly defined to include time deposits and wholesale deposits, and is held only by genuine non-bank private sector agents. It is not to include balances held by the government and its affiliates, or by banks and quasi-banks.[12] In the UK context this measure can be equated with M4x, as calculated nowadays on a regular basis by the Bank of England.[13] The M4x aggregate, like all broad money aggregates, is dominated by bank deposits. Indeed, it is not going too far to regard "the quantity of money" and "the quantity of bank deposits" as more or less synonymous in today's world. An awkward and tiresome issue is that in the UK during the period under review banks had subsidiaries ("conduits", also known as "intermediate other financial corporations" or IOFCs) that were on the border line between quasi-banks and non-banks. They were allowed inside the old M4 definition, but were excluded – correctly, in the author's opinion – from M4x. The matter is discussed further at the end of the third section.

Some economists think that the key aggregate in monetary economics is the monetary base by itself.[14] This is just wrong. In the UK QE was very large relative to the level of the monetary base in early 2009. Indeed, the monetary base rose by more than five times between the start of 2009 and mid-2013. The five-fold surge in the base provided the rationale – or rather the bogus rationale – for Liam Halligan's forecasts in *The Sunday Telegraph* that QE would provoke a dramatic leap in inflation and eventually culminate in a Zimbabwe-style currency debasement. Such forecasts – and the "theory" behind them – have been invalidated by events.[15]

Secondly, many people are baffled about how a large increase or decrease in the quantity of bank deposits can affect anything in the economy.[16] At a 2014 press conference shortly before standing down from the chairmanship of the Federal Reserve, Ben Bernanke remarked that "QE works in practice, but doesn't work in theory". This may have been intended as a wisecrack, but it resonated in the world's media and even in some university economics departments as if it were a serious remark. In fact, the processes that connect money and expenditure have figured prominently in the history of economic thought.[17] Despite Bernanke's sneer, they have been discussed countless times by many undoubtedly well-reputed authorities in a large body of literature.

One of the best accounts is to be found in Keynes's 1930 *A Treatise on Money*, which differentiates between transactions in "the industrial circulation" (roughly speaking, those in the income–expenditure–output circular flow) and "the financial circulation" (which can be interpreted as transactions in titles to existing assets).[18] As Keynes realized almost 90 years ago, the value of total transactions in an advanced economy is vast, being a multiple both of national income and of transactions involving the extension of new bank credit.[19] Given the insignificance of new bank credit relative to the value of transactions, the fame accorded to Bernanke because of his allegedly important research on the "credit channel" must be seen as an aspect of wider bewilderment about these topics.[20]

Two paragraphs can quickly arrive at the heart of the matter. (See also the author's discussion of the hot potato argument on pp. 38–9 in Chapter 1.) With their money demand functions defined, and with the non-income arguments in the money demand function given, agents have one and only one desired ratio of their money holdings to income. (With tastes and relative prices given, people have one and only one desired ratio of expenditure on Weetabix, red socks and holidays in Spain to their income.) Suppose that – for whatever reason – the actual money holdings of *all* agents (that is, the aggregate quantity of money) are above this level. They therefore *all* want to reduce the ratio of money to income. What happens?

Suppose that one agent spends above income in order to send the excess money elsewhere. That boosts expenditure, but it does not rid the economy as a whole of the excess money, because the money is credited to another agent. This other agent may also try to unload the excess money by spending above income, but the money again stays in the economy, now in yet another bank account. The condition of an excess *supply* of money is associated therefore with an excess *demand* for commodities. The desired ratio of money to income is restored when this excess demand has raised the price of commodities by enough to eliminate the excess money holdings. Given the stability of the money demand function, and the assumption of certain unchanged values of the non-income arguments in that function, the rise in the price level of commodities has to be equi-proportional with the rise in the quantity of money (that is, of bank deposits). The value of the transactions involved in the adjustment processes, which include transactions in existing assets, is a high multiple of national income and expenditure, as the notions of "national income and expenditure" are understood in the Keynesian textbooks.

Let it be repeated that the argument of the last two paragraphs – which puzzles many people, including apparently a much-admired Fed chairman – has been developed by many other economists, beginning with David Hume and Richard Cantillon in the eighteenth century, running via Leon Walras and Knut Wicksell in the nineteenth century, and then through Alfred Marshall, Irving Fisher, Arthur Pigou, John Maynard Keynes, Don Patinkin and Milton Friedman in the twentieth. One point must be hammered home time and again. In the two-paragraph cameo just given, the tendency of agents to spend above income arises solely because of the divergence between their actual and desired money holdings. Equilibrium is restored when agents' actual and desired money holdings are the same. (That is that, finish, full stop, end of story. This is the proposition many people find strange. It is basic.[21])

For clarity, the tendency of agents to "spend more" and unload excess money has nothing necessarily to do with any of the following:

- "the rate of interest", whether that is to be understood as the money market rate, the corporate cost of capital or the government long bond yield;[22] or
- the quantity of new bank credit to the private sector;[23] or
- "credit availability", or
- the spreads charged by banks on loans to the private sector.[24]

Of course, movements in "the rate of interest" (whatever this deeply ambiguous notion means), new bank credit (which is relevant to money creation) and credit spreads (also relevant to the pace of money creation) are relevant to macroeconomic trajectories. But the movements of these variables, and their impact on demand, output and so on, are conceptually distinct from the actions of people, companies and financial institutions when they equilibrate (or try to equilibrate) the demand to hold money with the quantity of money created by the banking system.

None of "the rate of interest", bank lending and credit spreads is directly pertinent to the transmission mechanism from money to the economy, as this mechanism is understood in the present chapter, and in a voluminous and classic body of literature.[25] Far too many supposed authorities think that the purpose of QE was "'to reduce interest rates", "to boost bank credit" or "to narrow credit spreads", as if bank lending to the private sector were the whole story. At its simplest, the purpose of QE was to raise the quantity of money and thereby the equilibrium level of nominal national income. The key motivating force in the transmission mechanism was the equilibration of agents' actual and desired ratios of money to income, after a positive exogenous shock had been delivered to the quantity of money.

The pervasiveness of agents' attempts to establish that equilibrium is fundamental to understanding the centrality of the banking system to economic analysis and policy-making. The centrality of the banking system arises above all because the bulk of its liabilities are money. The composition of its assets, and even large shifts in asset composition, may be of considerable interest and importance to other topics, but they are secondary issues in the determination of national income and wealth.[26] The relationship between the quantity of money and nominal national income holds in a situation where money is a commodity (so no bank credit to the private sector exists by definition), or where banks' assets consist totally of either cash and government securities, or cash and so-called "seasoned" securities issued by the private sector.[27]

III

In late 2008, in the weeks following the Lehman crisis, macroeconomic and regulatory officialdom in the principal economies decided that banks must be made safe. The people involved were in such a tizzy that they resolved that "the tidying-up of bank balance sheets" – and especially a major recapitalization of the banking system – had to be done once and for all, definitely and quickly.[28] They repeated to themselves the mantra that they should "never let a serious crisis go to waste".[29] (The phrase, "the principal economies", means here the G20, more or less. It seems that the discussions, held in English, were driven by the USA and the UK. In terms of individuals and at the intellectual level, they were piloted by Ben Bernanke and Mervyn King.)[30]

Banks across the advanced world were therefore required to shrink their risk assets and to raise more capital. The effect of the official injunctions was:

- to make the banks sell off non-core assets, such as securities, to non-banks;

- to oblige the banks to stop new bank lending (which would increases risk assets) and to pull in low-quality loans (even if normally banks are very reluctant to do this, except as a last resort); and
- to issue securities (both new equity capital and bonds) to investors.

All three courses of action led to a fall in the level of bank deposits relative to what would otherwise have happened. They all caused the destruction of money balances.

The mechanics of money creation and destruction are critical to the analyses in this volume, and are discussed in other chapters. At the risk of repetition, some amplification is needed now. When a bank sells anything to a non-bank, the non-bank pays for it by a deduction from his/her bank deposit, which then falls; when a bank loan is repaid, a money balance in a deposit is used to cancel the loan, and both the loan and the deposit disappear from the bank's balance sheet and the economy; and, when someone subscribes for a new issue of securities by a bank, the investor's bank deposit falls by the value of the newly issued securities that are being bought. In short, in late 2008 and early 2009 compliance with the official injunctions implied contraction of banks' assets and the quantity of money.

Over the five years from autumn 2008 banks in the advanced countries tried hard to meet the new, much tighter regulatory standards. The result was that money growth was negligible or very low in all the countries involved, and so was the rate of increase in nominal GDP. That may sound worrying or even bizarre, given that the G20 meetings in late 2008 were concerned to combat the threat of global recession. Indeed, the statement just made – that officialdom caused a collapse in money growth by its regulatory squeeze – may astonish readers who regard officialdom as blameless and the bankers as "banksters". But the statement is pivotal to the argument of this chapter and as a preliminary to understanding why QE was imperative in early 2009.

The Italian economist, Rainer Masera, has pointed out that "a fallacy of composition" may have been at work in official thinking. It is of course true that, when a particular bank boosts its capital and liquid assets relative to its competitors in the same economy, that particular bank is stronger in relative terms and more resilient to shocks. The result is benign in that sense. But, if all the banks in an economy try to boost capital and liquidity as a proportion of assets, and if they do so by cutting assets, the result is a credit crunch that may be totally inappropriate in a depressed macroeconomic conjuncture. The raising of banks' capital/asset ratios, as one item in an agenda of so-called "macro-prudential regulation", can be mishandled. To quote Masera's words, it can culminate in "a negative perverse loop" where "economic activity falls with a further deterioration in the credit quality of banks' portfolios".[31] Masera did not refer to the quantity of money, but – of course – if banks' assets fall, in practice their deposit liabilities are likely to fall too.

How much did bank lending weaken after 2008? As far as the UK is concerned, the relative significance of different influences on changes in the quantity of money can be identified from official data on the so-called "credit counterparts" to broad money growth. The information in the next section relates to the M4 aggregate in the UK, even though – as was remarked earlier – M4x is the right aggregate in the context.[32] M4 was appreciably larger (by about a third in the Great Recession years) than M4x, because it included money balances held by so-called "inter-mediate other financial corporations", which are not genuine non-banks. Figure 2.1 shows the levels of M4 and M4x since 1998. The concluding section will suggest that the credit counterparts for M4 provide a suffi-ciently reliable guide to the situation, despite the differences between M4 and M4x.

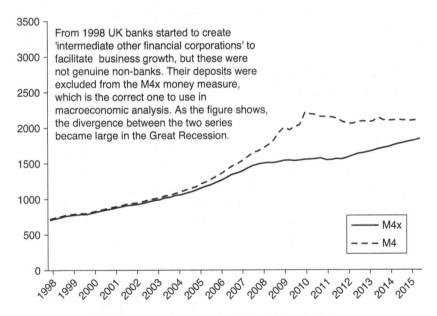

From 1998 UK banks started to create 'intermediate other financial corporations' to facilitate business growth, but these were not genuine non-banks. Their deposits were excluded from the M4x money measure, which is the correct one to use in macroeconomic analysis. As the figure shows, the divergence between the two series became large in the Great Recession.

Figure 2.1   The divergence between the UK's M4 and M4x money measures (levels of M4 and M4x, in £ billions, quarterly data from the Bank of England)

IV

The majority of banks exist in order to generate profits for their share-holders. They grow their balance sheets by adding assets on one side of the balance sheet and financing these assets by incurring liabilities on the other side. The profits come of course from charging a higher interest rate on the assets than is paid on the liabilities, as well as levying fees for arranging loans and providing other services. Liabilities are dominated by deposits, but they are not exclusively deposits. It follows that:

> The growth of deposits = the growth of banks' assets minus the increase in non-deposit liabilities.

Non-deposit liabilities are mostly banks' capital, notably the equity capital which belongs to the shareholders, but also include bond liabilities. Assets can be claims on the domestic public sector ("the state"), the domestic private sector and the external sector. So the growth of deposits can be seen as reflecting changes in banks' claims on the three sectors minus the increase in non-deposit liabilities.

The bar chart in Figure 2.2 shows the size of these influences on M4 in the five years to mid-2008 (that is, the five years before the radical upheaval in bank regulation which followed the Lehman crisis). Figure 2.3 shows the same set of numbers, but for the five years after mid-2008 (that is, as banks responded to the regulatory onslaught on their businesses). A comparison of the two charts shows the radical difference between the two periods. In the first five-year period banks were expanding their loan portfolios aggressively, with total new claims on the private sector increasing by almost £1000 billion.[33] The growth of bank lending *exceeded* the growth in the quantity of money, which was a bit more than £700 billion. The main factor explaining this gap was that banks had to increase their capital, evidenced in the £186 billion increase in their non-deposit liabilities. (Note that this is a *deduction* from M4, with a bar in Figure 2.2 that is negative and lies beneath the zero line.) Meanwhile the public sector contribution to money growth was small, but negative. From 1985 to 2009 UK official policy was to "fully fund" the budget deficit, so that public sector transactions had little effect on the quantity of money.[34] In this five-year period such transactions reduced M4 by £38 billion, a minor influence on the overall picture.

In the second five-year period the M4 quantity of money continued to expand, but at an annual rate of less than a third that in the previous five years. Although the growth of bank balance sheets was therefore much slower than before, the banks had to raise more capital because of the

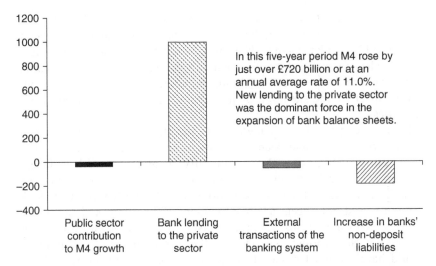

Figure 2.2   *Influences on the growth of money in the five years to mid-2008 (bars are of credit counterparts to cumulative change in M4 over five years to mid-2008, in £ billions)*

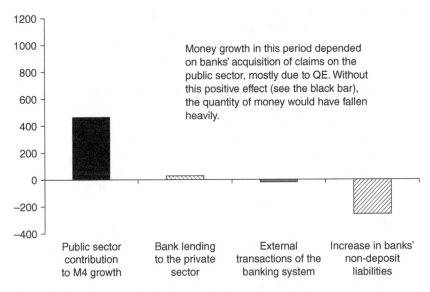

Figure 2.3   *Influences on the growth of money in the five years to mid-2013 (bars are of credit counterparts to cumulative change in M4 over five years to mid-2013, in £ billions)*

regulators' demands. In this five-year period non-deposit liabilities went up by over £257 billion. From late 2008 official disapproval of the amount of risk in UK banks' balance sheets was a major worry for their managements. They virtually stopped expanding claims on the private sector, which went up by a mere £29 billion. (Some new lending was made, but it was offset by the shedding of low-quality loans and so-called "toxic securities".)

Here we come to the key message. If the effect of the public sector's transactions on M4 had been the same in the five years to mid-2013 as in the previous five years, the M4 quantity of money would have fallen. Indeed, it would have fallen substantially, by hundreds of billions of pounds. The sum of the increase in non-deposit liabilities and new bank lending would have been negative by about £200 billion and the public sector's own transactions would have taken the figure down by a further £38 billion. Sure enough, a squeeze of the sort implied by these numbers would have attracted money balances to come in from the rest of the world. So M4 might not in the end have dropped by the full £200 to £250 billion indicated by the analysis.[35] But there would have been a big drop, all the same. Whereas M4 money growth in the five years to mid-2008 was 11 per cent a year, it would probably have been negative in the five years to mid-2013.

Happily, a major policy change occurred in early 2009, with the announcement of QE. The nuclear weaponry of macroeconomic policy was activated. The public sector's transactions were a large positive shock to the quantity of money, as the Bank of England bought gilt-edged securities (particularly medium- and long-dated gilt-edged securities) from the private sector, including private sector non-banks. According to the statistics, the public sector's transactions added £463 billion to M4 in the five years to mid-2013. The number is somewhat higher than the outstanding QE stock, officially put at £375 billion, but "in the same ballpark".[36]

A reasonable conclusion from the data is that the de-risking of bank balance sheets (the shedding of risk assets and the raising of large amounts of capital) from autumn 2008 cut the quantity of money drastically. If an offsetting force of some kind had not been at work, if the monetary megatons from QE had not been delivered, the fall would have been in the hundreds of billions of pounds. Although no one knows exactly the size of the fall that would have occurred in the counterfactual (that is, with no QE), a plausible initial hypothesis is that QE and related operations added more than £400 billion to M4 in the five years to mid-2013. So without QE and those operations M4 in mid-2013 would be about £400 billion lower than it actually was. As M4 was just under £2100 billion at June 2013, it would instead have been about £1700 billion. M4 in mid-2008 was about £2000 billion. The implied result is that, without QE, M4 would have declined by perhaps 10 to 15 per cent from its mid-2008 level instead of rising by about 5 per cent.

V

Let it be conceded that the use of credit counterpart data relating to M4, instead of to M4x, is imperfect. But analysts have to cope with official statistics as they are, and not as they might be in an imaginary utopia. For all the problems, enough information is in the public domain to be confident that credit counterpart analysis for M4x would yield much the same conclusion as that just drawn for M4. Helpfully and vitally, the Bank of England publishes figures for bank lending to the non-bank private sector excluding the irritating "intermediate other financial corporations".

The data for this aggregate, termed M4Lx for short, confirm that such lending was extremely weak – indeed negligible – after the regulatory tightening in late 2008. (Compare Figures 2.4 and 2.5.) In the five years to the third quarter 2008 M4Lx lending was cumulatively £924.1 billion;

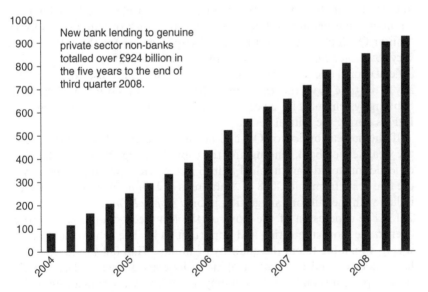

*Figure 2.4   Cumulative change in stock of M4x lending, in five years from
Q3 2003, in £ billions (bars are of change from Q3 2003 to
quarter shown in M4Lx in £ billions)*

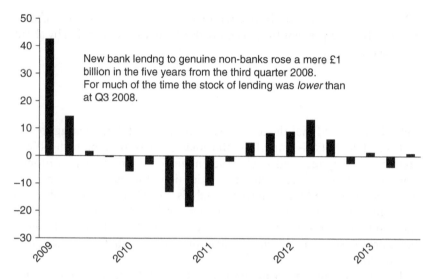

New bank lendng to genuine non-banks rose a mere £1 billion in the five years from the third quarter 2008. For much of the time the stock of lending was *lower* than at Q3 2008.

Figure 2.5   *Cumulative change in stock of M4x lending, in five years from Q3 2008, in £ billions (bars are of change from Q3 2008 to quarter shown in M4Lx in £ billions)*

in the five years from Q3 2008 M4 it was cumulatively a mere £0.9 billion. (In many quarters in that five-year period the stock of lending was lower than at Q3 2008.) Further, the capital requirements for the IOFCs were very low, since managements structured them with the aim of bypassing official capital adequacy rules. As the IOFCs are being closed down gradually at the time of writing (September 2016), the capital-raising of the main banking system must have been similar to that of the main system plus the IOFCs during the critical period.

If the nuclear option of QE had not been exercised from March 2009, the weakness of bank lending and the capital-raising efforts mandated by officialdom would have implied a drop in the UK's quantity of money in the five years from mid-2008 of "hundreds of billions of pounds". That is in line with the author's suggestion in his *Financial Times* letter of 22 July 2013. The conclusion of the work on the M4 credit counterparts carries over to the more interesting and important M4x. The achievement of QE was to stop a big fall in the quantity of money. That fall would otherwise have occurred and been catastrophic in its consequences.[37] The disinflationary pressures on the UK economy in the five years from autumn 2008 were harsh and unwelcome; they would have been even more ferocious if QE had not been implemented. Halligan's accusation in summer 2009 of "grotesque policy vandalism" was totally misguided, as were numerous other verbal bombardments against QE in the media. Contrary to the July 2013 article by Jonathan Davis, the information available allows rigorous and quantitative analysis that is every bit as objective as most work in macroeconomics.

But the successful implementation of QE does not justify any applause for the Bank of England. The Great Recession of late 2008 and early 2009 could have been avoided if central bankers and regulatory officialdom – including the top people at the Bank of England – had had a sufficient grasp of the pertinent areas of monetary economics. Key individuals with immense policy-making power, notably Ben Bernanke and Mervyn King, seem not to have recognized in late 2008 the likely adverse impact of the tightening of bank regulation on the growth of the quantity of money. In early 1936, just as his *General Theory* was about to be published, Keynes wrote in a letter to *The Times*, "no question is more important than the principles on which the Bank of England and the Treasury should fix the quantity of bank money. It has not been discussed lately as much as it deserves to be."[38] Over 80 years later that stricture remains applicable.

NOTES

1. Liam Halligan 'QE just acting as a sugar rush for insolvent banks that deserve to fail', *Sunday Telegraph*, 4 July 2009.
2. As late as October 2014, one of his columns ('Monetary policy: an unconventional tool', *Financial Times*, 5 October 2014) raised "questions about whether [QE] has worked". See also Dan Conaghan *The Bank: Inside the Bank of England* (London: Biteback Publishing, 2012), pp. 227–8 for a wider scepticism about monetary policy.
3. Michael Woodford 'Bernanke should clarify and sink QE3', *Financial Times*, 2 August 2011.
4. Jonathan Davis 'The art and artifice of Fed-watching', 15 July 2011.
5. The joint letter ('Theories look flimsy if they are misunderstood', *Financial Times*, 1 September 2011) carried the signatures of Jamie Dannhauser, Michael Oliver and Gordon Pepper. Oliver and Pepper are discussed below in Chapter 8, pp. 193–4. The other letter – which in fact related to American monetary policy – was Tim Congdon 'Quantitative easing in the USA was both desirable and necessary', *Financial Times*, 22 July 2013.
6. Tim Congdon and Liam Halligan 'The debate: is there an inflation bubble?', an exchange in *The Sunday Telegraph*, 15 February 2014.
7. The definition of QE is beset by ambiguity, inconsistency and muddle. For present purposes QE is understood to consist of operations by the state (either the central bank or the government) to purchase assets from genuine private sector non-banks with funds borrowed from the commercial banking system. Such operations boost the monetary base when conducted by the central bank, which credits sums to commercial banks' cash reserves with it. However, if the government makes the asset purchases, no effect on the base occurs. The important effect for the macroeconomic outlook is the increases in money held by private sector non-banks, that is, the quantity of money broadly defined. The subject is covered in Chapter 4 of Tim Congdon *Money in a Free Society* (New York: Encounter Books, 2011). The phrase "quantitative easing" was first

used by Richard Werner in commentary on Japanese monetary policy in the mid-1990s, notably in the title of an article in *Nihon Keizai Shimbun* on 2 September 1995. Werner used the phrase to refer to central bank operations to boost the monetary base in order to stimulate bank lending. It is clear from his work that he was interested in the effect on bank lending, not on the quantity of money. It is also clear that the Bank of England's QE exercise from March 2009 was intended to increase the quantity of money, broadly defined, as stated by Mervyn King in an interview (with Stephanie Flanders) for the BBC at the time. In effect, there are two notions of QE, a UK-style QE and a Japanese-style. The inspiration for QE operations of the UK kind – where the asset purchases were of long-dated government bonds from non-banks with an immediate impact on the quantity of money – can be found in Keynes's work, notably in the advocacy of monetary policy *à outrance* at the end of *A Treatise on Money: 2. The Applied Theory of Money*. (Elizabeth Johnson and Donald Moggridge [eds] *The Collected Writings of John Maynard Keynes*, vol. VI [London and Basingstoke: Macmillan for the Royal Economics Society, 1971, originally published 1930], p. 347.) The author – who was a vocal supporter of UK-style QE in early 2009 – acknowledged his debt to Keynes in this area of economics in, for example, Tim Congdon 'What is to be done about Japan's financial crisis?', *Central Banking* (London: Central Banking Publications), May 2002, vol. xii, no. 4. In his view Keynes is the true originator of the ideas behind the Bank of England's QE exercises. See Tim Congdon 'Who invented QE?', *Economic Affairs* (London: Institute of Economic Affairs), October 2012 issue, vol. 32, no. 3. In qualification, Keynes's thinking about the most aggressive forms of monetary easing was influenced by Ralph Hawtrey at the Treasury. Hawtrey also advocated deliberate expansion of the quantity of money to combat severely depressed economic conditions in, for example, his *Trade Depression and the Way Out* (London: Longman, Green & Co., 1931, 2nd edition, 1933). (Note that the phrase "monetary policy *à outrance* is sometimes criticized as not being idiomatic French. The correct phrase is said to be "monetary policy *à l'outrance*". In fact, both usages are acceptable.)

8.   See pp. 38–42 above in Chapter 1.
9.   This part of the theory of monetary policy suffers from a common fallacy, which seems to have begun with Nicholas Kaldor in a 1982 pamphlet, *The Scourge of Monetarism* (Oxford: Oxford University Press). Kaldor accepted that equality of money demand with the quantity of money balances created by the banks is one of the economy's equilibrium conditions. One feature of an economy with bank credit is that a divergence between money demand and supply can be eliminated by a change in the quantity of money. For example, someone with an excess money balance might repay a bank loan, which both reduces the aggregate quantity of money and restores this individual's money equilibrium. Kaldor's fallacy is the proposition that changes in the quantity of money (as a result of adjustments to agents' bank borrowings) are the *only* way in which monetary equilibrium is maintained in a modern economy with fiat money. (Kaldor's idea is obviously inapplicable in a commodity-money economy.) The proposition is associated not just with the correct statement that the quantity of money can be and much of the time is "endogenous" (that is, the result largely of processes in the banking system not under direct official control), but also with the implausible claim that the quantity of money is determined by national income, where national income is to be viewed as set by other entirely non-monetary means. (In the crudest versions national income is a multiple of investment, which depends on the private sector's "animal spirits".) The easiest way of dismissing Kaldor's ideas is to note that new bank credit is a tiny fraction (usually less than a quarter per cent) of the value of all transactions, while the levels of transactions and national income are positive whether new bank lending is positive, negative or nil. Basil Moore's *Horizontalists and Verticalists: the macroeconomics of credit money* (Cambridge: Cambridge University Press, 1988) is sometimes regarded as the best volume-length discussion of endogenous money. For a sympathetic critique of the more extreme statements about endogenous money, see Sheila Dow 'Endogenous money: structuralist', pp. 35–51 in Philip Arestis and Malcolm Sawyer (eds) *A Handbook*

of *Alternative Monetary Economics* (Cheltenham, UK and Northampton, MA, USA: Edward Elgar Publishing, 2006), particularly p. 44. Also interesting are several papers in Victoria Chick *On Money, Method and Keynes* (London and Basingstoke: Palgrave Macmillan, 1992) and Victoria Chick *Macroeconomics after Keynes* (Cambridge, MA, USA: MIT Press, 1983). Chick and Dow notice that, if Kaldor and Moore were right, Keynes's liquidity preference theory of the rate of interest – and indeed virtually all of Keynes's monetary thinking – would need to be abandoned. According to Chick, "one concludes that money is neither purely exogenous nor purely endogenous. Which is the better description depends on circumstances" (Chick *Macroeconomics after Keynes*, p. 236).

10. Like so much of monetary economics, the precise status of the idea of "monetary disequilibrium" is debated. The idea clearly implies that agents are "off their money demand curves", which upsets some economists who are wedded to the view of the world as populated by rational individuals who always fulfil plans. (To be "off a demand curve" implies that a person's or company's behaviour is not fully in accordance with that implied by a well-specified demand function, which at least superficially is irrational. But the person or company may not be irrational. They may simply be having difficulty in reaching a preferred situation.) Papers were written in the 1970s and early 1980s on "disequilibrium" or "buffer-stock" money, almost as if the problem of eliminating imbalances between money demand and supply were a new topic. See, for example, 'Disequilibrium money: a note', pp. 254–76 in Charles Goodhart *Monetary Theory and Practice: the UK experience* (London: Macmillan, 1984).

11. The critique of the present argument in Chapter 3 by Ryland Thomas turns on two ideas, that the impact effect of QE operations on the quantity of money can be diluted by second- and third-round effects, and that changes in the velocity of circulation disrupt the equi-proportionality of changes in the quantity of money and national income.

12. See the Introduction pp. 7–8 for more on the significance of a broadly defined money aggregate. Government balances are excluded because the government is so creditworthy that its spending behaviour is little affected by the size of its money balance, which is usually maintained at the central bank. See note 12 to the Introduction for more on the adoption of the M4x aggregate in the UK.

13. See Norbert Janssen 'Measures of M4 and M4 lending excluding intermediate other financial corporations', pp. 1–4, *Monetary & Financial Statistics* (London: Bank of England), May 2009 issue. The Bank of England seems to be exceptional in the care it has taken to exclude IOFC balances from money. Other central banks have paid the topic less attention, and apparently not realized the serious distortion that such balances can cause in the interpretation of money data.

14. As noted in the Introduction (pp. 10–11), the monetary base consists of the liabilities of the central bank, including the cash reserves lodged with the central bank by the commercial bank, and Milton Friedman and others believed in a fairly mechanical link between the monetary base and the quantity of money.

15. In the 2014 exchange Halligan's words were, "Once our banks have 'fixed' their balance sheets (by writing down bad debts or, more likely, shoving them on to taxpayers), I believe they will use their QE-bolstered reserves to lend excessively, so boosting broad money and, therefore, inflation." But he never – in all his other commentary on the wickedness of QE, which extended over more than five years – mentioned actual trends in broad money growth as relevant to inflation. It is important to realize that Halligan was by no means alone in thinking that the several-fold expansion in the monetary base – in the USA as well as the UK – would result in higher inflation. See Alan Greenspan *The Map and the Territory* (London and New York: Allen Lane, 2013), p. 281, and Allan Meltzer *Why Capitalism?* (Oxford: Oxford University Press), pp. 121–43.

16. The classic reference here is to Eugene Fama 'Banking in a theory of finance', *Journal of Monetary Economics* (North-Holland Publishing Company), vol. 6 (1980), pp. 39–57. The central point is that banks' assets and liabilities must always be equal. So the

expansion of the deposit liabilities (or so-called "inside money"), which make up most of banks' liabilities, cannot make anyone better off. Money growth therefore does not represent a positive wealth effect and, according to Fama, cannot affect anything. Of course, if this argument can be made about commercial banks' liabilities, it can also be made about the central bank's liabilities ("outside money"). Fama seems not to have appreciated this, but it is obvious. If central banks' assets are entirely claims on the private sector (such as the mortgage-backed securities now held in large amounts by the Federal Reserve) and central bank liabilities are also held 100 per cent by the private sector, the private sector cannot be better off if the central bank expands. The situation might appear more promising if central bank assets are claims on government. But – if Barro's contention that public debt is not net wealth in the hands of the public is accepted – then again an increase in the monetary base as a result of central bank acquisition of government debt is not a positive wealth effect. (Robert Barro 'Are government bonds net wealth?' *Journal of Political Economy*, vol. 82, no. 6 [Chicago: University of Chicago Press, 1974], pp. 1095–117.) In short, if the thesis of Fama's 1980 article were right, monetary policy – understood as the consequences of changes in the balance sheets of either the central bank or the commercial banks – could not affect anything. "Fama's attack on the problem of integrating monetary theory and value theory is radical: he simply abolishes monetary theory" (Kevin Hoover *The New Classical Macroeconomics: A Sceptical Enquiry* [Oxford, UK and Cambridge, MA, USA: Basil Blackwell, 1988], p. 5). The conclusion is peculiar, even crazy. Evidently, something has gone wrong. Might one make the modest suggestion that an increase in the quantity of money influences the economy by a mechanism other than a wealth effect? In an interview for a *New Yorker* journalist in 2009, when asked about the causes of the downturn, Fama replied, "We don't know what causes recessions ... We've never known" (Philip Mirowski *Never Let a Serious Crisis Go to Waste* [London, UK and New York, USA: Verso, 2013], p. 179).

17. Mark Blaug *Economic Theory in Retrospect* (Cambridge: Cambridge University Press, 4th edition, 1985), p. 633. Despite the power of the quantity theory to explain nominal national income in the long run, it plays no role in short-run macroeconomic forecasting, which is instead based on the Keynesian income–expenditure model. See note 21 below.

18. The implications of this point for the income–expenditure circular flow, as taught in elementary textbooks, are unsettling, as explained in Tim Congdon 'A critique of two Keynesian concepts', pp. 44–76, in Steven Kates (ed.) *What's Wrong with Keynesian Economics* (Cheltenham, UK and Northampton, USA: Edward Elgar Publishing, 2016).

19. Keynes *A Treatise on Money: 1. The Pure Theory of Money*, chapter 15, pp. 217–30.

20. The standard reference is Ben Bernanke and Mark Gertler 'Inside the black box: the credit channel of monetary policy transmission', *The Journal of Economic Perspectives*, vol. 9, no. 4 (autumn 1995), pp. 27–48. The word "creditist", implying the noun "creditism", appeared in Ben Bernanke and Alan Blinder 'Credit, money and aggregate demand', *American Economic Review*, vol. lxxviii, no. 2, pp. 435–9. (See p. 438.) Bernanke and Blinder apparently believed that what they termed "credit shocks" had a direct effect on national income and expenditure. In fact, most credit is extended to purchase existing capital assets. Credit transactions are therefore part of Keynes's "financial circulation". They have no direct, first-round effect on his "industrial circulation", which comes to the same thing as the income–expenditure circular flow. As Keynes's "effective demand" (which affects output and employment in the textbooks) arises inside the income–expenditure circular flow, the overwhelming majority of credit transactions have no direct, first-round effect on aggregate demand or national income.

21. Most economists are taught the Keynesian theory of national income determination, which says that national income is a multiple of investment. The theory originates in Keynes's 1936 *The General Theory of Employment, Interest and Money*, but most

instruction is not from Keynes's book, which is barely readable except to specialists, but from a textbook in the tradition of Paul Samuelson's 1948 *Economics* (York, PA: McGraw-Hill). A surprisingly high proportion of them come to believe that this is the *only* such theory. It is in fact a theory of the determination of *real* national income *in the short run*; it is not a general theory at all. It is useless in understanding both the many-fold changes in national income in nominal terms that occur over the long run, and the impact of banking and changes in the quantity of money on expenditure and incomes in the short run. Economists indoctrinated in the Keynesian approach realize, when faced with events like the Great Depression or the Great Recession, that banking and money must be integrated into the analysis somehow. But they attempt this integration by appealing to categories ("the rate of interest", most obviously) that are part of textbook Keynesianism, and just cannot see the significance of the stability of agents' desired ratio of money to income and wealth in the transmission story. Of course the two paragraphs in the text could be expanded enormously in analyses where that stability is crucial. See, for example, Tim Congdon *Money and Asset Prices in Boom and Bust* (London: Institute of Economic Affairs, 2005).

22. Michael Woodford's work – and that of the Swedish economist, Lars Svensson – are examples of an exclusive focus in macroeconomic analysis on "the rate of interest", meaning just one rate, the instrument rate or policy rate set by the central bank. By assumption, agents' attempts to keep actual money balances in line with the demand to hold them cannot matter in the Woodford–Svensson account of how the economy works. *Indeed, they cannot even appear in that account.* For Woodford's influence on European monetary policy in the years before the Great Recession, see Chapter 4, pp. 112. For an example of Svensson's approach, see his paper 'Monetary policy and real stabilisation', National Bureau of Economic Research, working paper no. 9486 (Cambridge, MA: NBER, February 2003).

23. See note 20 above for "creditism". For another example of a much-cited pundit who sees everything in terms of the rate of interest and bank lending, see Richard Posner's *The Crisis of Capitalist Democracy* (Cambridge, MA, USA and London, UK: Harvard University Press, 2010). On p. 36 the "monetarist fallacy" is said to be that the Fed can always reduce the Fed funds rate to a sufficient level "by increasing the amount of lendable funds that banks have", when of course monetarism in fact focuses on the quantity of money; on p. 282 the level of bank deposits is said to matter because it determines "the amount of lendable money", which is a complete misunderstanding. (Extra loans create new deposits, and national income and wealth adjust to the deposits thereby created.)

24. For the claim that in the USA "unconventional monetary policy", which was dominated by QE, was concerned to narrow credit spreads, see Chapter 9, pp. 237–60, in Alan Blinder *After the Music Stopped* (New York: Penguin Press, 2013).

25. The author of course accepts that the price of bonds (and hence bond yields) may adjust to a mismatch between money demand and supply. So "the rate of interest" in the sense of the level of bond yields is a monetary variable, as Keynes's liquidity preference theory argues. But an economy can be imagined with money and equities and real estate, and no bonds. In that economy the relationship between money on the one hand and national income and wealth on the other will survive, but – by assumption – it cannot have anything to do with the rate of interest in the sense of bond yields. The point, which is obvious, is explained also on pp. 327–8 of his *Money in a Free Society* (New York: Encounter Books, 2011).

26. In 1945 claims on the British state represented over 83 per cent of the assets of the London clearing banks, where the deposit liabilities of these organizations were the dominant constituent of the UK money supply. By contrast, in 2006 – just before the Great Recession – claims on the British state were less than 1 per cent of the UK banking system's total assets. But this vast change in banks' asset composition had no bearing on banks' ability to honour payment instructions or on the role of bank deposits in transactions. The monetary theory of national income determination holds

regardless of banks' asset composition, as long as banks are able to honour their obligations to depositors.

27. Chick noted that banks could create money by the purchase of existing securities (or "seasoned securities") in Victoria Chick *Macroeconomics after Keynes* (Cambridge, MA, USA: MIT Press, 1983), p. 235. In that event money creation could occur with no new overall credit extension in the economy.

28. The British prime minister in late 2008, Gordon Brown, believed that bank recapitalization was essential to ending the crisis. See below, pp. 173–4 in Chapter 7. This belief in the prime importance of bank recapitalization may have reflected conversations with Mervyn King, governor of the Bank of England. See note 30 below.

29. This even became the title of a book, Philip Mirowski *Never Let a Serious Crisis Go to Waste* (London and New York: Verso, 2013).

30. Mervyn King believed that bank recapitalization was a precondition of financial recovery in late 2008. Further, if the private sector were not prepared to inject new capital, the state should do so on terms that might be punitive to existing shareholders. He has claimed ownership of these ideas, saying that American policy-makers picked them up from the UK example. See note 57 on pp. 384–5 of Mervyn King *The End of Alchemy* (London: Little, Brown, 2016). The notion that much more bank capital was needed in late 2008 was related to the proposition that additional bank lending to the private sector was essential to boost private spending. (It is related therefore to the "creditism" espoused by Bernanke and discussed in note 20 above.) But no new bank capital is needed if banks expand their balance sheets (and so create money) by acquiring default-risk-free government securities or extra cash reserves. In the author's view the UK's Great Recession could have been avoided entirely if QE on a sufficient scale had been announced in October 2008 instead of bank recapitalization. The argument has been made in several places, but see Tim Congdon 'Bank recapitalisation and the Great Recession', *Standpoint* (London: Social Affairs Unit), December 2015, pp. 42–5.

31. Rainer Masera 'Six paradoxes of Eurozone economic policies', mimeo, presentation given at the XXVIII Villa Mondragone International Economic Seminar, June 2016. The quotation is from p. 5. Masera has prepared other research in a similar vein with colleagues at the Banca d'Italia. Their work should be compared with the Bank for International Settlements' November 2015 paper on *Assessing the economic costs and benefits of TLAC implementation*. (TLAC stands for "total loss-absorbing capital".) According to the BIS, the purpose of having more capital is that banks are more robust in facing cyclical shocks. But the study says specifically on p. 3 that it is not concerned "to predict what will happen at implementation", overlooking entirely the "negative perverse loop" about which Masera, the author of this chapter and many others have been and remain worried.

32. The trouble stems from the Bank of England's limited funding for its statistical unit. Numbers have been compiled for the credit counterparts to M4 for several decades back into the past, but they are not available for M4x, simply because of cost.

33. Remember that this includes claims on "intermediate other financial corporations", many of which were in fact bank subsidiaries. Another problem is that the statistics in the Bank of England's database are often revised. The statement in the text, and the data used in Figures 2.2 and 2.3, are from the database at June 2013, when the first version of this chapter was written. The data used in Figures 2.1 and 2.4 are from the database at August 2016, when the revised version was prepared.

34. For decades until 1985 the UK authorities varied the maturity profile and instrument composition of its debt sales (and occasional purchases) to influence monetary conditions. This stopped with the announcement of the full funding rule. Thereafter the short-term interest rate became, in effect, the *factotum* of UK monetary policy. The announcement of QE in March 2009 represented a return to the pre-1985 position, although most policy-makers would have struggled to identify the rationale for their actions. Mervyn King at the Bank of England had some awareness of the historical background. See King *End of Alchemy*, pp. 182–3.

35. A body of theory known as the monetary approach to the balance of payments is relevant here. The key contention – first enunciated in the eighteenth century by Adam Smith and David Hume in their critique of mercantilism – is that economies' need for real money balances is related to real incomes and output, and is unaffected by exchange controls, trade policy or a credit squeeze. A credit squeeze reduces the amount of money created by domestic agents. The effect of a credit squeeze is therefore to attract money balances from abroad, to make good the shortfall in real money balances. One reference is Jacob Frenkel and Harry Johnson (eds) *The Monetary Approach to the Balance of Payments* (London: Allen & Unwin, 1976). If Bernanke's creditism were valid, the monetary approach to the balance of payments – a core element in traditional monetary economics – would have to be abandoned.

36. The main reason for the excess of the public sector contribution to M4 growth over the stock of QE assets is that the continuing budget deficit from 2009/10 onwards was financed to a significant extent by the issuance of short-dated gilts that were attractive to the banks.

37. The analysis in this chapter has been extremely critical of Ben Bernanke and Mervyn King. To give King his due, he was the key protagonist of QE in the Bank of England in early 2009. See Conaghan *The Bank*, pp. 202–3. Bernanke also proved effective in backing the right policies from early 2009 onwards. Nevertheless, the author sticks to his view that neither of them appreciated how the mandatory bank recapitalization and tightening of regulation in late 2008 would damage money growth in the two economies where they were responsible for the key high-level banking policy decisions.

38. Johnson and Moggridge (eds) *Activities 1931–39: World Crises and Policies in Britain and America* in *Collected Writings of Keynes*, vol. XXI (London and Basingstoke: Macmillan for the Royal Economics Society, 1982), p. 381.

3. UK broad money growth and nominal spending during the Great Recession: an analysis of the money creation process and the role of money demand*

Ryland Thomas

In the UK the annual rate of broad money growth slowed from double-digit figures in mid-2007 to a rate of just under 1 per cent in early 2010, the weakest number since the Selwyn Lloyd squeeze in the early 1960s (see Figure 3.1). Nominal spending during 2008 and 2009 fell in absolute terms for the first time since the Great Depression of the 1930s and at a rate not seen since the extraordinary nominal contraction of the early 1920s. It is therefore an attractive hypothesis to attribute the Great Recession of 2008–09 to a large fall in the growth rate of broad money. The argument would echo the celebrated thesis of Chapter 7 of *A Monetary History of the United States 1857–1960*, in which Milton Friedman and Anna Schwartz argued that an almost 40 per cent fall in broad money was the cause of the USA's 1929–33 Great Depression.

This chapter discusses the behaviour of broad money and nominal spending in the UK during the recent financial crisis, and considers the extent to which the recession can be given a monetarist interpretation. A monetarist interpretation is understood as one in which movements in aggregate demand can be convincingly ascribed to shifts in money supply and money demand. The label "monetarist" has become inescapable in recent decades for analysis of this sort, with monetarism and Keynesian sometimes seen as antagonistic towards each other. However, Keynes remarked in *The General Theory* that changes in national expenditure and income could be motivated by agents' attempts to equilibrate the demand to hold money with the actual quantity of money in existence. Indeed, he described the requirement that money demand be equivalent to the money supply at the equilibrium levels of national income and wealth to be "the fundamental proposition of monetary theory".[1]

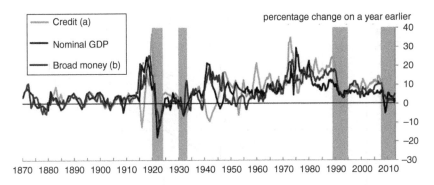

Notes:
(a) M4 lending 1963–98, M4 lending excluding "intermediate other financial corporations" (IOFCs) 1998–2012. Data are adjusted to exclude the impact of securitizations and loan transfers. Pre-1963 data from David Sheppard *The Growth and Role of UK Financial Institutions 1880–1962* (London: Methuen, 1971).
(b) M3 1945–63, M4 1963–98, M4 excluding intermediate "other financial corporations" (IOFCs) 1998–2012.

Sources: Sheppard (1971); Forrest Capie and Alan Webber *A Monetary History of the United Kingdom, 1870–1982*, Vol. 1 (London: Allen & Unwin, 1985); Sally Hills, Ryland Thomas and Nicholas Dimsdale 'The UK recession in context – what do three centuries of data tell us?', *Bank of England Quarterly Bulletin*, 2010, vol. 50, no. 4, pp. 277–91; and Bank of England.

Figure 3.1   Money, credit and nominal GDP since 1870

First, the chapter considers the key drivers of the fall in money growth over this period and, in particular, the role of banking system behaviour and various policy measures. The focus is on a broad measure of money including (nearly) all bank deposits. Second, the chapter looks at the behaviour of the demand for money and the path of broad money velocity. The main contention will be that an analysis of the changing determinants of money demand is as important to explaining the weakness of aggregate expenditure as an understanding of the causes of the slowdown in the rate of money growth.

I

At the simplest level, standard monetary theory says that nominal spending in the economy must be consistent in equilibrium with equivalence between the supply of and demand for money. In an elementary treatment the demand for money can be viewed as exclusively for transactions purposes, with the quantity of money demanded as changing in proportion to

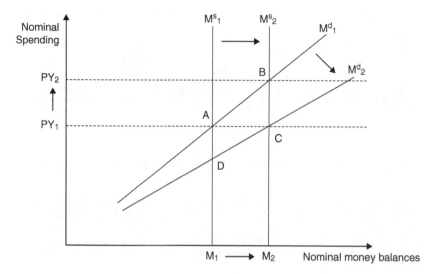

Figure 3.2   Changes in the money supply and nominal spending

nominal spending. So an increase in the money supply (M^s), other things equal, must at some stage lead to higher nominal spending in order that the demand for money (M^d) increases in line with the higher supply. This is demonstrated in Figure 3.2 by the movement from point A to B. But underlying shifts in money demand that are unrelated to the transactions motive, due to changes in the arguments in the money demand function (for example, the return on money relative to other assets) or even to shifts in the money demand function (such as Keynes's changes in "liquidity preference"), might occur at the same time as ups and downs in the money supply. That will alter the desired amount of money held at a given level of nominal spending, and also raise or lower the equilibrium velocity of circulation.[2] (See point C in Figure 3.2.) By implication, if the money supply falls in conjunction with a rise in liquidity preference – which is arguably a plausible combination during a financial crisis – the economy may be hit by a "double whammy". Both the drop in the money supply and the decline in velocity undermine demand, with nominal spending falling proportionately more than money.

That theory is all very well. But an important task here is to decide which assets count as money. Where should the line be drawn between money and non-money assets? Traditionally, economists have used money concepts that include notes and coin in circulation with the public and bank deposits. But are all bank deposits to be viewed as money? And is it always sensible to privilege the liabilities of banks as definitely "money", and to draw a sharp distinction between them and the liabilities of non-banks?

At least two approaches to these questions have been discussed in the literature. One is to take an "effective money supply" approach which argues that there are a whole host of different assets that at any one time might serve as money. But the "money-ness" of those assets varies over time and with the state of the economy. For example, the observing economist might want to derive a measure of money in which its various components have different weights, with the weights based on how much interest the components pay. The thinking would be that the lower the interest paid on a particular money balance, the more likely it is that people are holding it because it offers transaction services and therefore the more "money"-like it is. This is known as the Divisia approach, with some economists contending that such measures are good at forecasting macroeconomic outcomes.[3]

Alternatively, binary either–or decisions can be taken about which assets count as money at any one point in time. For example, before the financial crisis various debt instruments – such as Treasury bills and very highly rated mortgage-backed securities – might have been treated as so predictable and certain in value, and so low cost to buy and sell, that they had the same properties of "liquidity" as money itself. However, in the Great Financial Crisis of 2008–10 no mortgage-backed security could serve that role, as confidence in markets' ability to value those securities collapsed. A more sophisticated version of this approach is to propose that the "money"-ness of certain instruments depends mainly on their ability to serve as collateral in various transactions, particularly when securing a loan. The analyst can then use the size of "haircuts" on that collateral and the length of collateral chains to attach weights to the different possible components of a money aggregate, with the weighted sum of the components constituting an effective measure of the money supply.[4] A problem here is to obtain sufficient data on the various assets being used as collateral, particularly on the characteristics that are deemed to make them "money-like". The information may not be readily available, especially in the form of a long time series in periods when new "money-like" instruments are being created (and sometimes destroyed).

The second approach is to draw the line under a set of assets that rarely lose their ability to serve as money such as cash and bank deposits. Any reduction in the supply or "money-ness" of other assets that fall outside that definition will typically show up as a structural increase in the demand for those assets which fall inside the definition. In each approach the outcome for the economy will be contractionary. But the argument in favour of the "draw the line" approach would be that it may be easier to anticipate or detect that contraction by analysing shifts in the supply and demand for an established measure of money. An established money measure has a long time series of data and a well-trodden path of empirical research behind it.

In this chapter I will adopt the "draw the line" approach. Following Congdon's persuasive analysis of the Lawson boom, I will focus on the broad measure of money, represented in the UK by M4 before 1998 and by M4x afterwards.[5] The M4/M4x series, which includes currency (that is, notes and coin) and bank deposits held by genuine non-bank private sector agents, was shown in Figure 3.1.[6] One motivation for using a broad measure of money is the existence of a well-recognized framework that explains how the *supply* of broad money is determined. As discussed in McLeay and others in a 2014 Bank of England paper, which built on analyses dating back to the 1950s, the supply of broad money can be seen as determined by transactions between the banking sector (including the central bank) and the non-bank private sector.[7] The most important of these transactions during peacetime has usually been the provision of credit by the banking sector to the non-bank private sector. But, more generally, any transaction between the banking sector and the non-bank private sector, notably purchases and sales of assets between them, will involve the creation or destruction of banking sector deposits and will thus affect the supply of broad money. The logic of money creation and destruction – which turns on the credit counterparts identity mentioned in the Introduction to this volume – will form the analytical basis of the second section of the chapter. (See p. 9–10 above for more on the credit counterparts identity.)

Monetary economics also has a tradition, stretching back many decades, of estimating the empirical determinants of the *demand* to hold broad money. This exploits the availability of long time series for *both* currency and bank deposits *and* the variables (income, an interest rate term for the opportunity cost of money, and so on) that are standard arguments in money demand functions. The research agenda has not been without its problems, with much criticism being made of attempts to exploit empirical estimates of *aggregate* money demand during the period of money supply targeting in the 1970s and 1980s. The conventional wisdom is that empirical estimates of the demand for money "broke down" in these years, in part because more or less contemporaneous steps towards financial liberalization had macroeconomic effects that the estimation procedures were not designed to capture. But since the 1980s more has been learned about agents' motivations to hold money in a financially liberalized economy, while the literature has also investigated data on *disaggregated* holdings of money (that is, of money holdings in different sectors of the economy, households, companies and so on). In principle, research at the sectoral level may make it easier to detect shifts in broad money demand. An initial exercise on these lines is attempted in section IV of the current chapter, but see also two Bank of England analyses – one in a 2007 paper by Berry and others, and the other in a 2011 paper by Bridges and others – for more detail on the pre- and post-crisis periods.[8]

II

What caused the weakness in broad money growth over the crisis? The crisis was initially characterized by a large shock to the supply of credit in mid-2007, which stemmed from the so-called "sub-prime crisis", and the closely related jamming-up of the inter-bank and asset-backed securities markets. (The sub-prime crisis involved the collapse beginning in 2006 of the value of securities that had facilitated mortgage loans in the USA to low-quality [or "sub-prime"] borrowers. From 9 August 2007 banks with large portfolios of such securities found it increasingly difficult to obtain credit lines from other banks. See p. 170 in Chapter 7 for more discussion.) The collateral damage from the inter-bank malaise led to sharp falls in asset prices and economic activity, and ultimately to the failure of Lehman Brothers in September 2008. Anxiety about the wider implications of the Lehman default led to a concerted policy response by the world's leading economic policy-makers, including those from the UK. That involved monetary policy in two forms, substantial interest rate cuts and large central bank purchases of securities (known as quantitative easing or QE). In the UK such purchases were exclusively of government bonds and were to a considerable extent from non-banks. To the extent that purchases were from UK resident non-banks rather than banks or foreigners, they had the direct effect of boosting the quantity of money, regardless of whether banks were making loans or not.

But the monetary policy actions were only part of the story. In addition a set of macroprudential and regulatory policies were introduced internationally to help banks repair their balance sheets, so that they might again provide credit to the real economy. Amongst other things, that involved recapitalization of the banking system, through a mixture of direct government capital injections and the private raising of equity. There were also regulatory requirements for banks to hold more liquidity and to rely less on short-term funding.

Explaining the weakness of broad money growth over the crisis period requires understanding the interplay of these various factors, with both the closure of the inter-bank market and macro-prudential regulation being relevant. A key hypothesis of other chapters in this volume (see the

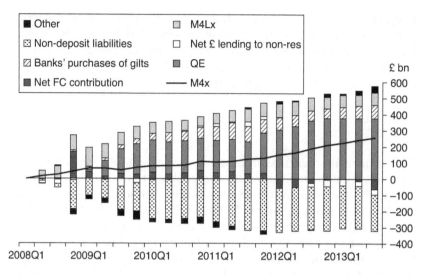

Figure 3.3   The counterparts to the increase in broad money since 2008Q1

contributions by Congdon and Ridley, and Hanke for the USA) is that the
weakness of broad money growth and, by implication, the contraction of
nominal spending during the crisis, were largely the result of misguided
capital and regulatory policies. In their view, higher capital and liquidity
requirements amplified the effects of the sub-prime crisis on bank lending,
as well as causing a direct reduction in the money supply through the issuance of long-term debt and equity by banks. Their claim is that the growth
of both broad money and credit would have been much stronger in the
absence of the new constraints, after October 2008, from the tightening
of macro-prudential regulation. They think that, without this regulatory
tightening, the sub-prime crisis would have played out in a much more
benign way. Instead of suffering the Great Recession, the leading economies would have experienced mild macroeconomic setbacks similar to
those that had followed other credit crises in the post-war period.

On the face of it there is some evidence for the Congdon–Hanke–Ridley
position. Figure 3.3 presents an accounting decomposition of the credit
counterparts to broad money growth in the five years from 2008. It
shows – in other words – how the cumulative increase in broad money over
the crisis can be accounted for by movements in the other items on the
consolidated banking system's balance sheet given that total assets must,
by definition, equal total liabilities.[9]

The figure shows that in the first three years of the crisis, between the start
of 2008 and the end of 2010 the stock of broad money increased by just £100

billion, or by about 6.5 per cent – an average rate of increase of only 2 per cent a year – well below the rates seen pre-crisis. For the following three years it increased by £150 billion, an average annual growth rate of 3 per cent.

In an accounting sense the figure suggests the weakness in broad money is largely driven by anaemic lending growth in the wake of the crisis (shown in the light gray bars) and a large increase in non-deposit liabilities (the dotted bars), reflecting issuance of equity and long-term debt by banks. Such issuance reduces broad money as the purchasers of bank instruments in the non-bank private sector have to pay for them, at least in the first instance, by relinquishing bank deposits held in the UK banking system. Pushing in the opposite direction are purchases of government debt by the Bank of England (the medium gray bars) and by the banks themselves (the cross hatched bars) from asset managers in the UK non-bank private sector. These purchases boost broad money, because the ultimate sellers of the assets receive a bank deposit in settling the exchange.

The Congdon–Ridley argument is that in the UK the observed weakness in lending growth and destruction of money (as long-term debt and capital liabilities replaced deposits) were largely the result of a misguided capital and regulatory policy response. But would credit and money growth have been materially stronger if the regulatory changes had not been carried through? Congdon and Ridley take a strong stand on the counterfactual behaviour of broad money, which rests on two key unstated assumptions. The first is that other actions being taken by the authorities, such as QE, had no influence on bank lending, banks' acquisition of gilts or their issuance of long-term debt and equity; the second is that, in the absence of a regulatory response, the sub-prime crisis would have had little adverse effect on lending, or at least that the adverse effect would have been no bigger than in previous crises. Both assumptions can be challenged.

First, take QE. The accounting decomposition in Figure 3.3 suggests that asset purchases have a one-for-one impact on broad money. But an essential element in the QE transmission mechanism is that central bank asset purchases add to the quantity of money, so that the private sector has an excess supply of money and an excess demand for assets. The excess demand for assets prompts portfolio rebalancing, notably by institutional investors, which lowers bond and equity yields, boosts asset prices in capital markets, and increases spending in the economy. The process of portfolio rebalancing is likely to have effects on more than one item in the credit counterpart identity. Analyses in a 2011 paper by Bridges and Thomas, and a 2012 paper by Butt and others, identify three main indirect effects of QE-induced portfolio rebalancing on the counterparts.[10]

First of all, QE may have actually induced some of the debt and equity issuance by banks. Of obvious relevance here would have been reductions in yields on bank debt and equity attributable to the QE operations. Paradoxically, some of the negative effect of banks' capital-raising on the quantity of money may have been the result of QE. The negative effect may not have been entirely the result of regulatory policy. Secondly, by creating reserves and forcing down gilt yields QE may have dissuaded banks from buying such large quantities of gilts (to meet their liquidity requirements) as they might otherwise have done. So, in the absence of QE, banks' purchases of gilts from non-banks (which increase non-banks' deposits and hence the quantity of money) would have been higher. Finally, by reducing yields in capital markets QE may have induced companies to issue more bonds and equities, and then to use the proceeds of the capital issues in part to repay bank debt. In other words, QE may have had a negative effect on bank lending through a capital market substitution effect.

The estimates from this analysis suggest that these "leakages" from QE amounted to around 40 per cent in each episode, although the mix was slightly different in each. Figure 3.4 shows how this counterfactual analysis affects the simple accounting explanation of money growth. The medium gray bars now show, with the leakages discussed above netted out, that QE boosted broad money by around £230 billion (or 60 per cent of the total amount of assets purchased) rather than £375 billion. Correspondingly, the other counterparts where these leakages occurred now show either a more positive contribution or a less negative contribution to the increase in broad money.

This offers a different perspective from Figure 3.3. The increase in broad money over the period is now equivalent to the estimated *net* impact of QE

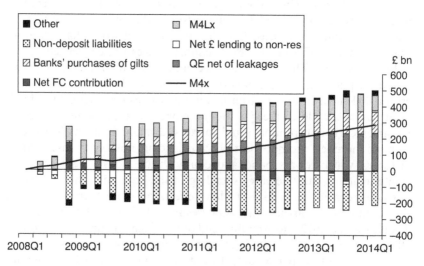

Figure 3.4   The counterparts adjusted for QE leakages

on broad money. The drag on broad money from issuance of long-term debt and bank recapitalization is smaller, being exactly offset by both the lending that banks would have carried out in the absence of QE and the purchases of gilts they would have made. So, once we strip out the impact of QE, one might argue that regulatory policy probably had at worst a neutral effect on the quantity of money. Liquidity and capital regulation were pushing in opposite directions on broad money, while lending to the private sector in the absence of QE would have been slightly positive to make up the difference. The other implication is that QE leakages are a key reason why money growth was not stronger over this period. Without those leakages broad money growth would have stabilized at a reasonably healthy 6 per cent in 2009 and 2010.

The second unstated assumption in the Congdon–Ridley position – that the sub-prime crisis itself would have had a much smaller effect on lending in the absence of tighter macro-prudential regulation – can also be challenged. If that were true, the analyst might expect bank lending in the recent crisis to have been weaker than in similar credit crises in the past. After all, previous crises saw less drastic shifts in regulation or sometimes no change at all. In particular, previous crises should exhibit much less of a slowdown in bank lending. In fact, Figure 3.5 compares *real* lending growth (that is, the increase in lending *adjusted for inflation*) in three episodes in

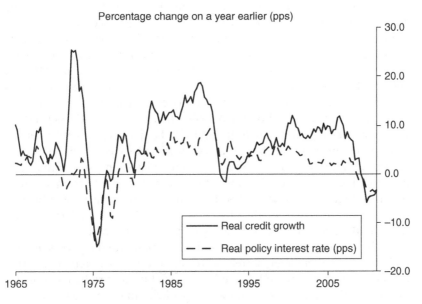

Figure 3.5   Credit growth in previous crises

modern times. The growth of real lending slowed in the Great Recession by a similar pace to that recorded in the credit crunch of the early 1990s and by considerably less than that which followed the secondary banking crisis of the mid-1970s. It might be argued that the context of monetary policy was very different in the 1970s and 1990s, with – for example – much higher real interest rates in the two earlier crises. But this does not seem to be the case when one compares the behaviour of real short-term policy rates over each period. Alternatively, the severity of the slowdown in bank lending in the mid-1970s might have been due partly to the introduction of Supplementary Special Deposits, a scheme which often goes by the more familiar label, "the corset".[11] Any multi-causal interpretation will be open to debate. Overall, the evidence here suggests that the slowdown in lending in the latest crisis was no worse than in previous crises, even though the latest crisis was the only one to have been accompanied by a major change in bank regulation. By implication, the underlying fragility of the banking system – which was made evident by the sub-prime crisis – was the chief cause of the slowdown in lending. The regulatory upheaval was not the dominant influence at work.

The argument can be taken further. It is surely plausible that the funda-mental size and scope of the sub-prime crisis was many times worse than crises in the mid-1970s and early 1990s, given the sheer scale of support required from central banks.[12] The finding that lending growth in real terms slowed only to the same extent as in those previous crises might be advanced as prima facie evidence that regulatory and other policies served to prevent a much more catastrophic fall in lending growth than actually occurred. One undoubted feature of financial markets needs to be empha-sized. Following the recapitalization of the banking system in 2008 and 2009 and other emergency measures, two recognized markers of inter-bank lending premiums and bank funding costs fell.[13] (The two markers were the spread between London inter-bank offered rate [LIBOR] and the overnight indexed swap rate [OIS] and UK banks' average credit default swap premiums.) On this basis, banks felt more relaxed about lending to each other and non-bank investors were happier to invest in bank debt, both of which supported the loosening of monetary policy from late 2008 onwards. Figure 3.6 shows that both premiums had increased significantly during the early stages of the crisis and had pushed up the banking sys-tem's funding costs relative to lending rates. It is hard to believe, first, that the falls in inter-bank lending premiums and bank funding costs in 2009 and 2010 were completely unrelated to the balance sheet repair resulting from regulatory policy, and, second, that such falls in turn had no positive impact on the banking system's ability to lend and preparedness to cut loan rates in response to policy rates. It is true that both premiums rose

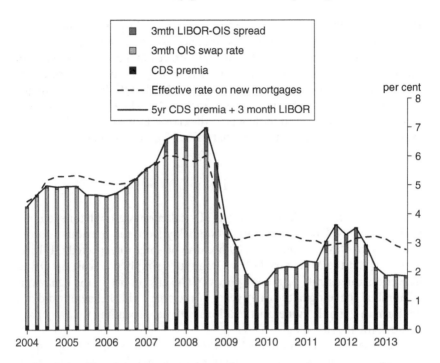

Figure 3.6   Floating mortgage rates and a representative measure of funding costs

again in 2010 and 2011, but arguably that should be seen as a by-product of the mounting crisis in the Eurozone. Strain in the Eurozone, rather than a delayed response to the changes in capital and liquidity policy implemented from October 2008, was the cause of renewed inter-bank tensions.

It is of course impossible to know what the counterfactual behaviour of the economy would have been in the absence of the sub-prime crisis and each of the various individual policy measures that occurred in response. But the evidence above suggests that macroeconomic conditions would have been even more unsatisfactory if nothing had been done by the authorities to repair banks' balance sheets. Without enough capital to reassure counterparties in the inter-bank market, banks would have been hard pressed to fund new assets and that would have had potentially catastrophic consequences for the supply of lending to the private sector. Overall, when looking at the causes of weak money and credit growth in the early stages of the financial crisis, the evidence suggests bank regulation probably prevented a much bigger collapse of the banking system.

But an inevitable sequel was a period of weak credit growth while banks convalesced and adjusted. QE was designed to boost the money supply, independently of credit growth, through direct purchases of assets from the non-bank private sector, particularly from large financial intermediaries such as insurance companies and pension funds. QE did make a major contribution to the recovery. But our analysis has shown that "leakages" from QE depressed broad money growth relative to what might have been expected based simply on the nominal value of purchases made.

III

This section examines the implications of weak money growth for spending in the economy. One question follows quickly from the previous section. If money growth was weak in 2009 because of some unexpected QE leakages, why did the Monetary Policy Committee simply not scale up QE to deliver a stronger rate of money growth? The answer lies in the behaviour of nominal spending in the early years of the crisis. This behaviour did not conform to a simple monetarist relationship where spending follows broad money growth with a lag.

One observation from Figure 3.1 is that the historical data do not display a stable relationship where contractions in money lead contractions in nominal GDP with a lag. In many periods broad money growth appears to move contemporaneously with or even to lag nominal spending. The main exception to this is the late 1960s and early 1970s, which corresponds to the period when monetarist confidence in the reliability of a money–income relationship was reaching its peak.[14] But in general the relationship between money and spending within and across business cycles is complex. The difficulties were appreciated in the classic 1982 study by Friedman and Schwartz, and extensive investigations into long-run data by, for example, Capie and Mills, and Capie, Mills and Wood in 1991 papers.[15]

This lack of a simple relationship between money and nominal spending throughout the entirety of the recent crisis is obvious in Figure 3.7. In fact, two phases are worth distinguishing. The first phase, between the end of 2007 and mid-2010, roughly corresponds to the height of the sub-prime crisis, the collapse of Lehman Brothers and the first round of QE in the UK; the second phase runs from the middle of 2010 onwards, a period which was dominated by the Eurozone crisis that began in spring 2010 and developed thereafter, and which also saw in the UK the second and third instalments of QE.

In the first phase the four-quarter growth rate of broad money and credit contracted from 10 per cent to 4 per cent (or by 6 percentage points)

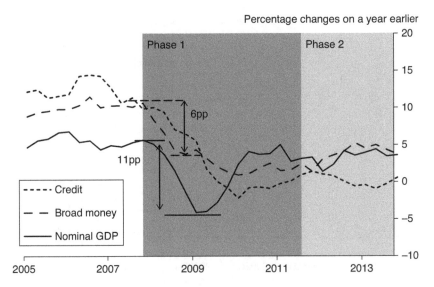

Figure 3.7 Broad money and nominal spending growth during the crisis

between the middle of 2007 and early 2009. During that period nominal spending growth fell broadly in tandem, but by an even larger amount of around 11 percentage points, falling from a positive rate of just over 5 per cent a year to a negative rate of minus 5 per cent. A closer exami-nation of the quarterly data might suggest some evidence of a leading relationship between money and spending in the early stages of the crisis between 2007Q3 and 2008Q2. But after the Lehman crisis nominal spend-ing growth fell rapidly over the following three quarters, while broad money growth remained positive, albeit at a low rate. As a result of these movements, the velocity of broad money fell rapidly throughout 2008 and early 2009 (see Figure 3.8). So it is not obvious that the slowdown in broad money growth preceded or was the entire explanation for the slowdown in spending over this period. Furthermore, from mid-2009 onwards nominal spending growth recovered very rapidly to just over 5 per cent on annual terms, whereas money growth weakened further to an annual rate of around 1 per cent. So, even if regulation was the cause of weak money and credit growth in the early stages of the crisis, this does not appear to be the whole story. The sluggishness of money did not prevent a rapid recovery in nominal spending in late 2009 and early 2010.

The recovery in nominal spending in 2010 despite a weakening of money growth leads to a distinct V shape in velocity over Phase 1 as a whole (see Figure 3.8 again). The divergence between money and spending needs

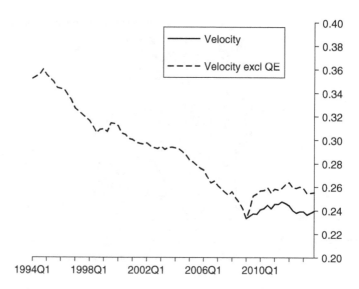

Note: Velocity calculated as quarterly nominal GDP at market prices divided by M4 excluding intermediate OFCs.

Source: Bank of England and ONS.

Figure 3.8   Broad money velocity: the effect of QE

explaining, with the role of money demand shocks perhaps offering useful insights about this period. A further point is that the upturn in nominal spending mostly took the form of higher inflation – which rose well above the Monetary Policy Committee's 2 per cent target – rather than of faster real growth. Above-target inflation was undoubtedly a key factor underlying the MPC's decisions to pause QE at this moment, despite weak money growth.

In phase 2 of the crisis a more traditional monetarist relationship developed. From mid-2010 the developing Eurozone crisis had significant implications for UK banks, with renewed upward pressure on bank funding costs, as shown earlier in Figure 3.6. The nascent recovery in money and credit growth in early 2010 stalled, and nominal spending began to decline. But at this stage in the crisis little money destruction was attributable to long-term debt and capital issuance, because such issuance was deterred by the higher cost of raising long-term debt and equity. In fact, for the relevant quarters the main effect of regulatory policy was positive for broad money as banks purchased substantial amounts of gilts. The banks' gilt purchases, in addition to the QE implemented in late 2011 and throughout

2012, were able to boost annual money growth to around 5 per cent. The 5 per cent figure was achieved despite the continuing weakness in bank credit to the private sector. Indeed, a healthy rate of money growth persisted into 2013, in part because private banks kept on buying gilts. The money revival presaged the recovery in nominal spending growth during 2013, establishing a more traditional monetarist pattern over this phase. Overall, our analysis suggests that the V in velocity during Phase 1 of the crisis was the real puzzle. The V in velocity must be explained if a monetarist account of the crisis is to be compelling.

IV

So, what does explain the V in velocity during the crisis? One factor that might be thought to have contributed to the V shape in velocity is QE. QE itself should lead to an increase in the money supply, followed by an increase in nominal spending some time later as portfolio rebalancing works its way through the economy. That would imply a temporary fall in velocity followed by a subsequent increase as the effects of QE on spending come through with a lag. In a counterfactual sense that might explain why money growth fell by less than nominal spending in the early stages of the crisis. But the timing does not work. QE began in March 2009 well after the fall in velocity. Indeed, when we strip out the effects of QE on broad money and nominal spending using the estimates from the Bridges and Thomas 2012 paper, the V shape becomes even more pronounced (Figure 3.8).[16] It also reveals a further more general drift upwards in velocity in 2010 and 2011. So we need to look for other causes to account for the behaviour of velocity.

The most likely cause for the fall in velocity throughout 2008 and early 2009 was suggested earlier in this chapter: increased liquidity preference reflecting a higher precautionary demand for money. That may have been because of uncertainty and a general aversion to risky assets. A range of uncertainty measures picked up over this period (see Figure 3.9). Some evidence can be assembled for switches, by both households and companies, away from sight deposits into time deposits during 2008 and early 2009. That may represent an increase in precautionary demand at the expense of the transactions demand for money (Figure 3.10). But care must be taken in making too much of movements between sight and time deposits over this period as the two became close substitutes at the low interest rate levels observed in and after 2009.

Increased money demand may also have been because of worries about future credit availability (see Figure 3.11). This may have led companies

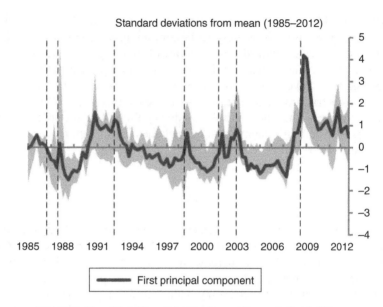

Standard deviations from mean (1985–2012)

First principal component

Source: Abigail Haddow, Chris Hare, John Hooley and Tamarah Shakir 'Macroeconomic uncertainty: what is it, how can we measure it and why does it matter?', *Bank of England Quarterly Bulletin*, 2013, vol. 53, no. 2, pp. 100–109.

Figure 3.9   A time series of uncertainty indicators

and households to hold higher money as a precaution, to anticipate the future withdrawal of credit facilities. More generally, we also know that trade credit and other settlement mechanisms deteriorated in this period. Bank deposits may have been even more favoured as a means of settlement, implying a higher ratio of money to spending and reduced velocity during 2008 and early 2009. The charts show that all these factors reversed quickly during 2009 and early 2010. As they look plausible potential candidates to explain the V shape in velocity, the series in the charts should form the basis of future empirical research into the demand for money over this period. Regulatory policy may have played a beneficial role here. It both reduced imminent fears about a collapse in credit availability and countered the need to hold precautionary cash balances. By implication, agents had lower liquidity preference than would otherwise have been the case, allowing nominal spending to recover in late 2009 and early 2010.

Other influences may have been at work in the recovery in velocity observed in 2010 and 2011. One may be *disintermediation*, understood as the transfer of financial business from intermediaries (such as the banking system) to other channels (like the capital markets). The higher credit

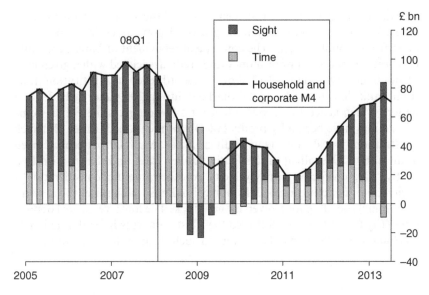

Source: Bank of England.

Figure 3.10   Sight and time deposits

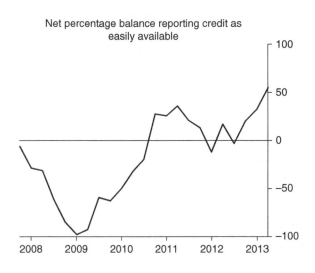

Source: Deloitte CFO survey.

Figure 3.11   Deloitte's CFO survey of corporate credit availability

spreads associated with the financial crisis and the accompanying increase
in banks' loan margins may have provoked companies into borrowing
more from capital markets. The consequent repayment of bank debt could
have lowered the amount of money and credit associated with a given level
of nominal GDP. Figure 3.12 shows a record level of substitution away
from bank debt towards capital markets during 2009 and early 2010, a
pattern which lasted to a lesser extent for a few quarters thereafter. Some
of that may have been a by-product of QE, as mentioned earlier. But such
substitution typically occurs in credit crunches. A similar pattern occurred
in the early 1990s, albeit on a slightly smaller scale, and that too led to a
gently rising profile of money velocity. Another potential consideration is
dishoarding, an activation of idle money holdings which raises the amount
of nominal spending for a given money stock. The low level of real deposit
rates (Figure 3.13), which followed the substantial cuts in bank rate in late
2008 and early 2009, may have induced such dishoarding via two mecha-

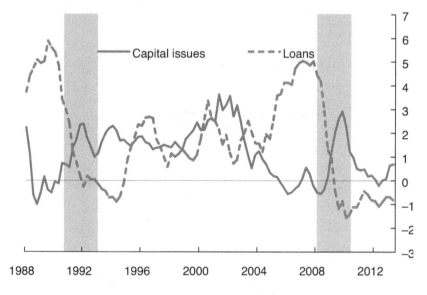

Notes:
(a) Shaded regions denote recessions in the UK.
(b) Lending series is sterling net lending to PNFCs excluding the effects of securitization.
(c) Capital issuance is given by the net amount raised from sterling issuance of equity, bonds
and commercial paper by UK private non-financial companies.

Source: Bank of England.

Figure 3.12   Capital market substitution

nisms. Either households and companies switched out of money into real goods such as durables and investment goods, or they switched into financial assets with a higher return than the nominal zero interest available on deposits (and the consequent negative real interest).

In summary, the range of policies introduced in response to the financial crisis may have reduced precautionary money demand, lowered the financial incentive to hold idle money balances and reduced fears about a collapse in credit availability. All these developments promoted the recovery in nominal spending seen towards the end of Phase 1 of the crisis. So, even though the policy response to the crisis may not have delivered strong money growth, it did result in a rise in money's velocity of circulation. Nominal spending growth recovered in 2010 and remained positive thereafter.

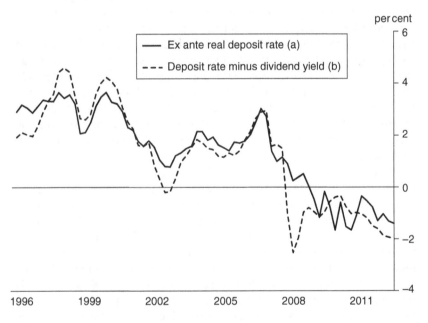

Notes:
(a) Ex ante real deposit rate is defined as the quoted rate on 1-year fixed rate bonds minus 1-year-ahead household inflation expectations from the Barclays Basix survey.
(b) Quoted rate on 1-year fixed rate bonds minus the quarterly average dividend yield on the FTSE all share index.

Source: Bank of England.

Figure 3.13 Relative rate of return on deposits

V

What are the main conclusions? These fall into the two discussion areas highlighted at the outset, namely the need to explain the pattern of broad money change in the crisis period, and the need to understand why demand and output did not respond mechanically in proportion to variations in broad money growth.

On the first topic, two reasons can be adduced for the weakness of broad money growth in the early stages of the crisis, despite the extensive policy response. First, bank balance sheet repair, only in part driven by regulatory policy, entailed a period of weak credit growth. Further, institutions' money holdings were drained as they subscribed for the long-term debt and equity issued by the banks. But arguably these adjustments were necessary to prevent a much more catastrophic collapse in bank lending. Meanwhile official demands that banks hold more liquidity encouraged banks to purchase gilts from non-banks, which boosted broad money. This countered the negative effect of higher capital and long-term debt issuance on broad money. Second, although QE was designed to boost the money supply independently of credit growth, leakages from QE meant that broad money growth was lower than might have been expected. Our analysis suggests that the positive effect of QE on broad money was much less than the value of the Bank of England's asset purchases. The critiques of official UK policy by Congdon and Ridley in the current volume have superficial plausibility, but rest on counterfactual assumptions that can be challenged.

But explaining the crisis is not all about the quantity of money and changes in its growth rate. To understand the trajectory of nominal spending over the crisis requires an interpretation of *both* the marked changes in the velocity of circulation between 2008 and 2011, *and* the role that policy played in influencing velocity. Changes in broad money and nominal national income were not equi-proportional, as some statements in the monetarist tradition require. Nevertheless, monetarist thinking helps in assessing the shifts in money-holding behaviour that complicated the relationship between money and spending in the UK's Great Recession. Such thinking must be retained in future empirical research and will surely be an aspect of any convincing future interpretation of the crisis.

NOTES

*   Any views expressed are solely those of the author and so cannot be taken to represent those of the Bank of England or to state Bank of England policy. This chapter should therefore not be reported as representing the views of the Bank of England or members of the Monetary Policy Committee, Financial Policy Committee or Prudential Regulation Authority Board.

1. John Maynard Keynes *The General Theory of Employment, Interest and Money*, vol. VII in Donald Moggridge and Elizabeth Johnson (eds) *Collected Writings of John Maynard Keynes* (London and Basingstoke: Macmillan, 1973, originally published 1936), pp. 84–5.

2. For more on the notion of the velocity of circulation, see pp. 188 in Chapter 8 below in a discussion of money and asset price determination.

3. See for an example of a Divisia analysis Michael Belongia and Peter Ireland 'Interest rates and money in the measurement of monetary policy', National Bureau of Economic Research Working Paper (Cambridge, MA: NBER), no. 20134, May 2014.

4. See, for example, Manmohan Singh 'Collateral and monetary policy', IMF Working Paper (Washington, DC: International Monetary Fund), no. 13/186, August 2013.

5. In a series of newspaper articles (mostly in *The Times*) Tim Congdon criticized the acceleration of money growth in the UK from 1985 to 1988, and forecast correctly that it would lead to asset prices excesses, and eventually to an inflationary boom and bust. He used broad money measures in all his analyses. The articles were collected in his 1992 *Reflections on Monetarism* (Cheltenham, UK and Brookfield, MA, USA: Edward Elgar Publishing, 1992).

6. For further discussion of the reasons for using M4x, rather than M4, in post-1998 analysis, see Stephen Burgess and Norbert Janssen 'Proposals to modify the measurement of broad money in the United Kingdom: a user consultation', *Bank of England Quarterly Bulletin* (London: Bank of England), vol. 47, 2009 Q3 issue.

7. A recent treatment is provided by Michael McLeay, Amar Radia and Ryland Thomas 'Money creation in the modern economy', *Bank of England Quarterly Bulletin*, vol. 54, 2014, Q1 issue, pp. 14–27.

8. See Stuart Berry, Richard Harrison, Ryland Thomas and Iain de Weymarn 'Interpreting movements in broad money growth', *Bank of England Quarterly Bulletin*, vol. 47, 2007, Q3 issue, pp. 376–88, and Jonathan Bridges, Neil Rossiter and Ryland Thomas 'Understanding the recent weakness of broad money growth', *Bank of England Quarterly Bulletin*, vol. 51, 2011, pp. 22–35.

9. See Bridges, Rossiter and Thomas, *BEQB*, 2011, and Nicholas Butt, Silvia Domit, Lewis Kirkham, Michael McLeay and Ryland Thomas 'What can the money data tell us about the impact of QE?', vol. 52, 2012, Q4 issue, pp. 321–31.

10. Key references are to the 2011 Bridges et al. paper and 2012 Butt et al. paper, both in the *BEQB*, and mentioned in note 9. Bridges, Rossiter and Thomas (2011) 'Understanding the recent weakness in broad money growth', *Bank of England Quarterly Bulletin*, Vol. 51, No.1, pp. 22–35. See also Jonathan Bridges and Ryland Thomas 'The impact of QE on the UK economy – some supportive monetarist arithmetic', *Bank of England Working Paper*, 2012, no. 431.

11. For more on "the corset", see Forrest Capie *The Bank of England: 1950s to 1979* (Cambridge: Cambridge University Press, 2010), pp. 521–3.

12. See Michael Cross, Paul Fisher and Olaf Weeken (2010), 'The Bank's balance sheet during the crisis', *Bank of England Quarterly Bulletin* (London: Bank of England), vol. 50, Q1 issue, pp. 34–42.

13. In a 2010 paper Button et al. discussed why three-month LIBOR ("London inter-bank offer rate") plus the five-year credit default swap premium was a good proxy measure of marginal funding costs for banks. See Richard Button, Silvia Pezzini and Neil Rossiter 'Understanding the price of new lending to households', *Bank of England Quarterly Bulletin*, vol. 50, Q3 issue, pp. 172–82.

14. Here the relationship is complicated by the presence of various disruptions to output caused by industrial unrest in the early 1970s. But, when the data are corrected for these influences, a 2012 paper by Ed Nelson identifies a correlation between changes in broad money and nominal spending. See Edward Nelson 'The correlation between money and

output in the UK: resolution of a puzzle' (Federal Reserve Board: Washington, DC, 2012), mimeo.

15. Milton Friedman and Anna Schwartz *Monetary Trends in the United States and the United Kingdom* (Chicago, IL, USA and London, UK: University of Chicago Press, for the National Bureau of Economic Research, 1982) remains the leading work in this field, but see also the three papers on pp. 71–138, of Forrest Capie and Geoffrey Wood *Money over Two Centuries: Selected Topics in British Monetary History* (Oxford: Oxford University Press, 2012).

16. See Bridges and Thomas 'The impact of QE on the UK economy', *Bank of England Working Paper*, 2012, for more discussion.

4. Have central banks forgotten about money? The case of the European Central Bank, 1999–2014

Juan E. Castañeda and Tim Congdon

The role of monetary policy in modern liberal democracies is controversial, but everyone agrees that central banks should prevent macroeconomic shocks rather than cause them. A policy regime should be designed to minimize macroeconomic instability. Ample empirical evidence, based on a well-established body of economic theory, identifies consistent medium- and long-run relationships between, on the one hand, growth of the quantity of money and, on the other, increases in nominal national income.[1] This chapter will argue, from the experience of the Eurozone from the introduction of the single currency in 1999, that maintaining steady growth of a broadly defined measure of money is crucial to the achievement of stability in demand and output. Monetary analysis is effective in interpreting the cyclical upheaval in the Eurozone's Great Recession in late 2008 and 2009. Further, over the last decade monetary instability in the Eurozone periphery's member states has been of exceptional severity. Oscillations in the rate of change in the quantity of money have been fully comparable with those seen in other notorious episodes of macroeconomic trauma, including the USA's Great Depression between 1929 and 1933 as documented in Friedman and Schwartz's 1963 classic study, *A Monetary History of the United States 1867–1960*.

The chapter is structured as follows. The first section recalls key points of the relevant body of theory, and reviews the empirical relationship between money growth and increases in nominal national growth for the Eurozone as a whole. The second section sketches the role of money (meaning "the quantity of money") in the evolving monetary-policy strategy of the European Central Bank. A salient message is that in the Eurozone's first four years the ECB monitored broad money growth as part of a "two-pillar" strategy, in accordance with the Bundesbank's long-standing and successful practice. It may not, strictly speaking, have targeted a money aggregate, but a "reference value" for M3 was set and followed. However, even this diluted kind of money-based policy-making was dropped in 2003. The loss of the quantity-of-money "pillar" was followed by a sharp acceleration in money growth, and a marked and consequent upturn in asset price inflation.

Although the Eurozone was initially less affected than the USA and the UK by the paralysis in wholesale money markets from August 2007, in autumn 2008 the tightening of bank regulation under G20 auspices led to a plunge in money growth.[2] The quantity of money actually fell in the year from the second quarter of 2009. Even five years later – in mid-2014 – it was little more than 5 per cent higher than it had been at the worst point in the Great Recession. The imposition of more rigorous bank regulation was far more important in policy-making than recognition that the quantity of money might affect macroeconomic conditions. The narrative suggests that three distinct sub-periods with markedly different policy-making approaches can be identified in the decade and a half under discussion. They are from January 1999 to May 2003, from May 2003 to October 2008, and from October 2008 to the start of 2015.[3] The different approaches reflected a lack of consistent thinking in the ECB leadership, and money growth and macroeconomic conditions were affected by this incoherence.

The third section of the chapter examines money trends in two specific Eurozone member states, Greece and Ireland. As will emerge, very large swings in money growth occurred, with catastrophic repercussions on output, employment and living standards. The final section concludes that the Eurozone's macroeconomic experience confirms the validity of a monetary interpretation of national income and wealth. By implication, the abandonment of the monetary pillar in 2003 was a serious mistake. Consideration should be given to the restoration of a money reference value or even to the introduction of a formal money target. At the least, ECB officials need to clarify their understanding of the relationship between regulatory actions on the one hand, and the growth of bank balance sheets and the quantity of money on the other.

I

As noted elsewhere in this volume, the relationship between money growth and the change in nominal national income has been thoroughly studied and confirmed in many countries over numerous long runs. A widely held view is that "excess" money growth – growth in the quantity of money that is well ahead of contemporaneous growth in real output – leads to inflation. Treatments by Irving Fisher, Patinkin, Friedman and many others share the common background of the quantity theory of money. A stylized argument assumes that the demand-to-hold-money function is stable, and that the arguments in it apart from national income and wealth are constant.[4] Given this assumption and starting from an equilibrium in which money demand equals the quantity of money actually in existence, a step increase in the quantity of money must be followed in due course by an equi-proportional increase in both national income and wealth.

This comparative-static result ("the proportionality thesis") is fundamental to the subject and familiar from a large body of literature. It has been accompanied by an unsettled and rather disorganized discussion of the processes by which the economy returns to equilibrium after the shock. In Friedman's papers, some of which now command almost iconic status, an initial jump in the quantity of money provokes a range of portfolio adjustments by companies and individuals. The prices of assets and goods rise, and keep on rising, in transactions that, taken together, are a multiple of national income in value.[5] The increase in the price level (and perhaps some advance in real output too) continues until the desired ratios of money to incomes and wealth are achieved.

The practical meaning of the assumed stability of money demand is that, once the period of adjustment is over, the desired ratios ought to be the same after and before the shock. Money and nominal national income must therefore rise together with, more or less, the same percentage increase. Since the adjustment processes take time, the real-world relationship between money and national income should be evaluated over the medium to long term. Of course, in order to make the analytical approach manageable, the appropriate measures of money, national income and the price level need to be chosen. A particularly important issue is the extent to which the prices of assets should be incorporated in the overall price level, since asset prices and such well-known inflation yardsticks as the consumer price index are not correlated in the short run.[6] These questions are not trivial, and the answers to them will determine both the scope and the limits of the current analysis. For reasons discussed elsewhere in this volume, a broadly defined concept of money (M3) is used throughout the current chapter.[7]

In real-world applications of the theory numerous difficulties and complications confuse the issue. The arguments in the money demand function other than income and wealth, notably the relative attractiveness of money and non-monetary assets, are forever changing. Meanwhile banking institutions and arrangements, which affect behavioural parameters, evolve in response to new technologies and regulations. If standard theory were the whole story, the velocity of circulation would be much the same decade after decade, but that is rarely a verdict allowed by the

Table 4.1   Key features of Eurozone monetary trends, 1999–2015

	Levels, in billions of euros	
	Quantity of money (M3)	Nominal gross domestic product
1999 Q1	4459.60	6337.80
2014 Q4	10 313.60	10 174.50
Average annual growth rate, %		
1999 Q1–2014 Q4	5.4	3.2
Ratio of money to nominal GDP:		
1999 Q1	0.704	
2014 Q4	1.032	

Source: IMF database and authors' estimates.

data. Instead careful scrutiny of banking and macroeconomic information is required to identify new influences on the demand to hold money
balances. In Friedman's words, "on an empirical level, [the quantity
theory] has increasingly become the generalization that changes in desired
real balances [that is, changes which will affect equilibrium velocity] . . .
proceed slowly . . . [S]ubstantial changes in prices or nominal income are
almost always the result of changes in the nominal supply of money."[8] A
further warning has to be given. For the Eurozone in the period under
examination, analysis is beset by problems, partly because the introduction of the single currency in 1999 was a remarkable experiment. As it
was the first time in the late twentieth century that several countries had
pooled their monetary sovereignty by sharing the same money, statistical
data became subject to series breaks, while many new institutional and
behavioural uncertainties were created.

At any rate, abundant data are available for the quantity of money and
nominal national income, and permit an initial appraisal. Table 4.1 gives
key information on the changes in the quantity of money and nominal
GDP for the Eurozone over the whole period. It is immediately evident
that hopes of an almost constant velocity of circulation are disappointed.
The ratio of money to GDP (that is, the inverse of velocity) rose appreciably in the almost 16 years under review. In a typical year the ratio of
money to GDP increased by over 2 per cent, not much less than the average
annual growth rate of nominal GDP of 3.2 per cent. On the face of it, the
change in the desired ratio of money to income was not much less important than money itself in accounting for the behaviour of nominal GDP.
But can the rise in the ratio of money to income be explained in choice-

theoretic terms, as a response to institutional developments and changes in the opportunity cost of money holding? If so, the central contention of the quantity theory of money – the proportionality thesis – might remain valid in an underlying sense.[9]

An important influence on the rise in the money/income ratio may have been that the introduction of the euro in the 1990s constituted a major deregulation of the entire European banking system. Preparations for the new currency were accompanied by the abolition of exchange controls, the ending of bank regulations that had once been specific to member states and the harmonization of central bank cash reserve requirements at a much lower cost to the banks than before.[10] This deregulation encouraged more intense competition, and hence a narrowing of margins between deposit and lending rates. As many businesses (and even some individuals) simultaneously hold deposits and have outstanding bank loans, the narrowing of margins enhances the attractiveness of banking services and raises the equilibrium ratio of bank intermediation to GDP. The effect applies particularly to non-bank financial institutions, the profitability of which is much influenced by the terms that banks offer. In the UK and other countries financial liberalization has been associated with both significant rises in the ratio of bank intermediation to GDP and markedly higher expansion of money balances in the non-bank financial sector than in other parts of the economy.[11] If these arguments were correct, two patterns might be expected. First, the rise in the money/income ratio would be expected to be most pronounced in the early years of the single currency, as agents took advantage of the opportunities created by banking liberalization. Secondly, the money holdings of companies – especially financial companies – ought to have risen more rapidly than the money holdings of households. Can supporting evidence be found?

Figure 4.1 shows the timing of the rise in the ratio of money to income. Clearly, more than all of it occurred between 1999 and 2008, with a peak value (of just over one) in the fourth quarter (Q4) of 2008. This is consistent with the hypothesis that the increased competitiveness of the banking system after the euro's inception lay behind the change in the money/income ratio, even if it is not a rigorous proof of that hypothesis. Table 4.2 gives numbers for the change in the money holdings of different types of agent, although – unfortunately – the statistics (which come from the ECB's database) begin in January 2002 rather than in January 1999.[12] Again, the facts agree with the possibility that the new currency represented a major deregulation, which promoted more money holding. As expected, non-financial companies increased their money holdings relative to turnover (that is, to nominal GDP roughly speaking) more rapidly than

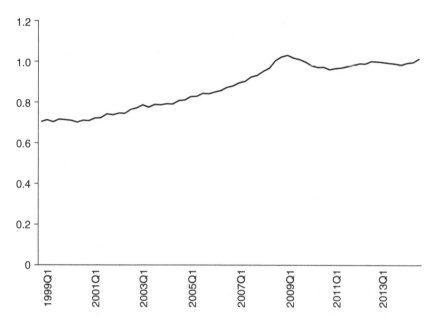

Figure 4.1   Ratio of quantity of money (M3) to nominal GDP in Eurozone, 1999–2014

households increased theirs relative to incomes, while financial companies' money balances climbed even more quickly relative to GDP.

The increase in financial companies' money may have reflected a widely noticed long-run tendency for financial assets (which is usually the relevant variable in determining financial sector money demand) to grow faster than national income and output. This tendency is sometimes denigrated as artificial "financialization", on the grounds that the financial sector adds less genuine value added than indicated by the incomes received by its workforce.[13] Whatever the truth of the allegation, the behaviour of Eurozone financial sector money accords with the notion that an intensification of banking system competition may have stimulated the propensity to hold money. To anticipate discussion in the next section, it is worth pointing out that the years 2003–08 not only saw unduly high money growth for all Eurozone people and companies, but were also characterized by extremely rapid rises in the financial sector's money balances. If pension funds and insurance companies are excluded, the compound annual growth rate of financial sector money between January 2003 and October 2008 was an extraordinary 17.9 per cent. This was well above the compound annual growth rate in the same period of household money which, at 6.9 per cent, was quite high enough.[14]

Table 4.2   Growth rates of different sectors' money holdings, 2003–14

M3 money, in billions, of euros, held by

| | Households | Companies: | | | |
		Non-financial	Pension funds & insurance companies	Financial, excluding PFICs	*All companies*
January 2003	3815.2	1095.9	204.1	454.0	1754.0
January 2015	6377.7	2085.4	376.4	1039.3	3501.1
% annual compound rates of change, Jan 2003–Jan 2015					
	4.4	5.5	5.2	7.1	5.9

Source: ECB database and authors' calculations.

One final body of information may be of interest in this context, the comparative experience of the Eurozone's member states. Doubts might be raised about the meaningfulness of national money data in a multi-nation currency union, because – for example – currency passes from hand to hand between residents of several member states. The notion of the "residence" of a money-holder becomes elusive. The difficulties are likely to be greatest for nations known to have disproportionately large financial centres, since such centres may be the location of so-called "brass-plate companies" of which the beneficial owners are non-residents. However, starting from January 2002 the International Monetary Fund has compiled broad money estimates for Eurozone states. As far as the IMF is concerned, these states still have identifiably national banking systems, and distinct governments that are accountable for bank regulation and deposit protection on a local basis. Table 4.3 sets out information for the 2002–14 period on the rates of growth of money and nominal GDP for the 12 member states that joined the Eurozone at its inception.[15] Table 4.4 shows the ratio of money to nominal GDP at the beginning and end of the period for the same countries.

The information in these two tables may still not convince economists sceptical about the quantity theory. Nevertheless, certain features of the data imply that money and national income are related, and that quantity-theory reasoning has analytical value. One message from Table 4.4 is that Luxembourg, the smallest nation in the Eurozone which has specialized in financial intermediation, was and remains an outlier, with an unusually high ratio of money to national income.[16] This conforms to expectations and warns that national money stocks could be affected by changes in the

Table 4.3   Growth of money and nominal GDP in Eurozone member states, 2002–14

	Average annual % rate of change	
	M3 quantity of money	Nominal GDP
Germany	4.8	2.3
France	5.6	2.5
Italy	5.7	1.6
Spain	5.3	3.1
Netherlands	5.5	2.5
Belgium	5.4	3.2
Austria	6.1	3.2
Greece	3.2	1.2
Finland	6.9	2.8
Portugal	2.1	1.7
Ireland	6.3	3.2
Luxembourg	3.0	5.8
Eurozone as a whole	5.2	2.6

Notes: Period is from Q1 2002 to Q4 2014. Data are from IMF database, with numbers in table estimated by the authors.

country in which companies (and hence their bank deposits) are registered. Italy presents an interesting contrast with Luxembourg. It is widely believed to suffer greater tax evasion than other countries, discouraging the holding of assets in places easily tracked by the authorities. At the start of the period under review the ratio of money balance to Italy's GDP was almost the lowest in the Eurozone and less than a fourteenth that in Luxembourg.

Despite these and other differences, all the Eurozone's nations (apart from Luxembourg) have seen an increase in the ratio of money to GDP in the single currency period. If Portugal, Greece and Italy are also excluded as being affected by special anxieties over their banking systems in the closing years of the 2002–14 period, the change in the ratio of money to GDP is close to the Eurozone average (of 37.4 per cent) for every Eurozone member state. There is also a reasonable correlation between the average annual rates of change of M3 broad money and nominal GDP in the 12 countries, although – once again – it is best to eliminate Luxembourg from the exercise.[17] A fair generalization from this and earlier information is that changes in the quantity of money have an important bearing on changes in national income in the Eurozone, in accordance with economic theory. While alterna-

Table 4.4   Ratios of broad money balances to GDP in Eurozone member states

	January 2002	December 2014	% change in ratio of money to GDP over 2002–14 period
Germany	0.659	0.895	35.8
France	0.658	0.950	44.4
Italy	0.550	0.893	62.4
Spain	0.844	1.091	29.3
Netherlands	0.838	1.165	39.0
Belgium	0.919	1.187	29.2
Austria	0.692	0.894	29.2
Greece	0.923	1.059	14.7
Finland	0.525	0.773	47.2
Portugal	0.908	0.948	4.4
Ireland	0.703	1.010	43.7
Luxembourg	8.124	5.155	−36.5
Eurozone as a whole	0.738	1.014	37.4

Notes: Period is from Q1 2002 to Q4 2014. Data are from IMF database, with numbers in table estimated by the authors.

tive views might be expressed, the hypothesis that macroeconomic developments can be interpreted from a quantity-theory perspective is legitimate.

II

The time has come to consider the role of money in the ECB's strategy. As adumbrated earlier, the discussion can be split into three, reflecting the changing emphases of the ECB's economics research team and Governing Council.

1.   A Successful Strategy: the Monetary Pillar Retained, from January 1999 to May 2003

Confidence in the relationship between a broadly defined money measure and nominal gross domestic product was basic to the design of the ECB's monetary strategy in its early years. In the post-war decades before the euro's introduction, Germany's central bank, the Bundesbank, had by far the most impressive record in the containment of inflation of all the

EU's central banks. It therefore set the intellectual pace in monetary policy thinking at the outset of the Eurozone. It had achieved its success by implementing a target for broad money growth, and was open and explicit about its methods in its publications. Given the background, it was logical that the ECB's first chief economist was Otmar Issing, who had previously been chief economist at the Bundesbank. In the late 1990s he played a vital role in the organization of ECB research and policy advice. His 2008 book, *The Birth of the Euro*, explained the preparations and options for the ECB's strategy.[18]

At its start the euro had no performance record, and it was essential to remove uncertainty and gain credibility. As noted above, the euro was a radical experiment. The Eurozone's member states shared the same money, but they did not share fiscal institutions. The powers to raise taxes and even to issue debt instruments were dispersed among the 11 nations. In this potentially fragile context with a wholly new configuration of powers and responsibilities, the decision to adopt the Bundesbank's much-admired monetary strategy was the safest option. It was widely expected that large behavioural shifts in the early stages of the new currency might be accompanied by high volatility in money growth. The ECB therefore announced not a binding target for broad money growth, but a "reference value". The reference value was for a rate of increase in broad money consistent with the ECB's definition of price stability. (This was for an annual rise of under 2 per cent in the harmonized index of consumer prices, over the medium term.)[19] Even though, in a formal sense the reference value was not a strict policy commitment, the exercise was intended with great seriousness. Issing and his colleagues were anxious to prevent unduly high M3 growth, as they believed it would be a reliable leading indicator of inflation trouble. As the ECB stated in the January 1999 issue of its *Monthly Bulletin*,

> substantial or prolonged deviations of monetary growth from the reference value would, under normal circumstances, signal risks to price stability over the medium term. This feature requires both that a stable relationship between money and the price level exists, and that monetary growth is a leading indicator of developments in the price level.[20]

Within this strategy the ECB pursued what it termed "two pillars" of analysis: one was the monetary pillar with its M3 reference value, and the other was more eclectic and included a range of data, including "the output gap".[21] The ECB's first President, Wim Duisenberg, said in 1998 that he could not indicate which of the two pillars was the "stronger" or "thicker", as they both mattered.[22] As announced by the ECB in December 1998, the first reference value (4.5 per cent) was the result of applying the money quantity equation, given expectations for output growth and money velocity in the Eurozone in the medium to long run. In the event, annual M3 growth in the opening years of the twenty-first century was well above 4.5 per cent, but the inflation numbers were pleasingly low and benign, and in accordance with the ECB's notion of price stability. In the years to January 2000, January 2001, January 2002 and January 2003, M3 advanced by 6.0 per cent, 6.6 per cent, 8.0 per cent and 7.0 per cent respectively. Critics of the monetary pillar pointed out that the expectations of inflation held in financial markets, as implied by bond yield differentials, were for inflation to remain in line with the ECB's objective. The money overshoot appeared not to bother market participants.[23]

2. A New Approach from May 2003: the Monetary Pillar Downgraded

In 2003 money growth decelerated, falling back towards the 4.5 per cent reference value. However, after reviewing its monetary strategy the ECB Governing Council decided in May 2003 to downgrade the role of the monetary pillar. Its statement was subtle and apparently even-handed, and said that the ECB was still pledged to the two pillars of analysis. Nevertheless, the publication of annual reference values for M3 was to be dropped. A shift in emphasis away from money and towards other indicators was under way. Issing remained on the ECB's executive board until 2006, but the tradition of Bundesbank-influenced broad money targeting was being de-emphasized.

Prominent academics praised the ECB's decision to snub money targeting and criticized the ECB for ostensibly retaining an analytical interest in M3 trends. The academic opponents of the money pillar came particularly from a New Keynesian position, which (as discussed elsewhere in this volume) is often represented in a three-equation model that nowhere mentions the banking system or the quantity of money.[24] New Keynesianism thus ignores the quantity of money, instead highlighting the importance of "the rate of interest" (usually meaning the money market rate set by the central bank in real terms) to the macroeconomic conjuncture.

An example of a paper advocating the elimination of the quantity of money from monetary policy-making and thinking was David Romer's much-cited 2000 contribution 'Keynesian macroeconomics without the LM curve' to the *Journal of Economic Perspectives*. Romer was particularly hostile to broad measures of money. While agreeing that central bank operations in money markets can impact on the amount of high-powered money and hence the money market rate, he said that "the appropriate measure of money is not clear" in textbook IS–LM analysis. He scorned the credit counterparts approach to the analysis of money growth. The new approach he favoured – of focusing on the real interest rate – would, to quote, allow the observer "to dispense with the confusing and painful analysis of how the banking system 'creates' money".[25]

The usefulness of monetary aggregates in policy-making had been denied in other influential academic articles just before and during the euro's introduction. In 1998 Michael Woodford, a celebrated monetary economist at Columbia University, published a paper on 'Doing without money: controlling inflation in a post-monetary world' in the *Review of Economic Dynamics*. According to the paper's abstract, economies would over time increasingly economize on the use of cash. In a supposed "cash-less limit" inflation would become "a function of the gap between the 'natural rate' of interest, determined by the supply of goods and opportunities for intertemporal substitution, and a time-varying parameter of the interest-rate rule indicating the tightness of monetary policy".[26] It followed that central banks, in the intellectual *avant garde* pioneered by Woodford and his associates, could target inflation without paying any attention to the banking system or the quantity of money. Woodford's 2003 book on *Interest and Prices* was widely hailed as a path-breaking work which might justify a future Nobel prize for its author. Its title recalled Wicksell's 1898 *Geldzins und Güterpreise*, which translates as *Interest and Prices*. The omission of the word "money" was seen as a deliberate slight to Patinkin's 1956 *Money, Interest and Prices*, a book often understood to be a classic development of quantity-theory ideas. In 2007 Woodford received the Deutsche Bank Prize in Financial Economics, which is awarded to "renowned researchers who have made influential contributions to the fields of finance and money and macroeconomics, and whose work has led to practical and policy-relevant results".[27]

The work of Woodford and other New Keynesians did indeed have practical, policy-relevant and far from negligible results. First, the communication policy of the ECB changed. The introductory statements of the President of the ECB at monthly press conferences (that is, those held after Governing Council meetings) increasingly gave priority to "economic" analysis and downgraded "monetary" research.[28] Second, and much more fundamentally, the downgrading of monetary aggregates led to monetary conditions that were too loose for too long. Figure 4.2 shows the annualized growth rate of M3 in six-month periods over the 13 years inclusive from the start of 2002 to the end of 2014. It is immediately apparent that the highest growth rates in these 13 years were from late 2006 to early 2008, when they were in double digits almost without interruption. As the trend growth rate of Eurozone output was thought to be little more than 2 per cent a year, a double-digit annual growth rate of quantity of money implied an acceleration in inflation to rates well above the 2 per cent price

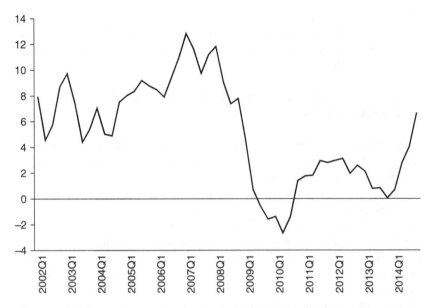

Figure 4.2   M3 growth in the Eurozone, 2002–14 (annualized rate of increase in last six months, %)

stability limit. That was true, even if a persisting rise in the ratio of money to income neutralized part of the risk.

Admittedly, inflation at the consumer level still remained moderate in 2006 and 2007. It needs always to be remembered that money is partly within financial portfolios, where agents are balancing money and non-money assets, while the lags between changes in money and in the prices of goods and services can be (in Friedman's phrase) "long and variable". The inflation pressure arising from excess money growth can surface in asset markets rather than in markets for goods and services. In practice, the high money growth of 2006 and 2007 affected asset prices most visibly and directly, and also boosted economic activity. House prices and stock markets soared, notably in the countries of the so-called Eurozone periphery, as will be discussed in more detail in the next section. Output in the Eurozone grew by 3.2 per cent in 2006 and 3.0 per cent in 2007. These were the highest figures so far in the twenty-first century and well above the numbers recorded in neighbouring years. The fastest money growth in the Eurozone's existence occurred in conjunction with marked asset price buoyancy, and above-trend growth in demand and output. This cannot be a coincidence. Critics of money targeting – such as Woodford and Romer – may have been right to question the precision of the relationship between changes in the quantity of money and changes in the price level of goods and services. But they went too far. The relationship between money and prices may have been less certain in the short run than expected, but that did not mean there was no relationship at all.[29]

3. The Response to Crisis: Tighter Bank Regulation Takes Precedence, from Autumn 2008 to end-2014

By mid-2007 the ECB Governing Council had become concerned about the medium-term dangers of above-target inflation. To the few observers who still tracked movements in the quantity of money, that could not have come as a surprise. But the focus of senior figures in international financial policy-making was about to shift towards a different and quite separate threat. In August 2007 the global wholesale money markets – the markets in which banks borrow from and lend to each other in many currencies, including the euro – closed down to new business. Senior bank executives were fearful that their counterparties had underestimated the fragility of some liquid assets, even including asset-backed securities carrying triple-A credit ratings. Banking systems in the advanced world seemed to be over-leveraged and, at least potentially, of doubtful solvency. As the euro-denominated inter-bank market had grown explosively since the start of the single currency in January 1999, and as banks in the Eurozone periphery were heavy new borrowers on this market, the ECB was anxious that some Eurozone banks might be hit by a sudden curtailment of credit lines.

The ECB reacted swiftly and effectively.[30] In the days following 8 August, which was the first to which the term "crisis" might be applied, it made borrowing facilities available on an immense scale to all Eurozone banks. The facilities were not at a penalty rate, but carried a cost close to the 4 per cent official minimum bid rate. The ECB's *Monthly Bulletin* called the extension of these facilities "a fine-tuning operation", but the numbers were vast, with €94.8 billion being provided on 9 August, €110 billion on 10 August, €310 billion on 13 August, and similar amounts on several days in the rest of the month. The aims – which were achieved – were to keep money market rates close to the official policy rate (that is, 4 per cent) and to ensure that all banks could fund their assets, even if inter-bank lines were being cut. The ECB was well aware that its conduct was exceptional and of an emergency kind, and the operations became known as the "non-standard measures".[31]

The non-standard measures involved transactions between the central bank and the commercial banks. They did increase the monetary base, but had no direct, first-round effect on non-banks' deposits (that is, on the quantity of money). However, the ECB's vigorous lending to cash-short banks did matter to monetary growth. If the ECB had not organized the non-standard measures, banks with net indebtedness to other banks would have been forced to shrink assets (by selling securities or cancelling loans), and that would have led to reductions in bank deposits on the other side of the balance sheet. In the event Eurozone banks, including banks in the Eurozone periphery, coped easily in late 2007 and early 2008 with their funding issues. Indeed, in the twelve months from September 2007 to August 2008 inclusive, new credit extended to the Eurozone's private sector was *higher* (€1329.2 billion) than in the previous twelve months (€1223.1 billion).[32]

Even as late as the autumn of 2008 the ECB expanded its lending to the banks by the implementation of the new fixed-rate lending facilities (with full allotment and no penalty rate), and by easing rules on the eligibility of loan collateral. Over the 18 months from August 2007 the ECB was a prompt and efficient lender of last resort. It is widely judged to have been better than, for example, the Bank of England in handling the inter-bank liquidity problems from August 2007.[33] It also prevented the failure of a large, specific institution, unlike the US Federal Reserve, which let Lehman Brothers go under in September 2008. For much of 2008 the global financial crisis was seen as a specific crisis of Anglo-American capitalism, while the Eurozone was better placed.

This favourable assessment turned out to be premature. The collapse of Lehman Brothers was followed by a sequence of high-level meetings under the auspices of the G20 nations, but with recommendations to the Bank for International Settlements (BIS), the International Monetary Fund and the European Commission (and so to all EU member states). The meetings arrived at agreements to enforce a tougher regulatory regime on the banks. In future banks were to operate with higher ratios of capital to assets, less inter-bank funding and higher proportions of liquid assets to total assets. (The changes taken together might be termed "the New Regulatory Wisdom". The NRW has costs as well as benefits, as discussed in Chapter 5 of the current volume.) The package of reforms was set out in a document known as "the Basel III Accord". This was finally approved in November 2010 by the G20, but already by then it was in the process of implementation. Indeed, Eurozone finance ministers decided at their Ecofin meeting in December 2008 that plans to recapitalize the banks should go ahead "without delay".[34]

No thought whatsoever seems to have been given to the implications of the regulatory upheaval for the rate of growth of the quantity of money. The monetary pillar had become invisible. Policy-makers' priority was to make the banks safe and robust, and less reliant on central bank support if inter-bank funding were interrupted again. Like Romer in his 2000 article, they may have found the discussion of how the banking system creates (or destroys) money "confusing" and "painful". In fact, the large-scale and hurried bank recapitalization endorsed by regulatory officialdom had catastrophic implications for money growth in the Eurozone, as elsewhere. Of course, senior officials were operating in panic conditions and some allowance might be made for that, but they seem to have lost altogether an understanding of relationships that are basic to monetary economics.

If banks' share prices are depressed by weak market confidence (as they certainly were in late 2008 and 2009), they are likely to react to demands for an increase in capital/asset ratios by reducing their assets or, at the very least, halting balance-sheet growth.[35] The asset reduction can be effected by sales of securities or by pulling in loans and cancelling them. If securities are sold to non-banks, non-banks pay for them by drawing on their bank deposits, which disappear from the economy; if loans to non-banks are repaid, the usual procedure is for non-bank borrowers to sell some assets, which initially adds to their deposits (at the expense of other agents' deposits), and then to use the deposits to pay off the loan. In both cases money balances are destroyed. Furthermore, the first-round effect of bank capital-raising is also to lower bank deposits and destroy money. (Investors typically pay for new securities issued by the banks by drawing on deposits. Payments from deposits of course reduce the level of deposits and hence the quantity of money.)

Contrary to Romer's claims, analyses of how banks create (and destroy) money are essential to good monetary policy-making. The ECB's actions had contradictory and paradoxical results. The ECB's lending facilities (the "fine-tuning operations" and the like) enabled the banks to operate despite the tensions in the inter-bank money markets. They "accommodated" existing bank business and were neutral or slightly positive for money growth. On the other hand, the European Commission and national financial regulators – acting in concert with the ECB – were increasingly requiring banks to maintain higher capital buffers and to fund assets more conservatively. Harsher bank regulation disrupted business models and was negative for money growth.

In practice, the negative forces overwhelmed the positive. Broad money growth collapsed. The month of October 2008 registered an exceptional 1.6 per cent upward blip in M3. But, from then on, the regulatory blitz led to a virtual cessation in Eurozone banks' new credit extension to the private sector. Whereas new credit had soared by €1329.2 billion in the twelve months to August 2008, it was to increase by only €195.5 billion in the twelve months to August 2009. Meanwhile, enforced bank capital-raising cut into money holdings, as investors acquired newly issued securities. In the six months from October 2008 M3 rose 1.0 per cent (that is, at an annualized rate of 2.0 per cent); in the next six months, from April 2009, M3 dropped by 0.8 per cent (that is, at an annualized rate of 1.6 per cent). Broad money growth of almost 9 per cent in the year to October 2008 contrasted with money growth of little more than nil in the year to October 2009.

The Eurozone's macroeconomic conjuncture changed drastically. Stock markets, and indeed asset markets in general, came under downward pressure. Eurozone residential property increased in value at a compound annual rate of 5.9 per cent in the first nine years of the single currency and reached an all-time peak in the third quarter of 2008. But between the second quarter of 2008 and the first quarter of 2010 it declined by 4 per cent, with much worse experience in some of the periphery economies. To the extent that loan collateral was provided by houses, these falls implied deterioration in the quality of banks' loan portfolios and were a further threat to their profitability and capital strength. The drops in asset prices, which were undoubtedly related to the squeeze on money balances, contributed to a deep contraction in Eurozone GDP of 4.4 per cent in 2009.

The ECB tried to alleviate persisting tensions in the inter-bank market by again expanding its lending facilities to the banking sector in May 2009, with the application of new twelve-month maturity repos. But a rethink about the wisdom of the "non-standard measures" seems to have begun at some point in mid-2009. The surge in ECB lending to Eurozone banks since August 2007 had been accompanied by a large increase in the monetary base. Jürgen Stark, who shared a Bundesbank background with Issing and had succeeded him as the ECB's chief economist in 2006, became concerned. His worry was that at some future date the rise in the monetary base would provoke a similarly large rise in the quantity of money and hence generate unacceptably high inflation. He managed to convince Jean-Claude Trichet, the ECB's President, and a majority of the Governing Council that the non-standard measures should be withdrawn. To quote from the editorial in the ECB's November 2009 *Monthly Bulletin*, "the Governing Council will make sure that the extraordinary liquidity measures [taken since mid-2007] are phased out in a timely and gradual fashion". That was necessary, according to the bulletin, "in order to counter effectively any threat to price stability over the medium to longer term".[36]

In a speech to the European Parliament on 16 March 2010 Stark said that the phasing-out of the non-standard measures had begun in December and would soon intensify. Very cheap borrowing facilities for the banks, at a mere 1 per cent rate, would soon disappear, while the term to maturity of the loans would be shortened. In Stark's words, "we decided to return to variable rate tenders in the regular three-month operations towards the end of April". For many banks in the Eurozone periphery the loss of the ECB credit lines was traumatic, since they still lacked the credibility in the interbank market to obtain enough funds to support their assets. If they asked their own customers (companies and households) to repay loans, they might breach legal agreements as well as forfeit goodwill. In effect, loan portfolios were illiquid. The banks therefore reacted to the withdrawal of the ECB loans by selling the most liquid assets they held, namely government securities. The spring of 2010 therefore saw substantial falls in the prices of bonds issued by governments in the Eurozone periphery, initiating what became known as "the Eurozone sovereign debt crisis". By far the most vulnerable country was Greece. Ahead of joining the single currency project in 1999 and 2000, it had deceived the European Commission and financial markets by understating its budget deficits and public debt. The drop in the price of its government bonds meant a surge in the yield, which then set the cost of servicing maturing debt. At the worst moments, in late April 2010, the yield of Greek government debt exceeded 30 per cent.

Whatever the uncertainties about its exact size, there was little doubt that the public debt was more than national income. Unless something was done, the debt interest on Greece's public debt would in due course move to above 20 per cent of GDP. This would be plainly unsustainable and indeed so intolerable that Greece would have to leave the Eurozone. On 10 May 2010 the ECB announced the Securities Markets Programme, which gave the Eurosystem (that is, the ECB working with the Eurozone national central banks) the authority to purchase large quantities of government bonds. Purchases of Greek sovereign paper came first, but over the next 18 months purchases were also made of Irish, Italian, Portuguese and Spanish government bonds. These purchases – which totalled over €200 billion by late 2011 – were not intended to boost the quantity of money, but to stabilize bond yields. On the Governing Council Stark and Axel Weber, attending as the President of the Bundesbank, voted against the Securities Market Programme, but were outmanoeuvred and outvoted.[37] Representatives from France and the Mediterranean countries had little interest in the Bundesbank tradition of monetary targeting, and were instead anxious to keep their banks afloat. The danger was that banking systems would have losses running into tens of billions of euros on assets – claims on European governments, after all – which only a few years earlier had been regarded as totally safe.

It can be argued that the sovereign debt crisis was precipitated by the withdrawal of the non-standard measures, even if the underlying problems were credit excesses and fiscal profligacy in the debtor nations. But

Stark, Weber and other senior figures from Germany were opposed to the restoration of large-scale credit facilities at easy terms from the ECB. A high proportion of the Eurozone's banks were nervous about their ability to fund existing assets, while the entire Eurozone banking system had to adjust balance sheets to the newly rigorous Basel III rules. The M3 measure of money fell by 2.5 per cent from April 2009 to July 2010, and had only just returned to its April 2009 figure by autumn 2011.

The debate within the ECB between representatives of German monetary thinking and a more widely held financial pragmatism became even sharper. Weirdly, the ECB increased its main policy rate twice (by 50 basis points in total) in April and July 2011, despite a depressed macroeconomic environment and while broad money growth was very weak. In countries on the Eurozone periphery persistent recession undermined tax revenues and widened budget deficits, exacerbating the sovereign debt crisis. Suggestions were made for a scheme of Outright Monetary Transactions to replace the Securities Markets Programme. The OMT involved, yet more frankly than the SMP, long-term central bank finance for governments, including governments of doubtful creditworthiness. On 9 September 2011 it was reported that Stark would leave the ECB, ostensibly for "personal reasons", but in fact because of disagreement with the OMT proposal. On 1 November Mario Draghi, governor of the Bank of Italy, replaced Trichet as ECB President. In December Draghi announced the return of massive, low-cost and long-term (three-year) ECB credit facilities for banks, up to an amount of almost €500 billion. In February 2012 the programme was enlarged to over €1000 billion, with the facilities becoming known as the "long-term refinancing operations" or LTROs. In the media they were dubbed more colloquially "the Draghi bazooka". The truth was that these were the non-standard measures in a new guise and on a larger scale.

The Draghi bazooka enabled most banks in the Eurozone periphery time to reorganize their affairs and to survive, but for many of them the three years to the end of 2014 were a difficult period of balance-sheet contraction and incomplete recapitalization. M3 grew, but only sluggishly. It went up by 3.0 per cent, 1.0 per cent and 3.6 per cent in the years to December 2012, 2013 and 2014 respectively. But – as will soon emerge – these figures concealed severe monetary retrenchment in the weakest states on the Eurozone periphery, and an extreme contrast between these states and a relatively comfortable situation in the Eurozone core. The ECB research department continued to monitor the behaviour of money, although the weight of monetary analysis as distinct from more general economic analysis declined over the years. Much of the research was of great complexity, showed no understanding of the importance of money to the determination of national income and wealth, and failed altogether to recognize the simplicity and power of the basic theory at work.[38] The intellectual muddles were associated with often bitter wrangling between the representatives of different monetary-policy traditions and banking constituencies. By the end of 2014 the Bundesbank's long commitment to the monetary pillar was far from dominating the ECB's research agenda or policy thinking.

* * *

The time has come for a quick summary of the money growth outcomes in the three sub-periods discussed above. Table 4.5 shows the money growth rates for the Eurozone as a whole for all three sub-periods, and for the core and periphery nations as a group in the last two sub-periods, and also for Germany and the rest of the core.

Money growth in Germany was stable during the first decade and a half of the single currency, and Germany enjoyed satisfactory macroeconomic performance. But in the periphery the annual rate of M3 growth ran at a compound 10.3 per cent in the five years (that is, our second sub-period) in which the monetary pillar no longer had a reference value on which policy-makers could focus, and slumped to virtually nil during and

Table 4.5   Money growth patterns in the Eurozone

All figures are of % compound annual rates of growth of M3 in the sub-periods under review, apart from length of sub-periods.

	From Q1 1999 to Q2 2003	From Q2 2003 to Q3 2008	From Q3 2008 to Q4 2014
Length of sub-period (in quarters)	*17*	*21*	*25*
The entire Eurozone	7.0	8.4	1.8
Seven nations of Eurozone core		7.8	2.8
Five nations of Eurozone periphery		10.3	−0.2
Germany		5.5	3.8
Core, ex-Germany		9.2	2.2

Note: M3 money stocks in countries were added together to obtain M3 measures for the core and periphery. The core nations were Germany, France, the Netherlands, Belgium, Austria, Finland and Luxembourg; the periphery nations were Italy, Spain, Greece, Portugal and Ireland.

Source: IMF database and authors' calculations.

after the Great Recession (our third sub-period). A fair verdict is surely that ECB policy-making was pro-cyclical rather than anti-cyclical, with money growth too expansionary in the years immediately before the onset of crisis in late 2008. The experience of two particularly hard-pressed nations on the periphery – Ireland and Greece – will now be considered in more detail.

III

The Introduction to this volume noted the importance of Friedman and Schwartz's *A Monetary History of the United States 1867–1960* to thinking about the Great Depression. Despite the disagreements that followed its publication, a great majority of economists accept that the extreme instability in money growth in the USA's Great Depression ought never to be repeated.[39] It will now be shown that the amplitude of fluctuations in the annual rates of change in broad money were larger in Greece and Ireland in the run-up to and during the Great Recession than in the USA in the run-up to and during the Great Depression.

The sources for the comparison are the monthly series for the quantity of money in the appendices to Friedman and Schwartz's 1963 volume, and the monthly M3 data from the IMF database for Greece and Ireland. The American money concept chosen for the current exercise is the sum of currency held by the public and commercial bank deposits, that is, broad money as usually understood. 1927 and 1928 were the final years of "the Roaring Twenties", with marked appreciation in share prices amid general prosperity. The plunge in the USA's quantity of money, as defined here, began in November 1929, just after the first crash in the stock market. It continued until spring 1933, when broad money stabilized for about a year ahead of very rapid growth in 1934, 1935 and 1936. So the boom–bust period associated with "the Great Contraction" (to use Friedman and Schwartz's term) might be seen as falling in the seven years 1927 to 1933 inclusive. As the exercise under consideration is concerned mostly with *changes* rather than *levels*, and as it should start from a relatively strong period for the economy, the level of broad money is obtained for these seven years. Annual changes are then calculated with the first value being for January 1928. The resulting series is shown in Figure 4.3.

Like other Eurozone countries, Greece and Ireland were little affected by the global crisis in 2007 and early 2008. As in the USA in 1927 and 1928, asset prices enjoyed marked appreciation amid general prosperity. Nevertheless, Greek and Irish money growth in 2007 and 2008 was much higher than in the USA in the 1920s. At any rate, M3 numbers can be

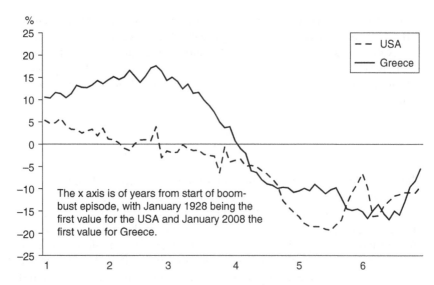

Figure 4.3 *Two episodes of extreme monetary instability: the USA's Great Depression and Greece's Great Recession (annual changes in broad money, monthly data, %)*

assembled for the seven years 2007–13 inclusive, and annual changes calculated for the six years 2008–13 also inclusive. The resulting series for Greece and Ireland are presented in two graphs, in Figure 4.3 and Figure 4.4, and contrasted with the annual changes in broad money in the USA over the 1928–33 period of exactly eight decades earlier. The main point is obvious from visual inspection. Instability in money growth was far more pronounced in Greece and Ireland in the Great Recession than in the USA in the Great Depression. More formal calculation delivers the same result. The standard deviation of the annual rates of change of US broad money in the six-year 1928–33 period, using monthly data, was 7.48. On the same basis and over the six-year 2008–13 period, it was 12.17 for Greece and 16.35 for Ireland. On this criterion, monetary mismanagement in these two Eurozone member states was more severe in the Great Recession than in the USA in its most notorious episode of central bank incompetence. Of course, all sorts of excuses and special factors can be invoked. Even so, the money data had a grim message for the citizens of the two nations.

One pointer to the wider misery was a surge in youth unemployment, which exceeded 30 per cent in Ireland at the worst of the crisis and was much worse in Greece. In 2014 fewer than 15 per cent of Greeks between the ages of 15 and 24 had a job, while over a half of those in the 25–29

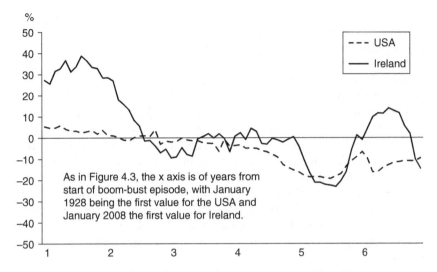

As in Figure 4.3, the x axis is of years from start of boom-bust episode, with January 1928 being the first value for the USA and January 2008 the first value for Ireland.

Figure 4.4   Two episodes of extreme monetary instability: the USA's Great Depression and Ireland's Great Recession (annual changes in broad money, monthly data, %)

year age bracket were still not in employment.[40] In 2014 the House of Lords published a report with the title, "Youth unemployment in the EU: a scarred generation?", with the Eurozone periphery being the focus of attention.[41]

IV

The quantity of money matters in the design of a monetary policy regime if that regime is to be stable or even viable on a long-term basis. The passage of events in the Eurozone since 1999 has shown, yet again, that excessive money growth leads to both immoderate asset price booms and unsustainably above-trend growth in demand and output, and that big falls in the rate of change in the quantity of money damage asset markets, undermine demand and output, and cause job losses and heavy unemployment. This is nothing new. The ECB did not sustain a consistent strategy towards money growth and banking regulation over its first decade and a half. The abandonment of the broad money reference value in 2003 was followed in short order by three years of unduly high monetary expansion and then, from late 2008, by a plunge in money growth to the lowest rates seen in European countries since the 1930s. The resulting macroeconomic turmoil was of the sort that would be expected by quantity-theory-of-money analyses, including such analyses of the USA's Great Depression as in Friedman and Schwartz's *Monetary History of the United States*.

Three lessons might be drawn from these developments. First, the stance of monetary policy cannot be assessed merely from the level of interest rates. Apart from a few months in late 2011 when an ill-judged increase in interest rates was engineered by the ECB, the three-month euro inter-bank rate has been under 1 per cent continuously from July 2009 to the time of writing (September 2016). Anyone trying to judge monetary policy from "the interest rate" (whatever that is) by itself would say that monetary policy has been exceptionally easy. But nations in the Eurozone periphery have been afflicted by a seemingly chronic malaise which again makes relevant Keynes's anxiety in his 1936 *General Theory* about a semi-permanent high-unemployment equilibrium. The behaviour of the broad money aggregate has been a better guide to the meaning of monetary policy.

Second, the monetary base *by itself* is also unsatisfactory as a measure of monetary policy. Many textbooks assert that changes in the monetary base are accompanied by equi-proportional changes in the quantity of money, and that the quantity of money then exerts its usual effects on financial markets and macroeconomic outcomes. But since 2008 large increases in the Eurozone's monetary base have had no follow-through into broad money, which – as just noted – has seen the lowest rates of increase that Europe has recorded since the 1930s. In 2011 Jürgen Stark appears to have lost credibility with his colleagues by adhering too dogmatically to a base-multiplier view of money supply determination. (As noted in the Introduction, other prominent monetarists – including even Milton Friedman – have alienated potential support for a quantity-theory approach by insisting on the rigidity of the link between the base and the quantity of money. No such link was found in the Eurozone in the 1999–2014 period.) The behaviour of the base and the money multiplier can of course account for changes in broad money in an arithmetical sense, but the Eurozone's experience confirms that this does not imply a causal connection.

Third, money targeting must be sustained over the long term if it is to work. Some economists – including, as we have seen, Romer and Woodford – repudiated money early in the single currency's existence on the grounds that a one-to-one relationship had not held between changes in money and nominal national income. But money is relevant to asset prices as well as to the prices of goods and services, while a change in the desired ratio of money to income does not mean that no relationship at all holds between money and income. As noted, by 2008 the fast broad money growth of the preceding three years had started to alarm the ECB about future inflation risks. The three-year lag may seem long, but it was not out of line with the UK's experience in its boom–bust cycles.[42] Occasional fluctuations in the velocity of circulation do not justify neglecting money data altogether.

The ECB did a good job in the period of most severe crisis with lender-of-last-resort loans (or "emergency liquidity assistance", as such loans now tend to be called) to banks that had dfficulty funding their assets.[43] The work continues to this day (September 2016), with large facilities still outstanding to banks in Spain, Italy, Greece and Portugal.[44] But top ECB officials did not seem to understand in late 2008 that a sudden demand for higher capital/asset ratios in the banking system would check the growth of banks' assets and hence cause a big decline in the rate of broad money growth. Their goal was to comply with demands from international regulatory bodies, such as the Bank for International Settlements and IMF. They were seemingly indifferent towards, or even ignorant of, the impact of the move to higher capital/asset ratios on the quantity of money. It is of the first importance that bank regulators become fully informed of the effect of their actions on the credit counterparts to money growth, no matter jibes from Romer and others that such analysis is "confusing and painful".[45]

The plight of the Eurozone periphery in the most problematic phase argues that some countries might have been well advised to leave the Eurozone for a few years, so as to facilitate the alignment of their costs and prices to those in the well-managed core nations.[46] But the implied currency devaluation would have had the immediate consequence of increasing the cost to banks (in Spain, Italy and so on) of repaying their loans to the ECB, as well as creating a tangled legal mess. In retrospect, it is clear that the paralysis in the global inter-bank market from August 2007 was an "asymmetric shock" which hit periphery nations (with many banks that were net debtors to other banks) much harder than core nations (where a majority of banks were creditors in the inter-bank market).[47]

Glaring imbalances between the macroeconomic performances of the core and periphery nations then emerged and perhaps were unavoidable to some extent. However, the decision to jettison the broad money reference value in 2003 was the prelude to the worst of the over-borrowing and financial excess in the 2005–08 period. Both the quantity theory of money and a large body of practical knowledge argued that a plunge from the explosively rapid rate of money growth to money stagnation from late 2008 onwards would result in macroeconomic agony. The ECB's Governing Council took the decisions both to drop the money reference value in 2003 and to move quickly to higher capital/asset ratios from 2008.

Friedman said of the Federal Reserve's conduct in 1930 and 1931 that it exercised its responsibilities "so ineptly as to convert what would otherwise have been a moderate contraction into a major catastrophe". At the start of the twenty-first century the ECB's research department had the benefit, compared with the Federal Reserve in the Great Depression, of over 70 years of advances in macroeconomic thinking. But monetary instability in some Eurozone member states in the 2008–13 period was greater than in the USA when the Fed was at its most criticized, unpopular and unsuccessful.

NOTES

1. See, for example, Michael Bordo and John Landon-Lane 'Does expansionary monetary policy cause asset price booms? Some historical and empirical evidence', NBER Working Paper no. 19585 (Cambridge: National Bureau of Economic Research, 2013).
2. In theory banks had several years to adjust to the new regulations, which were themselves only in draft form in late 2008. In practice they hurried to comply, leading to large-scale asset disposals and early balance-sheet retrenchment.
3. The paper ends with the adoption of "quantitative easing" in February 2015, which was accompanied by higher money growth and better macroeconomic conditions.
4. The body of literature is enormous and discussed elsewhere in this volume. Milton Friedman's entry on 'The quantity theory of money' in *The New Palgrave* would be widely viewed as a good attempt at a definitive treatment. See Peter Newman and others (eds) *The New Palgrave: Dictionary of Money and Finance* (London, UK and New York, USA: Macmillan and Stockton Press, 1992), pp. 247–64.
5. Again, the collection of literature is enormous, with the account of the so-called "real balance effect", pp. 3–33, in the second edition of Don Patinkin's *Money, Interest and Prices* (New York: Harper & Row, 1965) being a celebrated, if controversial statement of the position. For a more synoptic treatment, see Preface to Part Five, 'How does the economy work?', pp. 325–29, of Tim Congdon *Money in a Free Society* (New York: Encounter Books, 2011). The discussion of the effect of quantitative easing on the economy in Chapter 2 above is also pertinent.
6. Large but temporary divergences between movements in asset prices and goods prices are indeed intrinsic to some monetarist accounts of the transmission mechanism. See pp. 188–94 below in Chapter 8.
7. See pp. 7–8 in the Introduction.
8. See Friedman's entry in *The New Palgrave: Dictionary of Money and Finance*, p. 249.
9. The quantity theory allows equilibrium velocity to be changed by non-monetary forces, such as changes in payments technology. In the period under discussion, it would remain valid in an underlying sense if an average annual growth rate of, say, 10.4 per cent – 5 per cent higher than that actually recorded – would have been accompanied by an average annual rate of increase of 8.2 per cent – also 5 per cent higher than that actually recorded.
10. On 1 January 1999 banks in the Eurozone received interest on their cash reserves, whereas previously in some countries they had been required to maintain cash reserves on a non-interest-bearing basis at well above levels needed for bank settlement obligations.
11. An increasing ratio of bank intermediation to national output is indeed a characteristic of long-run economic growth in all economies. Asli Demirgüç-Kunt and Ross Levine

Financial Structure and Economic Growth: A Cross-Country Comparison of Banks, Markets, and Development (Cambridge, MA: MIT Press, 2004) is the usual reference today, but the idea goes back to Adam Smith.

12. The series began in January 2002, when euro-denominated banknotes were introduced. The first annual change is therefore for January 2003.

13. Critiques of "financialization" often come from left-wing, even Marxist sources. See, for example, Ozgur Orhangazi 'Contradictions of capital accumulation in the age of financialization', pp.248–65, in Turan Subasat (ed.) *The Great Financial Meltdown* (Cheltenham, UK and Northampton, MA, USA: Edward Elgar Publishing, 2016).

14. The tendency for financial sector money to grow faster than whole-economy money was also observed in the UK over several decades, reflecting the institutionalization of asset ownership. See Tim Congdon *Money and Asset Prices in Boom and Bust* (London: Institute of Economic Affairs, 2005), pp.32–7.

15. Apart from Greece (which joined in 2001), all 12 countries belonged to the Eurozone from the start of the euro (if only in scriptural form) on 1 January 1999. After 2007 seven further small or relatively small nations also joined: Slovenia, Cyprus, Malta, Slovakia, Estonia, Latvia and Lithuania. Because of their quantitative insignificance, the seven post-2002 members are not analysed here. Note that the IMF database publishes broad money series on a Euro-wide basis (that is, banks registered in one country have deposit liabilities across the Eurozone, which are included in the money concept for the country of registration) and on a residence basis. Apart from Luxembourg, the differences are small.

16. Luxembourg was once regarded as a centre of tax evasion. See p.183 of Stephen Valdez and Philip Molyneux *An Introduction to Global Financial Markets* (London: Palgrave, 8th edition, 2016) for a description of the stereotypical tax-evading "Belgian dentist". The introduction of the EU's Savings Directive in 2005 was intended to stop these practices.

17. If Luxembourg is excluded, a simple ordinary-least-squares regression of the numbers in Table 4.3 (with the changes in nominal GDP regressed on M3) yields a t-statistic on the regression coefficient of above 2.8 and a coefficient of determination (or r^2) of 0.47. If the intercept term is suppressed, the t-statistic on the regression coefficient rises to over 15 and the r^2 to 0.96.

18. Otmar Issing *The Birth of the Euro* (Cambridge: Cambridge University Press, 2008), pp.52–130.

19. See Issing 'The ECB's monetary policy strategy: why did we choose a two-pillar approach?', pp.260–69, in Andreas Beyer and Lucrezia Reichlin (eds) *The Role of Money: Money and Monetary Policy in the Twenty-First Century* (Frankfurt: European Central Bank, proceedings of the 4th ECB Central Banking Conference, 9–10 November 2006). See particularly p.262.

20. See the article 'The stability-oriented monetary policy strategy of the Eurosystem', *Monthly Bulletin* (Frankfurt: European Central Bank, January 1999 issue), pp.35–50. The quotation is from p.48.

21. The "output gap" (the difference between the actual and trend level of output, expressed as a percentage of trend output) was important to the economic analysis, as it played an important part in the New Keynesian model. But it had to be estimated by ECB research economists and was in fact not directly observable, unlike M3 and other money aggregates.

22. Issing *The Birth of the Euro*, p.99.

23. "For much of the 2001–04 period, the main reason for deviations of M3 growth from the reference value has been the impact of portfolio shifts, which are identified and quantified outside the money demand model. This has led to greater emphasis being placed on the M3 series corrected for the estimated impact of portfolio shifts in both the external and internal communication of the monetary analysis." See Bjorn Fischer, Michele Lenza, Hugh Pill and Lucrezia Reichlin 'Money and monetary analysis', paper presented at the 4th ECB Central Banking Conference on the role of money, 10–11

November, 2006. The quotation is from p. 10 of the paper. The estimates of the portfolio shifts can be found in the ECB's *Monthly Bulletins* for May 2003 and January 2005.

24. See pp. 195–6 in Chapter 8 below, by Philip Booth, for more on New Keynesianism.

25. David Romer 'Keynesian macroeconomics without the LM curve', *Journal of Economic Perspectives*, vol. 14, no. 2, spring 2000, pp. 149–69. The quotations are from p. 162.

26. Michael Woodford 'Doing without money: controlling inflation in a post-monetary world', *Review of Economic Dynamics*, vol. 1, no. 1, pp. 173–219. The quotation is from the abstract.

27. The quotation is from the Wikipedia entry, as at September 2016, on the Deutsche Bank Prize.

28. See the evidence in Helge Berger, Jakob de Haan and Jan-Egbert Sturm 'Does money matter in the ECB strategy?', *International Journal of Finance and Economics*, vol. 16, no. 1, pp. 16–31.

29. A common problem here is that statistical work finds that the quality of money demand functions deteriorated in the 1980s and 1990s, compared with earlier decades, at least partly because of financial deregulation. The functions' closeness of fit (as measured by the coefficient of determination and standard error of estimated equations) and the significance of coefficients (measured by t-statistics) were less satisfactory than before, although – almost invariably – the regression coefficient on the income term was positive and took a value not far from 1. Money relationships were then said to have "broken down", and advice was given to senior policy-makers, many of them naive about statistical methods, that they could ignore money. But the positive, almost unitary value of the regression coefficient on the income term still implied that large fluctuations in money growth would be associated with large fluctuations in the growth of demand, income and output. See Congdon *Money in a Free Society*, p. 319, for a discussion of the misunderstandings in this area.

30. See Brett Fawley and Christopher Neely 'Four stories of quantitative easing' *Federal Reserve Bank of St. Louis Review*, no. 95 (1), January/February 2013, pp. 51–88, for a detailed comparison of the programmes and facilities offered by the US Fed, the Bank of England, the Bank of Japan and the ECB, as they tackled the financial crisis from 2008 to 2013 in somewhat different ways.

31. The ECB's measures were in a well-established tradition that the central bank should act as lender of last resort to a solvent banking system subject to a run, as proposed by Bagehot's 1873 *Lombard Street*. Ironically, the central bank known as the most important historical sponsor of this approach, namely the Bank of England, was reluctant to adopt the Bagehot prescription in the Northern Rock crisis of September 2008. See pp. 170–74 in Chapter 7 below for further discussion.

32. The numbers are from the ECB's database, which differentiates between credit to "general government" and to "other Euro area residents". These "other residents" are taken to be equivalent to the private sector.

33. Timothy Geithner *Stress Test: Reflections on Financial Crises* (London: Random House Business Books, 2014), p. 132, and Ben Bernanke *The Courage to Act* (New York, USA and London, UK: W.W. Norton), p. 164.

34. The quotation is from the Ecofin meeting press release (2 December 2008). As discussed extensively elsewhere in this volume, notably in Part II, the rationale for the capital-raising programme was not obvious and lacked long-run historical precedent. Capie and Wood have shown that in the nineteenth century, well before the Basel rules had been introduced, banks did adapt their levels of capital to the level of risk in the markets. (Forrest Capie and Geoffrey Wood *Do We Need Regulation of Bank Capital? Some Evidence from the UK* [London: Institute of Economic Affairs, March 2013], 'Current Controversies' series, no. 40.) They question the purpose of the new, restrictive bank regulation. In their words, "The support of the British government, the EU and the Bank for International Settlements for higher capital requirements to prevent failure is . . . misguided . . . Talk of the separation of different types of bank recognises the importance of failure . . . Once banks are forced by the possibility of failure to take

responsibility for their actions, they are best placed to judge their own capital requirements. Under this new system, if they do not do so sensibly, they will not be in the business of banking for long."

35. The point does now seem to be understood in some parts of the ECB. To quote from
a recent research paper, "the effects of dampened credit and asset price growth on predicted crisis probabilities can be sizeable . . . During recession periods, an uncontrolled
asset-side deleveraging response to increased capital requirements could induce even
more recessionary pressure." See Markus Behn, Marco Gross and Tomas Peltonen
'Assessing the costs and benefits of capital-based macroprudential policy', ECB
Working Paper Series (Frankfurt: ECB), no. 1935 (July 2016).

36. ECB *Monthly Bulletin*, November 2009 issue, p. 6.

37. Hans-Werner Sinn *The Euro Trap* (Oxford: Oxford University Press, 2014), pp. 261–5.
See also Fawley and Neely, 2013, p. 81.

38. Of course, the phrase "the simplicity and power of the basic theory at work" is contentious. Nevertheless, the robustness of the link between money and other macroeconomic
variables in the first 15 years of the euro's existence is readily interpreted with the ideas
set out by Friedman, Patinkin and many others over centuries. See the references in
notes 4 and 5 above.

39. Randall Parker (ed.) *The Economics of the Great Depression: a Twenty-First Century
Look Back at the Economics of the Interwar Era* (Cheltenham, UK and Northampton,
MA, USA: Edward Elgar Publishing, 2007), p. 13 and p. 15, and see also Parker's subse-
quent interviews with 12 prominent macroeconomists.

40. Confederation of European Trade Union/ETUI *Benchmarking Working Europe*
(Brussels: ETUI, 2014), p. 37.

41. House of Lords EU Committee *Youth Unemployment in the EU: a Scarred Generation?*
(London: The Stationery Office), 12th report of the 2013/14 session.

42. See note 9 on p. 243 of Tim Congdon *Keynes, the Keynesians and Monetarism*
(Cheltenham, UK and Northampton, MA, USA: Edward Elgar Publishing, 2007).

43. For a recent discussion of the pros and cons of last-resort loans (or "emergency liquidity assistance"), see Forrest Capie and Geoffrey Wood 'Financial crises from 1803 to
2009: the crescendo of moral hazard', pp. 325–42, in their volume *Money over Two
Centuries* (Oxford: Oxford University Press, 2011).

44. The net indebtedness of banks in these four countries to the ECB was €722.2 billion in
July 2016, according to the Osnabruck University's Euro Crisis Monitor (www.eurocri
sismonitor.com).

45. It is perhaps worth noting that Romer is by no means alone in his aversion to credit
counterpart analysis. See Leland Yeager and Robert Greenfield 'Money and credit confused: an appraisal of economic doctrine and Federal Reserve procedure', pp. 179–95,
in Leland Yeager *The Fluttering Veil: Essays on Monetary Disequilibrium* (Indianapolis,
IN: Liberty Fund, 1997), reprinted from a 1986 article in the *Southern Economic
Journal*, for a critique of such analysis from economists with an avowed interest in the
quantity theory of money. The debate between the base multiplier approach to money
determination and credit counterpart analysis was mentioned above in the Introduction,
pp. 8–12.

46. Pedro Schwartz, Francisco Cabrillo and Juan Castañeda 'Saving monetary union? A
market solution for the orderly suspension of Greece', pp. 123–46, in Philip Booth (ed.)
The Euro – the Beginning, the Middle . . . and the End? (London: Institute of Economic
Affairs, 2013).

47. Concern about asymmetric shocks was one theme in the British Eurosceptic critique
of the single currency project in the 1990s. However, the risks of asymmetric shocks
in currency unions was noticed in the academic article usually seen as the intellectual
justification for currency unification, that is, Robert Mundell's 'A theory of optimum
currency areas' *American Economic Review*, November 1961.

PART II

The Financial System in the Great Recession:
Culprit or Victim?

Introduction to Part II

Tim Congdon

Part I of this book set out grounds for arguing that a sharp slowdown in the rate of broad money growth was the main cause of the global slump of late 2008 and 2009. The question naturally arises, "what caused the sharp slowdown in the rate of broad money growth?" The three chapters in Part II provide a possible answer to this question. A key issue is whether the financial system was a guilty malefactor or innocent bystander in the macroeconomic setbacks of the period.

In Chapter 5 Adam Ridley defines what he terms "the New Regulatory Wisdom" which emerged from the crisis. The NRW included large increases in banks' regulatory capital requirements. Ridley proposes that the NRW was responsible not just for a new aversion to risk in the banking industry. More fundamentally, the demand for extra capital implied a check to balance-sheet expansion that became (and remains) important to money growth trends. (Or perhaps one should say became so important to money stagnation.) In Chapter 6 Charles Goodhart also sees the demands for extra bank capital as having been at least partly responsible for the marked slowdown in credit extension and money growth. However, he believes that capital injections into the financial sector by G20 governments went some distance to mitigate the problems. In Chapter 7 Steve Hanke sides with Ridley in the debate. In a discussion where he develops points made in a January 2103 magazine article, Hanke describes the abrupt raising of banks' capital ratios as "the tried and true practice of bank-bashing". He notes that, paradoxically, "the drive to deleverage banks and to shrink their balance sheets, in the name of making banks safer, destroys money balances." (In the original article Hanke warned that, "if the political chattering classes continue to call for ever higher capital requirements for banks, expect to see tight credit, anaemic growth, and an unhealthy money supply picture for the foreseeable future." At the time of writing [September 2016] that looks right.)

The contention that mistakes by officialdom, not the commercial banking industry, were the main cause of the collapse in money growth that led to the Great Recession is controversial. Perhaps actual or looming loan losses meant that too many banks in mid-2008 lacked the capital to sustain new lending, so justifying the injection of new capital. With the capital/asset ratio given, it is true enough that extra capital should enable extra asset acquisition. But – if the reasoning behind that view is right – why did regulatory officialdom under G20 auspices press for a big increase in capital/asset ratios at the worst moment in the cycle? With capital given, a move to a much higher capital/asset ratio must lead to asset shrinkage and the large-scale destruction of money balances, while economic theory and a mass of evidence imply that the large-scale destruction of money balances must be deflationary. (In 2016 the Bank of England tried to head off a supposed post-Brexit referendum recession by *reducing* banks' capital/asset ratios. Can the logic behind its 2016 approach be reconciled with *raising* those same ratios in and after October 2008, to respond to the worst demand downturn since the 1930s?)

The claim that international officialdom caused the Great Recession, and did so with the full blessing of the G20 group of top nations, may startle. It should not be confused with the claim that in the run-up to the crisis bankers everywhere were saints, angels, geniuses or "masters of the universe". It also does not mean that bankers' role in the Great Recession was passive and neutral. In the critical years serious blunders were made by some financial institutions.[1] In such places as Greece, Ireland and Iceland these blunders too often involved not just folly, but also extreme greed and outright criminality. The banking sector pathologies experienced by Greece, Ireland and so on before and during the Great Recession have been seen in numerous other episodes of financial liberalization. Wild rates of growth in bank credit to the private sector and the quantity of money during the boom years, in association with crazy asset price increases, have been followed by violent slumps in credit, money and asset prices in the bust.

Given the frequency with which booms have been followed by busts, supporters of free-market capitalism have to wonder why businessmen and financiers are not more alert to the long-run implications of grossly unsustainable macroeconomic trends. (They might also point an accusatory finger at the political leaders, with attendant civil servants, central bankers and so on, who are ultimately responsible for the idiocies.) Obviously, such schools of thought as "rational expectations" – in which all agents are thought to take decisions in the light of the best available economic theory – have difficulty when confronted with the real-world chaos of Greece, Ireland and so on in the Great Recession. The rational expectations hypothesis, and the New Classical School with which rational expectations thinking is associated, have undoubtedly taken a hammering in the last few years. Robert Lucas' assertion in his 2003 presidential address to the American Economic Association, that macroeconomics' "central problem of depression-prevention has been solved for all practical purposes", looks plain silly today.[2]

Of course cyclical fluctuations in economic activity are man-made events, not Acts of God or accidents of nature. The question of the allocation of blame for the Great Recession cannot be shirked. It has to be asked why in late 2008 the top people at key international policy-making meetings pressed not just for injections of capital into banks (to remedy an actual or supposed lack of capital), but also for massive and wholly unexpected increases in banks' regulatory capital/asset ratios? Could they not see that such increases would be sharply deflationary? Further, is that the kind of policy-making that intelligent, well-informed private sector decision-takers could anticipate and pre-empt, if their behaviour did indeed conform to the rational expectations hypothesis propounded in the textbooks?

NOTES

1. Several books have been written about mismanagement in Britain's top banks. For the case of HBOS, see Ray Perman *Hubris: How HBOS Wrecked the Best Bank in Britain* (Edinburgh: Birlinn Ltd, 2013); for RBS, see Iain Martin *Making it Happen: Fred Goodwin and the Men who Blew up the British Economy* (London: Simon & Schuster, 2014); for Lloyd's, Ivan Fallon *Black Horse Ride* (London: Robson Press, 2015).
2. Robert Lucas *Collected Papers on Monetary Theory* (Cambridge, MA, USA and London, UK: Harvard University Press, 2013), p. 445.

5. The impact of the New Regulatory Wisdom on banking, credit and money: good or bad?

Adam Ridley

Output growth in the leading Western economies has been weaker since the Great Recession of 2008 and 2009 than at any time since the 1930s. According to the International Monetary Fund's database, advanced economies' gross domestic product was flat in 2008 and dropped by 3.4 per cent in 2009. Although 2010 enjoyed a rebound with 3.1 per cent growth, the next three years saw output advancing typically by a mere 1.5 per cent a year. This was well beneath the pre-2008 trend. Even now (September 2016), after slightly better years in 2014 and 2015 of 2 per cent increases in advanced economy output, it is uncertain whether future growth will be sustained or vigorous. A period of several years of morose and sluggish recovery is a distinct possibility. Is such mediocrity the inevitable result of the crisis and the best we can hope for?

By common consent, the Great Recession began with the banking disasters of 2007 and 2008. In the leading Western nations the official response to these disasters has had a number of well known and familiar common features, although policy has been far from stable or easy to predict. The elements of this response constitute what might be termed the "New Regulatory Wisdom" (NRW). How is this to be defined? What has been its impact so far? And what will its effects be if it is maintained into the future?

The next section defines the NRW in more detail, and the section after that discusses the official motives for its adoption during and after the Great Recession. The chapter then reviews the impact of the NRW on the quantity, quality and pricing of new bank credit, and the ability of capital markets to take the place of the banks in the extension of new credit. The conclusion is that regulatory actions that were ostensibly wise and necessary in microeconomic terms had drastic and very unfortunate macroeconomic results. Such actions reflected the exaggerated belief of most journalists and economic commentators, soon communicated to politicians, that the key issue was potential insolvency in the financial system. The result was an obsessive focus on an actual or supposed lack of capital. No one in the top regulatory bodies, the key international agencies and the governments of leading nations stopped to ask what the cumulative and aggregated effect of the regulatory upheaval would be on bank credit, the quantity of money and macroeconomic activity. These same agencies ought now to consider how best to restore stability and predictability in the regulatory environment, and to end the virtual "perpetual revolution" from which banking now suffers.

I

The NRW has several aspects. First, the family of controls imposed on banking and securities businesses ("banks" for short) by officialdom has become more unfriendly. Tighter requirements have been imposed on banks' balance sheets. They must keep more capital relative to assets and limit their leverage, they must maintain a higher proportion of assets in liquid form, they must have a lower proportion of risky loans and securities in their portfolios, and they must fund their businesses more conservatively from stable sources.

Second, several policy initiatives have put pressure on market participants to transfer over-the-counter (OTC) contracts into recognized exchanges, clearing houses and various post-trade registration businesses. In this process of "domesticating" OTC activity, these institutions – which specialize on the settlement of trades – have assumed greater significance relative to the banks. In effect, the banks are being "cut down to size" as part of the larger ambition in public policy to "deleverage balance sheets". As a result, the financing and growth of private sector activity hereafter will be tilted more towards the capital markets than in the past.

Third, new controls are being enforced on long-term savings institutions, particularly insurance companies and pension funds. Tough policies are being introduced to ensure a closer matching of assets to the risks implicit in their liabilities, which in practice has meant a reduction in the riskiness of asset portfolios and less management discretion in asset selection.

Fourth, policy-makers have shown their concern about the structure of the banking industry, with measures to separate so-called "utility banking" from "casino banking". Utility banking is to be understood as the provision of payments services to depositors, notably to retail depositors, combined with the matching of deposits to very safe assets, such as government securities. "Casino banking" is seen as including proprietary trading and "own account" business, traditionally undertaken in banks by the treasury team, often with input from top management. (It needs to be emphasized here that many risk exposures in banking arise from customer business and that a key management function has always been to manage the size of such exposures relative to bank capital.) The problem of separating "utility" banking from the casinos of high finance has been particularly serious in "universal banks". Universal banks have historically been a feature of continental European financial systems, and not of financial systems in the English-speaking world. They have combined commercial banking (that is, deposit-taking and lending) with investment banking (that is, the trading of securities, and the underwriting of securities issued by the corporate sector).

Fifth, one of officialdom's complaints during the period of intense crisis was that it lacked established procedures and institutions for dealing with novel challenges. So regimes have been introduced to "resolve" failing bank businesses. Of particular concern has been to reduce the alleged "too big to fail" risk (TBTF) and to regulate better the systemically important businesses which remain.

Sixth, the monitoring of risks in the financial sector relies on support from two powerful associates, the accountancy profession and the ratings industry. Top accountants have pressed for new and sometimes rather complex standards. In particular, they require financial institutions' accounts to be prepared on a "fair value" basis. (Under fair value accounting, assets are entered on balance sheets on a mark-to-market basis instead of according to their historical cost.) The consensus is that the rating agencies did an unsatisfactory job in the run-up to the crisis, by underestimating the loss probabilities in the riskier tranches of asset-backed paper. They have been criticized especially for being too soft towards dangerous underwriting practices in US housing finance between 2002 and 2006. But during and since the Great Recession they have over-compensated for such earlier failures by pre-emptive and often excessive downgrades of intrinsically strong financial businesses. That has aggravated the funding strains for such businesses, in an environment already beset by a systemic lack of confidence.

These six trends in financial industries' organization and regulation have been disruptive in their own right. But they have been at work while the peak regulatory institutions, both domestic and international, have been reshuffling their responsibilities and powers. (The upheavals have been greatest in the USA and the UK.) In effect, the financial sectors of major economies have been subject to a disorderly process of perpetual revolution. Year after year seemingly definitive measures are modified, almost always tightened and usually rendered more complex. Politicians, acting under the auspices of the G20 Group of leading nations, feel that they must "do something", and recommend new committees and institutions. This leads to the recruitment of an increasing number of ever more risk-averse regulators who, once they have been appointed, move into new policy areas and propose new initiatives. All too often, the initiatives emanate from a multiplicity of sources and may be inconsistent. For example, regulatory policy in EU member states reflects inputs from national, EU and global authorities, and these inputs often differ in both their priorities and substantive content.

II

The recurring pattern of the policy response to the crisis emerged soon after its intensification in autumn 2008. The authorities' first concern focused on the banking industry, seen as the prime culprit for the Great Recession. The key prescription was to require more banking capital from private sources or, where that was impossible, to mandate capital injections from the state. National regulators implemented recommendations from the Basel-based Bank for International Settlements, with a new set of regulations (Basel III) updating and reinforcing the standards contained in Basel I and II that had originated in the 1980s. The European Commission advanced the EU's own framework, in a Capital Requirement Directive that had begun hesitantly in 2006, but post-crisis was to become more respected, central and urgent in implementation. The years after the crisis saw progressive and remorseless tightening of target ratios for capital, liquidity and leverage. This was complemented by ever more demanding analyses of varying scenarios of market stress and failure, with capital and funding tests based on them.

The larger institutions faced a particular burden. Officialdom had been perplexed during 2008 by the potentially self-reinforcing downward spiral of system-wide confidence breakdown and market disintegration that seemed to be under way. Such system-wide pathologies were judged to be due to trouble only at large banking or financial businesses. Smaller banking businesses could therefore be allowed to close, because their disappearance would have only isolated effects and these would not be of systemic significance. But large businesses were deemed "too big to fail", because of their "systemic importance".[1] Officialdom decided that in future "global systemically important banks" (G-SIBs) should have advance plans about how their "resolution" would proceed in crises of various kinds. These plans had to be agreed with official institutions in several jurisdictions, such as the Prudential Regulation Authority in the UK, and the Federal Reserve and the Securities Exchange Commission in the USA. In the EU big banks – banks with operations in several European nations – had to negotiate their resolution strategies not only with national regulatory bodies, but also with the European Banking Authority. The EBA had been set up as recently as January 2011.

In the USA a veritable encyclopaedia of measures was launched by Dodd–Frank legislation in 2010. Indeed, Dodd–Frank was perhaps the critical post-crisis regulatory innovation for US capital markets. One of its main aims was to curb the supposed excesses of OTC derivation and trading. It even went so far as to specify initial and variation margins for certain categories of securities trading, as well as directing that OTC trading had to take place on organized platforms rather than between one stand-alone finance institution and its customers. Fund management was also regarded as an appropriate subject for more regulation, even though no economic theory identifies the fund management industry as capable of causing booms and busts in the economy as a whole.

The insurance industry posed specific issues. Like the fund management industry, it is not usually seen as having any bearing on business cycles. But the turmoil at AIG in late 2008 had suggested to some that, in the extreme, the solvency of big insurers and leading investment banks could be related. The EU therefore pushed national insurance industries to accept its Solvency II Directive, with risk-sensitive asset weighting used in assessing and fixing the regulatory capital of insurers. Solvency II is now [late 2016] widely adopted across the EU. It penalizes illiquid, high-yield and risky long-term assets (such as private equity, property and infrastructure), and favours liquid, low-yield and safe short-term assets with high credit ratings, notably short-dated government and public sector bonds.

III

The discussion so far shows that the NRW constituted a "regime shift" for banking systems in all the advanced economies. This regime shift is still not complete and remains far from certain in its eventual scope. But it has clearly had major effects already on virtually every aspect of banks' operations, notably:

- asset selection;
- costs and margins on loans and other products;
- market standing and credit ratings;
- ability to raise new capital; and
- capacity to lend.

Each of these may be considered in turn.

1. Asset Selection

The NRW can be viewed as a comprehensive attempt to make banks safer. It has involved constant regulatory pressure for banks to set their risk appetite at lower levels, both in general and specific terms. Pivotal to the process of de-risking bank balance sheets have been the requirements to hold more capital relative to assets. The banking industry has therefore been anxious about the critical, but little noticed implications for the return on capital, particularly on equity, and on both simple and risk-weighted bases.

The argument has revolved around a well-known formula for deriving bank profitability. Banks' assets (A) can be seen as split between safe and liquid assets (C), and relatively risky earning assets (or "loans"), L. The paradigmatic safe asset is of course cash and, for simplicity, the safe and liquid assets can be taken to yield nothing. The ratio of liquid assets to total assets may be assumed to be set by regulators at c. Total assets are $L + C$ or $L + c.A$. So $L = (1 - c).A$. Profits (P) are equal to the loan margin or profit "spread" on earning assets, s, multiplied by the quantity of earning assets, which is:

$$P = s.L = s.(1 - c).A$$

while the rate of return on capital (K), is P/K, which is:

$$P/K = s.(1 - c).A/K$$

It is evident that, if the loan margin (s) is given, the rate of return on capital is inversely related to the ratio of liquid assets to total assets and the capital/assets ratio. Alternatively put, if new regulation demands a doubling of the "leverage ratio" (that is, of the ratio of capital to assets), a bank's balance sheet must halve for any given level of capital. If the target return on capital is to be maintained, the net loan margin has to double. The proportion of private sector borrowers which can absorb this increased cost is limited. In practice, banks have reacted to the range of new regulatory intrusions by switching credit from high-risk, exciting clients to safe and boring ones.

The need for regulatory capital can be further reduced by eliminating or cutting back capital-intensive, high-risk products and services. Since 2008 banks have had to restrict or even to abandon specialized activities, such as private equity financings, shipping and aircraft leasing, and infrastructure and unsecured long-term lending. The de-risking of balance sheets has also been accompanied by a rise in the ratio of low-risk claims on the public sector to total assets. Overall, both commercial banks (with their loan portfolios) and investment banks (with their portfolios of securities and underwriting activities) have been forced to write less business at a lower return. Not surprisingly, in all the major economies the stock market capitalization of the banking sector has fallen heavily relative to that of other economic sectors.

2. Costs and Margins on Loans

As already explained, newly imposed official obligations to hold more capital and liquidity relative to total assets must either reduce banks' return on capital or force them to widen loan margins.[2] Of course, banks have for many decades faced downward pressure on margins from competition, so that much of the mainstream loan book before 2007 was of marginal profitability. One response was to seek profits in other parts of the balance sheet, notably by currency trading, and the origination, writing and trading of derivatives, all of which served customer needs. More extreme and adventurous was outright proprietary trading, on the back of banks' capital, regardless of customer requirements.

Banks – particularly large banks with their number and diversity of customers, and their access to numerous marketplaces – are well placed to manage risk on currency and derivative exposures. However, official-dom interpreted the late 2008 media alarm about credit default swaps and other products as justifying restrictions on banks' position-taking. More specifically, they saw it as providing a rationale for separating commercial banking from the kind of risk-taking seen in the proprietary trading of the investment banks. The "Volcker rule", that banks must not engage in proprietary trading divorced from customer business, was part of the USA's Dodd–Frank legislation and was publicly endorsed by President Obama in January 2010. The similar reforms recommended by the 2011 Vickers Report in the UK were part of the wider international trend. The Liikanen Report of September 2012, published under the impetus of the European Commission, applied the same thinking to the EU as a whole.

But – if banks cannot make profits from trading activities, whether customer-related or not – they must either accept a lower rate of return on capital or charge a wider margin on their loans. The official attack on proprietary trading was in this sense an attack on bank profitability. Over and above this effect, extra regulation has added an assortment of additional charges, costs and expenses. The expansion of regulation and the increased burden of compliance have been obvious sequels to the crisis, but talk of pre-funding deposit insurance schemes and a new EU-wide financial transactions tax have also been a worry for the banking industry. (In the first instance contributions to such schemes are straight deductions from banks' profits. Banks may try to recover them by charging their customers more, but then the ultimate effect of more regulation is again to widen loan margins.)

The drive for greater clarity about banks' resolution strategies has encouraged the issuance of new types of liability, such as the hybrid bail-in "contingent convertibles" (or COCOs). COCOs provide for investors to convert their bond-like claim on a bank into equity, if the unfortunate contingency occurs. This contingency is that the bank suffers losses that deplete capital beneath a regulatory capital/asset ratio minimum. As they are novel and untested, they create serious uncertainties for both the banks that issue them and the investors who buy them. The poisonous combination of risk and unfamiliarity makes COCOs an expensive form of capital, which again cuts into banks' profitability.

3. Market Standing and Credit Ratings

The impact of the post-2007 deterioration in banks' credit rating on their operations has been surprisingly little noticed and discussed. It is widely agreed that the credit rating agencies did not distinguish themselves in the period before the Great Recession, as they failed to spot the slide in credit standards in the American housing finance industry and wrongly gave triple-A ratings to securities that turned out to be unsatisfactory in the end. But their assessments of the banking industry from 2008 onwards – that it was much riskier and less creditworthy than before – were taken very seriously. The ratings agencies have marked down severely the credit standing of the vast majority of banks and insurance companies. The downgrading has not only reduced the market values of quoted banking groups, but also added to their difficulties in financing assets. Regaining strong ratings will be hard and take time.

Arguably, the setters of accounting standards have made matters still worse by pressing for early, comprehensive and conservative treatment of bad debts. Instead of taking a pragmatic and flexible view, banks are being obliged to over-provide when in doubt about the likelihood of loans being repaid. Such write-offs reduce capital, which then undermines banks' ability to extend new credit. (The traditional bank practice of forbearance on bad or doubtful debts has been condemned by those emphasizing the moral hazard supposedly implicit in it. This condemnation overlooks the large body of historical evidence, notably from the Third World debt crisis of the 1980s, which demonstrates the scope for asset values and loan collateral to recover in cyclical upswings.)

4. Ability to Raise New Capital

Given all the regulatory reforms, innovations and threats, and the perva-sive assumption that risk is bad and must be minimized, it is not surprising that the return on equity in most banks has fallen steeply compared with the pre-crisis period. (The return on equity is now widely seen as likely to be between 5 and 10 per cent a year for most banking groups, compared with a cost of equity commonly cited as over 10 per cent.) Logically, with the return on equity lower than its cost, the market value of quoted banks is beneath their book value. This makes it harder still to raise new equity capital and also adds to the cost of issuing such non-deposit liabilities as the COCOs that currently have regulatory blessing.

5. Capacity to Lend

Commercial banks' defining characteristics are that they provide settle-ment and money transmission services to non-banks, and that they extend credit to the private sector and (sometimes) the state. Relative to capital markets, which enable non-bank savers to transfer funds to corporate borrowers, their credit facilities are low-cost and flexible. (Capital markets cannot grant overdrafts to small- and medium-sized companies, whereas banks can.)

The NRW has undermined banks' ability to extend credit to the private sector. Three mechanisms need to be mentioned. First, the regulatory demands for more capital and liquidity have of course reduced the scope to lend to the private sector. With the quantity of banks' capital given, it is obvious that an increase in their capital–assets ratio means a reduction in assets. Since at the start of the crisis banks' assets were overwhelmingly claims on the private sector, a reduction in assets has in practice been syn-onymous with a reduction in loans to the private sector. Meanwhile liquid assets (such as cash reserves at the central bank and short-dated govern-ment securities) are mostly claims on the government. If they expand when total assets are given, loans to the private sector must drop further to accommodate them.

Secondly, as explained above, banks have responded to the regulatory assault by widening loan margins. That has made credit more expensive for borrowers. At the margin, some borrowers must have repaid loans or declined to seek new facilities.

Finally, officialdom's aversion to risk has affected the relative dynamism of different types of credit. As loans to small companies are risky com-pared with residential mortgages, it is plausible that the implementation of the NRW would raise the ratio of mortgage loans to small company

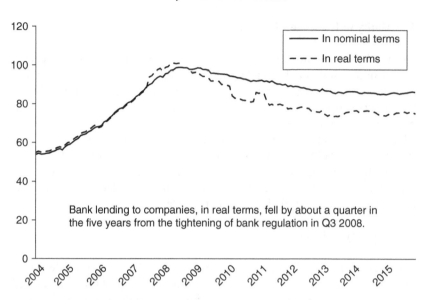

Bank lending to companies, in real terms, fell by about a quarter in
the five years from the tightening of bank regulation in Q3 2008.

Note: Graph shows monthly values of stock of loans (August 2008 = 100, just before the tightening of bank regulation), in both nominal and real terms.

Figure 5.1   UK bank lending to companies, before, during and after the
Great Financial Crisis

loans in banks' overall loan portfolios. The pressures to lend to safe, boring and low-risk businesses, and to dispose of high-risk capital-intensive services and activities, are intensifying. The quality of banking services will decline, as expertise is lost in understanding the credit requirements of sectors which are important to long-run growth and innovation. As Figure 5.1 shows, in the UK the stock of bank credit extended to companies fell in nominal terms, and more drastically in real terms, in the five years from autumn 2008 and remains sluggish even now (late 2016). Small- and medium-sized companies have been particular targets of the credit squeeze. (See Figure 5.2, which demonstrates that the trend in SME credit was even weaker than lending to corporates as a whole.)

IV

The "top-down" constraint of the regulatory pressures on leverage ratios, capital and liquidity in banking has had – and continues to have – a severely contractionary effect on all European economies. As Van Steenis,

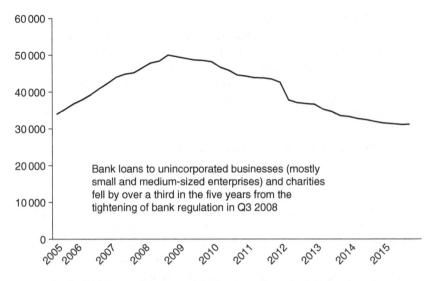

Note: Stock of loans to unincorporated businesses and non-profit institutions, £m, quarterly data from Bank of England.

Figure 5.2   Bank loans to small businesses and charities in the UK, 2005–15

a top analyst of the banking sector at Morgan Stanley, observed in a 2012 research paper, for the European economy "historical data . . . imply [approximately] €1 trillion of net new lending to support 1%–2% a year GDP growth to 2017". But Morgan Stanley's estimate was that, "banks in Europe will struggle to deliver more than €400 billion of new credit over the next five years given constraints on funding as well as leverage under [the Basel III regulatory framework]". Bluntly, "[b]alance sheet light competitors [that is, competitors not subject to the same capital rules as the banks] will attempt to disrupt and take share . . . [B]anks will be forced quickly to find a new model to deliver credit or lose relevance through disintermediation. We estimate a $5 trillion funding gap globally, $3 trillion of which is in Europe."[3]

What of the motivation of individual banks? Is there any commercial logic in providing credit on an ample scale in the new regulatory environment? Deutsche Bank reached sombre conclusions in another 2012 analysis for investment clients. In its view the challenges were particularly severe for European BBB-rated banks, since they had a higher funding cost than their better-rated competitors. Indeed, their high funding costs – in combination with all the new capital and liquidity rules – meant that they could not lend to any low-risk corporate counterparties and still be profitable. Even A-rated and AAA-rated banks found it difficult to make profits sufficient to meet target returns to capital. Only if they sold bank services to corporate customers in addition to extending credit could long-standing relationships with big corporates provide returns that might match the cost of equity. The message was that some banks running corporate loan books might be doing so in a value-destructive way. Undoubtedly, the NRW can choke off or cap credit expansion. To quote the Deutsche report, "So most lending should be dis-intermediated [that is, transferred] to the bond market. We have ... estimated top-down $2 trillion of corporate loan disintermediation ... We now think it could be $3 trillion [in the coming period of bank balance-sheet retrenchment]."[4]

Its critics claim that the banking system is not as capital-constrained as its spokesmen sometimes assert. They argue, for example, that staff costs and employee numbers are too high, and that a clampdown on inefficiency could lead to higher profits and more capital retention. Alternatively, the critics say that banks' balance sheets are replete with assets of little or no social value, such as loans to other financial intermediaries. In their view, public policy-makers are entitled to ask for the banks to focus on areas of most social and economic value to the economy (as these policy-makers regard the issue), and to demand a rebalancing of bank assets. Their assessment is that fewer loans to the finance sector can be accompanied by more to industry. Further, in their judgement, banks can comply with the officially approved "deleveraging" of their balance sheets and yet serve the wider economy successfully.

This smacks of dangerous optimism. Deleveraging is not a simple mechanical process which can be implemented swiftly and without cost to the bank, its clients or the wider market. When banks extend loans, they enter into legal contractual commitments to their borrowers. If they ask borrowers for early loan repayment in order to meet the supposed imperative of deleveraging, they may breach the terms of contracts and leave themselves open to challenge in the courts. They cannot discriminate against certain types of customer, merely because official policy (which is itself highly volatile) is in favour of rebalancing between different sectors of the economy.

It must again be emphasized that, certainly for the larger banks, the biggest challenge in capital raising today is the "permanent revolution" which the NRW embodies. Since 2008 the regulatory regime has tightened significantly and without interruption, year after year, to an unpredictable degree and in unforeseen ways. Senior bank executives have to expect that the regulatory assault is to continue into the medium term. If so, why should a rational fund manager invest in any banking institution?

Thus, in November 2015, a full seven years after the initial moves to a more rigorous regulatory regime, the Financial Stability Board issued new guidelines for G-SIBs' capital position. In this environment the notion that large amounts of new bank equity can be raised from market sources is unrealistic.

If banks are indeed so hemmed in by new regulation that they cannot expand their loan portfolios, is there any prospect that credit business can be transferred to capital markets? One view is that novel forms of financial business can develop rapidly and bypass the old-fashioned mainstream banks. In a 2013 article in *The Spectator* Andrew Haldane, the chief economist at the Bank of England, pointed out how many of banks' customers can now meet each other in cyberspace. To quote,

> New peer-to-peer entrants into most aspects of banking services – consumer financing, foreign exchange, IPO underwriting, invoice financing, small business lending and equity venture capital financing (so-called crowd-funding). . . . [These entrants are] . . . small and few but growing rapidly in size and multiplying in number.

Haldane's fundamental proposition was that, thanks to the information technology revolution, the new services would fill the so-called "Macmillan gap". Innovation on these lines is undeniable and welcome. But past experience suggests that the impact over the next few years will be patchy. Peer-to-peer lending cannot grow fast enough to take on the role of the banks. Another issue is how the regulatory authorities will view the risks involved in these new and still rather informal credit channels. Will there be the usual miserable early scandals and failures?[5] Will this new financial Wild West attract the outlaws or the responsible entrepreneurs for whom this should be a great opportunity? Will there be heavy-handed clampdown at any point?

Sure enough, some financial business will be diverted from the banking system to capital markets. Nowadays large British companies have access to the international bond market, where the best names can issue paper in any currency and convert the proceeds back into sterling. No doubt some "securitization" of bank finance will occur. Optimists might take comfort from the American example. In the USA about 70 per cent of corporate funding comes from the capital markets and only 30 per cent is provided by the banks. If the USA can do it, surely the UK and Europe can copy? A realistic reply to this question is that the gigantic upheaval envisaged might take place over a decade or two, but not in the course of a single business cycle (of five or seven years). An institutional and cultural revolution would be needed for a more rapid shift to capital market finance. In any case, the capital markets cannot readily deal with the financing needs of small- and medium-sized businesses. For SMEs bank finance is critical, and will remain so.

It must also be pointed out that big players in the capital market have also to cope with the regulatory distrust of risk-taking. Not only have underwriters and brokers to redirect business towards clearing houses, but they have also to allow for heavier capital loading than pre-2008 for assets held during the securitization process. This extra loading on securitization activity is over and above the more general move towards higher capital/ asset ratios in the banking industry. Moreover, because commercial banks have bowed to official pressure and cut their credit lines to the securities industry, investment banks have smaller books of securities than before. In bond markets they cannot deal with counterparties in the same size and with the same narrow dealing spreads as in 2006 or early 2007. A common complaint at present (late 2016) is that the secondary market in bonds is less liquid than pre-crisis. On this basis, the ability of the primary market to accommodate vastly increased bond issuance must be in doubt.

The markets through which so many of these processes must operate will also be under the same familiar pressures. The reforms imposed by officialdom require private sector profit-motivated businesses to operate with a larger capital burden. As already noted, banks are always competing with the capital markets as sources of funds for corporates. But they are less able to help corporates with their own financing needs, and both they and their customers must lodge extra collateral to conduct derivatives business. Morgan Stanley calculated that the USA's Dodd–Frank legislation led to an "industry-wide incremental initial margin requirement associated with the new regulations at $1.7 trillion".[6]

V

Where does the discussion lead us? As far as the past is concerned, it is plain that the NRW has acted not just to check the growth of banks' risk assets, but to cause large outright contractions in many banks' holdings of such assets. The further consequence has been to cause reductions, or at best stagnation, in banks' overall balance sheet size. At the aggregate level, this was most obvious in 2009 and 2010. The evidence strongly suggests that the NRW was one of the main reasons why the potentially manageable banking crisis of 2007 and 2008 turned into the disastrous Great Recession. Ostensibly microeconomic steps to reduce risk in the banking system had drastic macroeconomic results. They constituted, in reality even if not in intention, a ferociously contractionary monetary policy.

In the last few years many governments have pursued textbook programmes of fiscal austerity. The Greek default and related trauma argue that fiscal austerity has been necessary perhaps, but not sufficient. The authorities ought also to have offset the adverse effects of government cutbacks on demand and employment. The combination of fiscal and monetary stringency in Eurozone periphery countries has had devastating impacts on output and jobs. The authorities should have followed a monetary and regulatory policy which supported economic activity rather than curbing it. In the run-up to the crisis, commentators might reasonably have claimed that governments had learned how to achieve non-inflationary growth, but the private sector had not understood how to manage risk. Today the focus is so much on controlling risks that we can no longer bring about growth.

Economic history offers instructive precedents. In October 1987 the Black Monday stock exchange crash threatened to provoke a serious downturn. This was, indeed, forecast shortly after by a distinguished group of 33 top economists at a Washington meeting held under the auspices of the Institute for International Economics. However, in sharp contrast with officialdom's reaction to financial stress in the year to autumn 2008, in October 1987 governments adopted a conscious policy of sustaining credit, easing liquidity and supporting asset prices. The adroit handling of the 1987 crash followed international success in mitigating the effects of the Third World debt crisis (from mid-1982) on economic activity, and the UK's (and especially the Bank of England's) exemplary management of the secondary banking crisis in the mid-1970s.

A case can be made that the malign effects of the NRW on the banking industry are the dominant reason that the macroeconomic sequel to the financial difficulties of 2007 and 2008 has been so much worse than the setbacks suffered after comparable difficulties in the 1970s and 1980s. At the most fundamental level, questions must be asked about the rationale and scale of the capital demands and the regulatory crackdown.

As far as the UK is concerned, only two banks – RBS and Lloyd's – had significant losses in the crisis period, with those at Lloyd's arising from its officially blessed acquisition of HBOS. As Table 5.1 shows, cumulative losses in the loss-making banks in the six years from 2008 (almost £35 billion) were only a fraction of the main groups' combined shareholder funds (about £175 billion) at end-2007, while the losses at RBS and Lloyd's were outweighed almost threefold by the profits earned by their more successful rivals.[7] Some might argue that there is an obvious disparity between the loss figure (to repeat, £35 billion) and the requirement for extra capital. As Table 5.1 brings out, shareholders' funds at the UK's big banks rose by about £140 billion between end-2006 and end-2011, a figure that was four times the losses of RBS and Lloyd's over the entire crisis period. The dissimilarity between the severity of officialdom's response to the Great

Table 5.1 UK banks' profits and capital before, during and after the Great Recession

	Pre-tax profits of all four/ five banks, £m.	Shareholders' funds of all four/five banks, £m.	Total losses of banks with losses, £m.	Total earlier year shareholder funds of banks with losses, £m.	Pre-tax profits as % of shareholder funds for all banks, %	Losses as % of previous year shareholder funds for banks with losses, %	Losses (of all loss-making banks) as % of shareholder funds for all banks, %
2005	34259	134046	0	Not relevant	25.6	Not relevant	Not relevant
2006	36151	143304	0	Not relevant	25.2	Not relevant	Not relevant
2007	36171	174153	0	Not relevant	20.8	Not relevant	Not relevant
2008	5896	169073	−8534	53038	3.5	16.1	5.0
2009	−5114	247640	−12939	31242	−2.1	41.4	5.2
2010	19284	266365	0	Not relevant	7.2	Not relevant	Not relevant
2011	28342	279009	−2802	121193	10.2	2.3	1.0
2012	6861	268997	−3621	75367	2.6	4.8	1.3
2013	9588	263408	−6501	68678	3.6	9.5	2.5
2014	20862	287862	0	Not relevant	7.2	Not relevant	Not relevant
Totals in six years from 2008	64857		−34397				

Notes: The table relates to the four/five largest UK-owned quoted banks, excluding Standard & Chartered. Like Standard & Chartered, the bulk (about 75–80%) of HSBC's profits are from international operations. HBOS was a separate bank (i.e., the fifth bank) until 2008, when it was acquired by Lloyd's.

Source: Company reports and accounts, as collated by REFS. REFS is a company analysis service prepared for institutional investors and now published by JD Financial Publishing Ltd in London.

Recession and the leniency of its reaction to earlier shocks could hardly be more marked. One has to ask, "has society as a whole benefited from the changed attitude of governments, central banks and regulators?"

Looking to the future, at least two lessons suggest themselves. First, as a minimum, the authorities – central banks, finance ministries and regulatory bodies – must recognize that apparently microeconomic steps to curb risk can have "systemic importance". Regulatory upheaval must not be so drastic and abrupt as to cause macroeconomic instability. The growth rates of bank credit and the quantity of money must be such as to ensure satisfactory expansion of nominal demand and output. A slower pace of regulatory reform may be more prudent. Policy-makers must never forget that they have a responsibility to keep aggregate economic activity advancing steadily at a trend rate.

Second, the international and national authorities need to take a step back and work out a sound long-term collective strategy. New institutions and initiatives have proliferated in the last few years to such a degree that many practitioners in the financial sector cannot cope with the upheaval. The authorities must consider how best to restore stability and predictability in the regulatory environment. Sadly, those in the eye of the storm, whether regulators or regulated, are too preoccupied to be able to resist the perpetual revolution going on around them. They often seem not even to have asked themselves whether all the turmoil is necessary and sensible.

NOTES

1. The phrase "too big to fail" is sometimes thought to have originated in the Great Financial Crisis of 2008 and 2009. In fact, the notion has its origins in early capitalism. See Charles G. Leathers and J. Patrick Raines 'Some historical perspectives on "too big to fail" policies", pp. 3–27, in Benton Gup (ed.) *Too Big to Fail* (Westport, CT, USA and London, UK: Praeger, 2004).
2. The Bank of England's *Financial Stability Report* (London: Bank of England) for June 2015 confirmed these points. Table B.1 on p. 35 noted that UK banks' Basel III risk-weighted capital ratio had increased by 4.1 percentage points since end-2011, and ascribed 2.9 percentage points of the change to the "reduction in risk-weighted assets". The document published an Appendix 2, with 'Core indicators'. Spreads on new corporate lending in the UK were said to have averaged 107 basis points between 1987 and 2006, and to have been 100 basis points in 2006, just before the crisis. The latest value (for December 2014) was 237 basis points. An even larger increase had occurred in new lending to households. In 2006 the spread was 352 basis points, but in March 2015 it was 658 basis points. (See p. 55 of June 2015 *Financial Stability Report*.)
3. Morgan Stanley and Oliver Wyman *Wholesale & Investment Banking Outlook* (Blue Paper, 23 March 2012), pp. 18–19.
4. Deutsche Bank Markets Research *European Banks Strategy: Corporate Lending Structurally Unprofitable, Consequences for Banks* (London: Deutsche Bank), 20 June 2012 note, p. 1.
5. The original version of this chapter was written in early 2014. In February 2016

newspapers began to report numerous bankruptcies of companies financed by crowd-funding platforms. According to a report in the *Financial Times* ('Fall of Rebus sparks calls for protection', 6 February 2016), "Research by AltFI Data and the law firm Nabarro recently found that one in five companies that raised money on crowd-funding platforms between 2011 and 2013 had gone bankrupt."

6. Morgan Stanley *US Interest Rate Strategist: The Impact of Dodd–Frank* (New York: Morgan Stanley Research), 26 October 2012.

7. The data in the table have been compiled from the REFS handbook of company analyst reports now compiled by London-based JD Financial Publishing, using a methodology developed by Jim Slater. The company analyst reports themselves come largely from company reports and accounts. Official data on the UK banking industry's equity and bond capital, and its profitability, are available, but are opaque. Series published for the UK banking system's profits and losses, available for both UK- and foreign-owned organizations, are not easily related to the banks' equity capital. The Bank of England's Bankstats database has a Table B3.2 on 'Monetary financial institutions' annual profit and loss', with a column under the mnemonic B5RL for 'Pre-tax profits'. The numbers are different from those in Table 5.1, with the loss numbers in 2008 and 2009 being £20 942 m. and £10 559 m. However, over the whole five years to 2013 the loss totals in B5RL (£31.5 billion) and Table 7.1 (£34.3 billion) are similar. There is no question that the UK banking system's losses in this turbulent period were much less than its equity capital before the trouble began, and that the increase in capital mandated by the authorities was a multiple of the losses incurred.

6. Why has monetary policy not worked as expected? Some interactions between financial regulation, credit and money

Charles Goodhart

The behaviour of leading economies during and since the Great Recession has had surprising features. Since the crisis intensified in September 2008, with the failure and partial liquidation of Lehman Brothers, central banks have taken dramatic actions to stimulate their economies.[1] They have cut interest rates to virtually nil, reaching the so-called "zero lower bound", and thereafter taken unconventional measures of monetary stimulus. These have included purchases of assets not just from banks, as with standard open market operations, but also at the long end of the yield curve from non-banks. The purchases have had the effect, and have been partly for the purpose, of raising the size of their own balance sheets enormously, often by a factor of three or four times. This has raised the monetary base commensurately, while the cash reserve balances held by commercial banks with their central bank have climbed by an even larger multiple. But the impact on both the broader monetary aggregates and bank lending to the private sector over the same period 2008–12 has been much smaller. The "money multiplier" has just collapsed. (For an explanation of the money multiplier, see the discussion in the Introduction, pp. 10–12 above.) Whereas the relationship between the growth in the monetary base and in the broader monetary aggregates used to be roughly one to one (that is, 5 per cent growth in the base used to be accompanied by about a 5 per cent growth in the quantity of money), now the relationship has at times been nearer to 100 to 1. Had broad money expanded at the same rate as the monetary base, then the recession and deflation would have long since disappeared, and the danger would instead have become inflation. What happened and what went wrong? Why has the massive expansion of the monetary base had so little effect on the broader monetary and credit aggregates? The following discussion reviews in turn the roles of capital requirements and liquidity management in banks' balance-sheet decisions.

I

The term "macroprudential" dates back to the 1970s, when it was used in internal, unpublished documents of the Cooke Committee (the precursor of the Basel Committee on Banking Supervision) and at the Bank of England.[2] A 2009 Bank of England paper defined the goal of "macroprudential regulation" as being to reduce the risk and the macroeconomic costs of financial instability.[3] The measures involved, notably the specification of minimum capital/asset ratios in banking, are seen as filling the gap between macroeconomic policy and the micro-prudential regulation of individual financial institutions. How would a newly appointed member of a nation's financial stability authorities, such as the UK's Financial Policy Committee, react to a potentially unsustainable boom? In a review of possible counter-cyclical macroprudential instruments, the suggestion might be made that the authorities should have the ability to triple the size of required banks' equity-to-assets ratios. Would a step of this kind not only be more than enough to stop the boom dead in its tracks, but even to risk overkill?

Yet in their drafting and introduction of the Basel III rules this is more or less exactly what the regulators have required since the Lehman Brothers crisis. Regulatory capital ratios have increased significantly across major economies and regions since 2008. According to the BIS, "Between 2008 and 2011, large European, US and Japanese banks raised their common equity-to-total-asset ratios by 20 per cent, 33 per cent and 15 per cent, respectively". The tier 1 capital requirement for GSIFIs ("global systemically important financial institutions") has gone up from 4 per cent in 2007 to 12 per cent now (September 2016), and is still under review, with the possibility of further increases. Moreover, this tripling of capital requirements has occurred not in a boom when raising new equity in markets, or retaining profits, is relatively easy. It has instead taken place in the context, initially of the deep recession of 2009 and subsequently of a persistent semi-deflationary malaise. Bank managements, who had been incentivized in the pre-crisis years to maintain a high return on equity, have repeatedly disappointed their shareholders.[4]

Against this background, it should not have been unexpected that banks should seek the "deleveraging" of their balance sheets. Indeed, in the middle of a hue and cry about banks being too large, they have been encouraged by politicians and commentators to shrink. They have done so, and continue to do so, not just by restricting new credit expansion, but even by selling off existing assets (both securities and entire loan portfolios) or pulling in loans. They have been particularly challenged about the social responsibilities that some observers see as implicit in their lending function. Whereas they have been encouraged to reduce their leverage overall, they have been under external pressure (from central banks and regulators, but at a further remove from the media and politicians) to increase their lending to the non-financial private sector. Small- and medium-sized enterprises (or "SMEs") have been deemed worthy destinations for new loans. Another deserving cause, as much of the media and political class see the matter, is to focus lending on concerns that are headquartered in their own specific nations, and which are not foreign-owned and foreign-managed.

The consequences have been predictable. Cross-border bank lending had experienced remarkable and consistent growth in the era of globalization that began after the Second World War and continued until the Great Recession. As is evident from Figure 6.1, such lending collapsed in the two

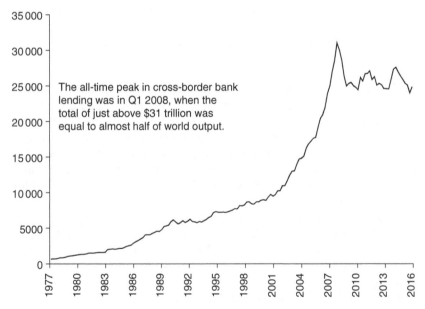

The all-time peak in cross-border bank lending was in Q1 2008, when the total of just above $31 trillion was equal to almost half of world output.

Source: Data from Bank for International Settlements.

Figure 6.1 *Cross-border bank loans both to other banks and non-banks (quarterly, in $ billions)*

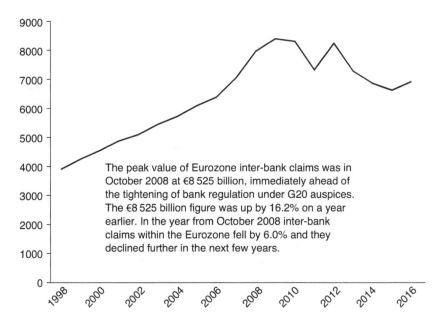

The peak value of Eurozone inter-bank claims was in October 2008 at €8 525 billion, immediately ahead of the tightening of bank regulation under G20 auspices. The €8 525 billion figure was up by 16.2% on a year earlier. In the year from October 2008 inter-bank claims within the Eurozone fell by 6.0% and they declined further in the next few years.

Notes: Figures are annual and for mid-year, data from ECB, in billions of euros.

Figure 6.2   Eurozone inter-bank claims (both loans and securities)

years from mid-2008 and since then has gone sideways. In the 1970s, 1980s and 1990s much of the cross-border lending boom was inter-continental, notably in the lending from North America, Europe and Japan to the developing nations of Latin America and Asia after the oil price rise of 1973. When the project for European monetary unification took off in the 1990s, there was a new surge in intra-European cross-border loans. Figure 6.2 demonstrates that the surge has now come to an end and has indeed gone into reverse.

Chapter 4 of this book mentioned the plight of banking systems in the Eurozone periphery since 2008, with market sources of funding no longer always available. Cross-border inter-bank lines have been replaced to a significant extent by credit and debit balances in the ECB's Target 2 payments system.

The latest data (for August 2016) at the time of writing report that the amount owed by the banks in the debit countries was almost €845 billion. Fears of the break-up of the Eurozone have so far proved misplaced, but the banking system in the single currency area is increasingly fragmented. (Temporary exchange controls were even necessary in one member,

Cyprus, after leading banks became insolvent and were unable to repay deposits in full in late March 2013.)[5] The pattern has been that banks in the Eurozone have sometimes been able to increase lending to the private sector in the nation where they are headquartered and where most of their shareholders reside. However, with overall asset totals fixed or declining, they have had to slash lending in foreign countries. To some degree the Balkanization of the inter-bank market reflects justified anxiety about the solvency of banks seeking funding from other banks. But also relevant is the process of deleveraging that has followed the jump in banks' regulatory capital/asset ratios, since loans to foreign entities are low priority in today's political environment.

It is clear that asset contraction and the reversal of the earlier growth in cross-border lending came after the official decision to engineer sharp rises in banks' equity-to-asset ratios in late 2008. But this does not imply that the decision was wrong. Too many European banks, with equity resources equal to well under 5 per cent of balance-sheet total assets, had patently too small and feeble a capital buffer to protect depositors against the large declines in certain key asset markets seen in late 2008 and 2009. Economists such as David Miles, an external member of the Bank of England's Monetary Policy between 2009 and 2015, and the co-authors of the 2013 book *The Bankers' New Clothes*, Anat Admati and Martin Hellwig, have persuasively argued that the optimal equity ratio remains well in excess of that now required by the Basel Committee on Banking Supervision and the Financial Stability Board.[6]

The mistake was not the decision to raise the minimum capital ratio, but allowing or even encouraging banks to meet the higher ratio by asset shrinkage and deleveraging. But how otherwise could such a higher ratio have been attained? Senior bank executives claim that, in the years of macroeconomic strain that followed the Lehman bankruptcy, they could not easily raise more equity in capital markets. Ultimately managements are answerable to shareholders and shareholders expect a positive rate of return on investments. Many institutional investors felt that the new regulations were so onerous that a satisfactory rate of return was not in prospect and refused to stump up the cash for new risk equity.[7]

But there is an answer, used in Scandinavia in the early 1990s, to some extent in the USA (with the TARP funds) in 2009 and 2010, and indeed in the UK in the crisis period.[8] The UK government could have recapitalized the banks by force-feeding them with additional loss-absorbing capital on terms which were expected to be beneficial, over the medium term, to the taxpayer. Indeed, in practice this was what the UK government did, although not perhaps on a sufficient scale. Of course, official readiness to inject capital in this way may raise the issue of "moral hazard", so strongly articulated by the governor of the Bank of England, Mervyn King, in his opposition to long-duration central bank loans to commercial banks. Are not government capital injections just another form of taxpayer bail-out?

The answer is "not necessarily". No increase in taxes is needed. The government could borrow from the central bank to invest in bank capital, and so structure the terms that it can reasonably expect to make a profit for the taxpayer as and when the capital injection is repaid. Moreover, until that repayment is made, the bank in receipt of government recapitalization should not be allowed to make payments to shareholders, in the guise of dividends or buy-backs, or to increase senior staff compensation either absolutely or as a percentage of total employee costs or of total costs. It might be felt that such constraints on top management are still too comfortable. If so, powers could be taken that, when the needed recapitalization exceeds some chosen percentage of initial equity, the government has the right either to take over the bank completely from existing shareholders, perhaps in exchange for warrants to buy back shares in future at current market prices, or to sack existing management, or both. The essence of moral hazard is the distortion to incentives that stem from too easy access to bail-out money. The source of the recapitalization funds (that is, whether the money comes from the government or the central bank) is not a material consideration here.

II

It is often stated that central banks can create liquidity, but not new equity capital for banks. Maybe, but they can lend to entities, such as governments and bodies like the Eurozone's European Stability Mechanism, which can make investments structured as equity. Be that as it may, central banks have since 2008 created huge volumes of liquidity, much of it now taking the form of commercial banks' cash reserves with themselves. But across the advanced world commercial banks have not used excess reserves to purchase assets, upsetting the textbook claim that such reserves are the base of a much larger credit pyramid. Indeed, as already noted, a widespread tendency in the main countries subject to the Basel rules has been for banks to contract their earning assets, particularly risky claims on the private sector.

Many commercial banks seem to be in a kind of "liquidity trap".[9] Adjusted for risk, the return on cash reserves at the central bank appears to be as good as on any other use of funds. Government sovereign debt is not subject to default risk (except in the Eurozone, where the Greek government agreed with many of its creditors a 50 per cent debt write-off in October 2011), but large rises in yield can cause capital losses on fixed-interest bonds. Meanwhile bank lending to the private sector requires the application of scarce capital and is subject to default risk. Further, since the 1999 introduction of the euro, which was accompanied by the payment of interest on banks' reserves at the ECB, it has become more common for central banks to pay interest on reserves. (The Bank of England went down this route in 2006 and the Federal Reserve in 2008.) It is surely obvious that – by making cash reserves more attractive – this now widespread central bank practice has worsened the liquidity trap in the commercial banking industry.

What can be done? One possibility would be to make the interest rate on banks' cash reserves negative, at least at the margin. Of course, the scope to inflict a penalty of this sort would be limited by banks' ability to hold liquidity (that is, legal-tender notes, particularly high-denomination notes) in their vaults and tills rather than at the central bank.[10] True enough, even this could be countered in principle by imposing a tax on banks' combined holdings of central bank cash reserves and vault cash. (Presumably the tax would apply only above some minimum figure which respected banks' needs to have enough cash to honour their obligations to customers.) In the extreme a sufficiently severe tax on banks' holdings of base money might prompt a sharp decline in the exchange rate and resultant inflation. Indeed, the authorities could drive the exchange rate down and inflation up to whatever level they wanted, although whether such a policy would be acceptable either domestically or abroad is dubious. (The discussion in the last paragraph might seem outlandish, but it bears comparison with Silvio Gesell's proposal that bank notes should have a carrying cost. Gesell's idea was picked up by Keynes in *The General Theory*.)

Since the first version of this chapter was prepared, negative interest rates on cash reserves have been tried in significant monetary jurisdictions, including the Eurozone and Japan. (The phenomenon has been called "NIRP", for "negative interest rate policy", in contrast to "ZIRP", or "zero interest rate policy", which applies when the central bank rate is zero. ZIRP was first adopted by the Bank of Japan in February 1999.) A fair comment is that the approach has been resented by the banks, which regard the tax as just another cost. Other approaches to stimulating lending to the private sector might be considered. The UK has introduced a "Help to Buy" scheme to promote mortgage lending and a "Funding for Lending" programme, where additional loans to the private sector are given preferential treatment in terms of funding and capital requirements.

In various ways it may be possible to reduce the capital requirements on lending, while still respecting the BIS (and ultimately the G20) commitment to successful macroprudential regulation. Given the importance of meeting the intellectual challenge, it is a pity that more was not done sooner.

NOTES

1. The Great Financial Crisis is usually dated as beginning with the closing of the whole-sale money markets in August 2007, but Japan has had a deflationary malaise since 1991.
2. Piet Clement 'The term "macroprudential": origins and evolution', *BIS Quarterly Review*, March 2010 issue, pp. 59–67.
3. Bank of England discussion paper 'The role of macroprudential policy' (London: Bank of England, November 2009).
4. If anything, this may be an underestimate of the added burden on the banks. In his recorded remarks at Davos, 21 January 2014, Mark Carney stated that, "Much has been achieved in recent years to repair the core of the banking system. Minimum capital requirements for the world's largest banks have been increased seven-fold. These banks are on course to meet these new requirements five years before the deadline . . ." (Mark Carney, 'Remarks given by the Governor of the Bank of England at Davos' CBI British Business Leaders Lunch, 24 January 2014, see http://www.bankofengland.co.uk/publi cations/Documents/speeches/2014/speech705.pdf).
5. In April 2013 the London law firm, Linklaters, published a note on the Cypriot exchange controls, *Eurozone Bulletin: Capital and Exchange Controls*, which was still available at the time of writing (September 2016) on its website (www.linklaters.com), although the controls were removed in April 2015. Losses for uninsured depositors at two of the nation's largest banks, Laiki Bank and the Bank of Cyprus, were sometimes over 50 per cent of deposits' face value.
6. See Anat Admati and Martin Hellwig, *The Bankers' New Clothes: What's Wrong with Banking and What to Do About It* (Princeton, NJ: Princeton University Press, 2013) and David Miles, Jing Yang and Gilberto Marcheggiano 'Optimal bank capital' *Economic Journal*, vol. 123, no. 567 (March 2013), pp. 1–37.
7. See p. 173 in the next chapter for UK banks' concern that they might be nationalized without compensation, as a result of the government's demands in October 2008 that they operate with more capital and that they allow capital injections from the state. See also Tim Congdon 'Central banking, financial regulation and property rights', pp. 29–39, in Eugenio Bruno (ed.) *Global Financial Crisis* (London: Globe Business Publishing, 2009) and Ivan Fallon *Black Horse Ride* (London: Robson Press, 2015).
8. TARP refers to the "troubled assets relief program" of 2008 and 2009, originally to a value of $700 billion, for which there is a Wikipedia entry covering the ground.
9. The phrase "liquidity trap" could refer to either banks or non-banks. In his original proposal of the idea in his 1936 *General Theory* Keynes was concerned that non-banks would not be willing to buy bonds at a higher price (and so at a lower interest rate) even as their money holdings were increased enormously by government or central bank asset purchases. The notion that banks might also be subject to a trap of this kind is of more recent lineage, as noted in, for example, Roger Sandilands 'Hawtreyan "credit deadlock" or Keynesian "liquidity trap"? Lessons for Japan from the Great Depression' in Robert Leeson (ed.) *David Laidler's Contributions to Economics* (Basingstoke: Palgrave Macmillan, 2010).
10. In a classic 1947 paper Pigou was one of the first economists to observe that bank notes

meant that they constituted an asset with a nominal return that could not fall beneath zero. (Arthur Pigou 'Economic progress in a stable environment', *Economica*, New Series no. 14 [1947], pp. 180–88. See pp. 186–7.) In non-bank hands legal-tender notes are almost impossible to tax as they are both easy to hide, and pass often and easily from hand to hand.

7. The Basel rules and the banking system: an American perspective*

Steve Hanke

At the height of the Great Financial Crisis of 2008 and 2009 and in its aftermath, movers and shakers in banking regulatory circles beat the drums for "recapitalization". Their theme was that, in order to avoid future crises, banks must be made more resilient to shocks. More specifically, banks should operate with higher ratios of capital to risk assets. Governments across the developed world therefore compelled banks to raise fresh capital to "strengthen their balance sheets". If banks could not raise more capital, they were told to shrink the risk assets on their books, notably their loans to the private sector. One way or another, banks were mandated to increase their capital–asset ratios. Virtually the entire international policy-making establishment jumped on the recapitalization bandwagon. In 2010 the world's central bankers, represented collectively by the Bank for International Settlements (BIS), handed down the Basel III rules. These rules constituted an international – indeed, potentially global – regulatory framework that, among other things, hiked the required ratio of equity capital from 4 per cent to at least 7 per cent of banks' risk-weighted assets.[1]

Little thought was given to an established feature of financial systems with fiat money. As banks create most of the money used in a modern economy, the imposition of higher capital–asset ratios would force banks to shrink their risk assets and hence their deposit liabilities. Such deposits are the main form of money nowadays. A squeeze on the quantity of money would therefore ensue.[2] In the middle of a slump this would be deflationary and wholly inappropriate; it would undermine rather than promote economic recovery. The squeeze on money would stifle the growth in aggregate demand at exactly the time when demand needed a boost. As can be seen from Table 7.1, worries about inadequate money growth were a legitimate cause for concern. In the USA, as well as in nearly all countries, the growth rates of the quantity of money, broadly defined, and nominal national income are closely related over the medium term.

In any event, banks did pare their balance sheets in compliance with

Table 7.1   *Money and nominal GDP in the USA, 1959–2012*
             (% compound annual increase over 10-year periods)

	Nominal GDP	M3
1960s	6.9	7.5
1970s	10.2	11.4
1980s	7.8	8.5
1990s	5.5	4.9
2000s	4.0	8.1
Decade to Q4 2012	3.9	5.6
Whole period	6.8	7.7

Over the 43-year period from the end of 1959 to the end of 2012 the USA's nominal GDP increased by almost 17 times and its money stock, broadly defined, by 24 times, but the ratio of money to GDP increased by under a half or at an average annual rate of under 1%.

Sources: Federal Reserve, Bureau of Economic Analysis and Shadow Government Statistics. See p. 326 of Tim Congdon, *Money in a Free Society* (New York: Encounter Books, 2011) for more detail on the preparation of the table.

the Basel III rules, which were supposed to have been largely implemented by 2013. Further, this paring of balance-sheet size was associated with, at best, stagnation in broad money of participating economies and miserable macroeconomic outcomes in the 2008–12 period. These results might have persuaded regulatory officialdom to look to undo their blunder or, at the least, to question the appropriateness of the recapitalization frenzy. But that was not on the cards. On the contrary, in 2013 and 2014 central bankers (at the BIS, the European Central Bank, the Bank of England, the Federal Reserve, and so on) joined forces with an alphabet soup of regulatory bodies, from Britain's Financial Conduct Authority (FCA) to the United States' Financial Stability Oversight Council (FSOC), and from the G20's Financial Stability Board (FSB) to the European Union's European Banking Authority (EBA). They all clamoured for yet another round of hikes in bank capital. In November 2014 the Financial Stability Board, working under the aegis of the BIS (and ultimately the G20 group of nations), called for a further increase in capital–asset ratios at "global systemically important banks".[3] When fully adopted in 2019, banks would need to have capital equal to 16 per cent of the total of outstanding loans, derivative portfolios, and other risky assets. This figure is dramatically higher than had been acceptable to regulators in the 20 years before 2008, a period – as it deserves to be remembered – of stable macroeconomic performance known as "the Great Moderation". To this day (September 2016) the BIS continues to make noises about even further increases in required capital–asset ratios, something to which banking associations in Europe, Japan and Canada have finally made formal objections.[4]

I

Why did regulatory officialdom in late 2014 want to saddle the global banking system with another round of capital requirement hikes, particularly when Europe had only just escaped a double-dip recession, and the UK and US were mired in growth recessions? Why had they for some years been pledged to go in this direction? Were they simply unaware of the devastating unintended consequences that would follow?

Let us recall the structure of bank balance sheets. Assets (cash, loans and securities) must equal liabilities (deposits, equity capital and bonds, all of which are owed to others – that is, to customers, shareholders and bondholders). In most countries, the bulk of the banking system's liabilities (roughly 90 per cent) are deposits. Since deposits can be used to make payments, they are "money". To increase their capital–asset ratios, banks can either boost capital or shrink risk assets. If banks shrink their assets, their deposit liabilities decline and money balances are destroyed. The other way to increase a bank's capital–asset ratio is by raising new capital, but this too destroys money in the first instance. When purchasing newly issued bank equity, investors exchange funds from bank accounts for new shares. This reduces the deposit liabilities of the banking system and wipes out money. So, paradoxically, the drive since 2008 to deleverage banks and to shrink their balance sheets, in the name of making banks safer, destroyed money balances.[5] At a further remove, it hit company balance sheets and asset prices. Bank deleveraging therefore reduced aggregate demand, in the Keynesian sense, relative to where it would have been without the official regulatory mandates for higher capital–asset ratios. These patterns are clear in the USA, the UK and other major economies where sharp discontinuities in bank credit creation and money growth are evident from autumn 2008.[6] The notable exception is China, where the authorities refused to join the recapitalization drive. The discussion in the next section focuses on the US by utilizing the International Financial Statistics database maintained by the International Monetary Fund. The third section reviews Britain's response to its own problems, which came before other countries in the form of the 2007 Northern Rock affair. These events in the UK went some way towards establishing a precedent for the conduct of policy in the US and elsewhere. Indeed, the UK punched above its weight in the G20 discussions during the crisis period. It had a disproportionate and untoward influence on the development of G20 policy in late 2008 and subsequently.

II

In all countries, the forces driving changes in the quantity of money can be identified from the credit counterpart arithmetic, which captures the behaviour of items on both sides of banks' balance sheets. While the US's own central bank and statistical agencies pay little attention to the credit counterpart data in the analysis of monetary policy, the US provides information to the IMF, which enables analysts to conduct credit counterpart arithmetic and to appraise the relative strength of the forces behind money growth, a topic of considerable interest in the Great Recession period.

In the five years to the third quarter of 2008, broad money, as defined by the IMF, rose at a compound annual rate of 8.3 per cent, which is somewhat faster than nominal GDP. The rate of broad money growth also had a tendency to accelerate in 2006 and 2007. Asset markets were generally buoyant. The main driver of the growth of bank balance sheets (and hence of broad money) was new bank lending to the private sector. Such lending rose by over $4500 billion in five years – also at a compound annual rate of 8.3 per cent (see Figure 7.1). On the other hand, banks reduced their claims

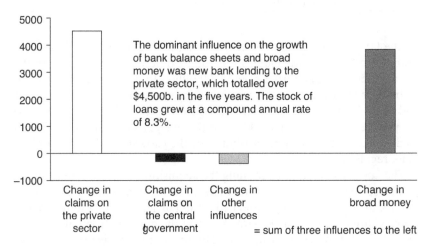

Source: Data from IMF and author's calculations.

Figure 7.1   Influence on the growth of broad money in the USA, in five years to Q3 2008 (in $ billions)

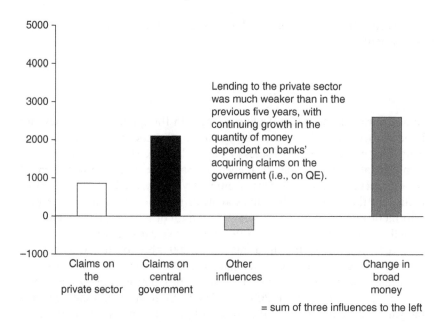

Source: Data from IMF and author's calculations.

Figure 7.2   *Influences on the growth of broad money in the USA, in five*
                years to Q3 2013 (in $ billions)

on the US government and the central bank during this period. In the five
years from Q3 2008, the pattern was totally different. New lending to the
private sector dropped from over $4500 billion to just above $850 billion,
or by over 80 per cent (see Figure 7.2). The contrast between Figures 7.1
and 7.2 – between the five years of vigorous growth in bank lending to
the private sector to autumn 2008 and the five years of stagnation in such
lending thereafter – can be attributed to the exogenous shock of tighter
bank regulation.

   The key consideration restraining the acquisition of more claims on the
private sector, which were of course risky, was the tightening of bank regulations, including officially mandated recapitalization. The resulting deflationary influence was particularly severe in the quarters from late 2008 to
mid-2012. But money growth was maintained at a positive rate as banks
grew their claims on the Federal government and the Federal Reserve via
the accumulation of Treasury bonds and bills, and cash balances at the
Fed. This growth in bank claims on the public sector was a by-product of
"quantitative easing" operations.[7] Without QE, money growth would have

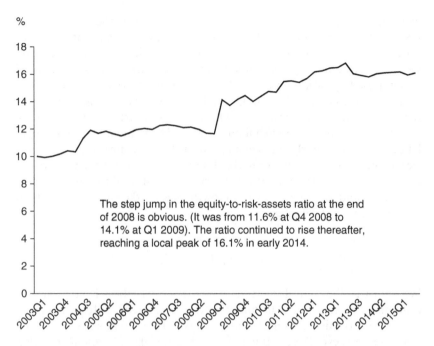

%

The step jump in the equity-to-risk-assets ratio at the end of 2008 is obvious. (It was from 11.6% at Q4 2008 to 14.1% at Q1 2009). The ratio continued to rise thereafter, reaching a local peak of 16.1% in early 2014.

Figure 7.3   Ratio of equity to risk assets in US banking, 2003–15

been negligible, implying greater strain in company balance sheets and lower asset prices than were actually observed. Almost certainly, the Great Recession – which was bad enough – would have been worse if the Fed had not organized the QE exercises.

Is there another way of monitoring the contrast between these two periods and identifying the timing of the change in the key influences on bank balance sheet growth? It has just been suggested that the turning-point came in autumn 2008, with the recapitalization of the banking system and the increase in capital–asset ratios. That ought to have caused, first, a step jump in the ratio of banks' equity capital to their risk assets (that is, to their claims on the private sector) as the new regulations came into effect and, second, a continuing rise in that ratio over the ensuing quarters. Figure 7.3 shows the series for that ratio, using the categories in the IMF database. (The "equity" numbers in the calculation were taken from a series called "shares and other equity". Risk assets were measured by "domestic claims", excluding claims on the federal government.)

The message of Figure 7.3 could hardly be clearer or more eloquent. US banks' capital position in the years running up to the Great Recession was stable and in fact highly robust by historical standards. (See pp. 32–7 in Chapter 1 for further discussion.) The change in the equity-to-risk assets ratio, at the end of 2008, was abrupt and out of line with previous experience; it was due above all to a regulatory upheaval that was unforeseen and unwanted by the banking industry.[8] The regulatory upheaval was imposed by officialdom. If US banks' equity-to-risk assets ratio had been the same in Q3 2013 as in Q3 2008, and the level of equity had been the same as actually prevailed at Q3 2013, risk assets would have been 37 per cent – or about $5000 billion – higher. The tightening of bank regulation, and particularly the demands from the government and its agencies for more bank capital, were the dominant reasons for the pro-cyclical credit crunch of 2009 and 2010, the torpor in bank credit in the following few years, and the plunge in the growth rate of the quantity of broad money from pre-2009 rates.

III

We return to the central question, "why was international financial officialdom so eager in late 2008 and indeed through 2009, 2010 and later, so committed to raising banks' capital ratios?" There is more to this story than meets the eye. The starting point for the global bank capital obsession is to be found in Britain and its infamous 2007 Northern Rock affair.[9] It was this British fiasco, rather than the September 2008 Lehman Brothers bankruptcy, that was the true beginning of the Great Financial Crisis and of the Great Recession which followed.

On 9 August 2007 the European wholesale money markets froze up, after BNP Paribas announced that it was suspending withdrawals on three of its money market funds.[10] These funds were heavily invested in US subprime credit instruments, which had suddenly become difficult to trade and to value. In the preceding two decades, many banks and financial intermediaries, in a number of countries, had financed their assets by borrowing from wholesale sources rather than from retail branch networks. In the UK Northern Rock, which had once been a cautiously managed building society in mutual ownership, was one of these organizations.[11] The ready availability of funds from the wholesale markets, which could be tapped by the issuance of securities, had facilitated Northern Rock's rapid expansion from its demutualization in 1997. However, in summer 2007 it did still have a significant branch network and hundreds of thousands of retail depositors.

With the wholesale money markets closed to new business, Northern Rock could not issue new securities or even roll over maturing debt. As significant liabilities were coming up for redemption, it faced a serious challenge in funding its business. In the years leading up to August 2007, Northern Rock had been consistently profitable, and had always had sufficient capital and liquidity to meet regulatory norms. However, by mid-2007, it was highly leveraged (with assets that were over 60 times equity capital), and its inability to secure new wholesale finance threatened the viability of its business model. Unable to secure the short-term funding it needed, Northern Rock informed its regulator (the Financial Services Authority) of its problems. Top FSA staff looked around for potential buyers of Northern Rock. They soon found one in the shape of Lloyd's Bank, which had been conservatively run in the credit boom of 2006 and early 2007, and was regarded as having good assets and adequate capital. But even Lloyd's Bank relied on the inter-bank market for financing to some degree. Given that the money market was paralysed by a lack of confidence, Lloyd's Bank's board was not 100 per cent certain that it could obtain sufficient retail deposits or an inter-bank line to fund the combination of its existing business and the purchase of Northern Rock. For the deal to go ahead, Lloyd's needed a standby loan facility which might have to be as large as £45 billion. With the money market closed, only the Bank of England could provide a facility of this sort. (Of course, if the money market were to return to normality, the Bank money might not be needed at all.)

By the end of the first week in September 2007, all of the FSA's senior staff and Paul Tucker, the Bank's senior executive for markets, wanted the Bank to provide Lloyd's with a standby facility to enable its takeover of Northern Rock. Although some haggling over the cost of the facility remained, everyone close to the negotiations wanted to avoid an intensification of the banking crisis. But there was an obstacle: the governor of the Bank of England, Mervyn King. At a fraught meeting on the afternoon of Sunday, 9 September, he said that the Bank would provide no help at all. When Hector Sants, chief executive of the FSA, set out the reasons that such help was essential to pre-empt worse funding strains at Northern Rock, King was belligerent. To quote from Ivan Fallon's book *Black Horse Ride*, "'No,' he said decisively and abruptly, 'I could not in any way support that. It is not our job to support commercial takeovers. I'm not prepared to provide any liquidity on that basis'".[12]

The next few days saw bad-tempered exchanges between King and top FSA and Bank staff. The antagonisms became bitter and personal. The truth is that King – who had come from a modest background in England's unremarkable West Midlands – loathed bankers and the City of London, and always had. The crisis gave King an opportunity to translate the loathing into action. Fallon quotes one banker as saying, "Mervyn saw his job as being to teach the banks and the markets a lesson".[13] Somehow or other, the tensions between the various players could not be kept quiet.

The situation became so desperate that Northern Rock had to be provided with an emergency loan facility from the Bank of England. Without that, it would no longer have been able to pay cash over the counter to retail depositors (or to transfer money to other banks via the online service at its website, which crashed because it received too many "hits"). However, the announcement of the facility was bungled, with the BBC over-dramatizing and exaggerating Northern Rock's difficulties. A massive run developed, so that the Bank of England was obliged to lend Northern Rock tens of billions of pounds to preserve the convertibility of bank deposits into notes, which is the touchstone of financial stability. Conditions became chaotic, with deposit withdrawals provoked by a media hubbub that was not proportional to Northern Rock's potential losses. On 17 September 2007, the Chancellor of the Exchequer, Alistair Darling, decided to announce a state guarantee on Northern Rock's deposits, which did indeed bring the run to an end.

The underlying issue raised by the Northern Rock affair was the eligibility of commercial banking organizations, which are profit-making (or at any rate profit-seeking), for loans from the central bank, which nowadays is almost everywhere state-owned. The traditional understanding in the UK before 2007 had been that solvent banks, and certainly solvent banks that had complied with regulations, could seek central bank help in funding their businesses if normal market sources (such as the inter-bank market) became unreliable.[14] Usually, they would have to offer good collateral and the central bank would be expected to charge a penalty rate. Despite the penalty, central bank finance was intended to promote the survival of any banks borrowing from it.[15] The larger aim was to protect depositors, but that meant keeping a bank in business until a more long-term solution was found. The standard vocabulary in these cases – that the central bank finance was "lender-of-last-resort lending" or "emergency liquidity assistance" – in no way implied that the central bank should be indifferent to the concerns of all stakeholders, including shareholders.

However, that was not Mervyn King's mindset. The truth is that he did not want the Bank of England to make any loans to commercial banks at all. His background was that of an academic economist, and he regarded the Bank's important task as being to organize high-quality economic research, and hence to inform and improve monetary policy. He did not think that a central bank should be a "bank" with an active balance sheet and constant interactions with commercial bank customers. Although in practice the Bank of England was involved in two big last-resort-lending episodes during his governorship (Northern Rock in September 2007, and RBS and HBOS in October 2008), King did his damnedest to keep loans to commercial banks off the Bank of England's balance sheet altogether.

In evidence to the Treasury Committee of the House of Commons on 11 September 2008, King maintained that it was not the central bank's role to lend to commercial banks on a long-term basis. In his view, that was a job only for the private sector or taxpayers acting via the government. By the phrase "on a long-term basis", King understood a period of six months, taking his cue from a European Commission "decision" of 5 December 2007.[16] (The British government asked the Commission for its view on whether its guarantee of Northern Rock deposits was state aid, since EU competition rules prevented such aid being extended for more than six months. The Commission's view was that a government guarantee on deposits was state aid, although a loan from the central bank was not.)

The implications of King's position are dangerous for banks and arguably for the entire financial system in a capitalist economy. If a bank cannot find alternative finance for its assets once a last-resort loan has lasted six months, that bank must either seek and find new money from the private sector or be taken into state ownership. By extension, the state would be entitled to seize the whole business with no compensation to shareholders, as it did both with Northern Rock on 17 March 2008, exactly six months after Darling's announcement of the state guarantee, and a similar organization, Bradford & Bingley plc, on 28 September 2008. In the weeks after the Lehman bankruptcy, much of the British banking system was in exactly the same position as Northern Rock had been in autumn 2007 and as Bradford & Bingley in 2008. They had had difficulty rolling over liabilities in the wholesale markets and might not have been able to fund their businesses. Meanwhile, because of the line being taken by the Bank of England under Mervyn King, they knew that any borrowings from it were time-limited, and might prove suicidal for managements and shareholders.

The only remaining private sector option was to raise new equity or bond capital, by the sale of securities to the long-term savings institutions. Here was the connection between King's attitude towards central bank loans to commercial banks and officialdom's insistence on extra bank capital as the solution to the crisis. Because in King's judgement central banks were not to lend to commercial banks except for a few months and even then on a frankly unfriendly basis, commercial banks would be obliged to raise more capital if they could not otherwise finance their loan portfolios. By this reasoning, bank recapitalization was a priority – indeed, an absolute priority – in the fraught circumstances of late 2008.

The Labour government in power during the crisis period, with Gordon Brown as Prime Minister and Alistair Darling as Chancellor, did have other sources of advice.[17] Nevertheless, as governor of the Bank of England, King was in an immensely powerful and influential position. It seems that his point of view managed to sway Brown, although possibly not Darling to the same degree.[18] At the G20 meetings in late 2008, Brown was fully committed to bank recapitalization as the right answer to the crisis. In the prologue to his book, *Beyond the Crash*, he recalled his reading of official papers in a flight back from Washington on 26 September 2008. He was "for the first time" fully apprised of the capital positions and prospective losses of Britain's banks. He judged that "doing nothing was not an option" and that "only one possible course of action remained". He almost glorified the moment when he underlined twice "Recapitalize NOW".[19]

Although Brown did not like King on a personal basis, he had plainly absorbed King's message.[20] Both men deemed loans from the Bank of England to the UK's commercial banks as a form of "taxpayers' money", and both were suspicious of banks and bankers. If extra capital was the correct response to banks' funding strains, and if the stock market was not prepared to buy newly issued securities from the banks, any large-scale official intervention had to take the form of capital injections from the state. If current managements and shareholders opposed such injections on the grounds that the new money diluted their interests, the British government could – and in fact did – threaten nationalization without compensation.[21] As Marcus Agius, Chairman of Barclays, told his shareholders, the banks faced "an existential threat".[22]

In short, Gordon Brown decided to indulge in a sophisticated form of bank-bashing. Perhaps surprisingly, he managed to attract many like-minded souls on the international financial scene. Indeed, Brown became the leader of the bank bashers. Hardly anyone among the politicians, regulators and central bankers in the peak supranational organizations (the BIS, the IMF and so on) offered a word of dissent as the British argument for bank recapitalization was introduced and developed at the G20 meetings in late 2008. As noted in Chapter 1 (see p. 31 above), Paul Krugman applauded the UK approach, which he attributed to Brown and Darling. To quote from his 12 October 2008 column in the *New York Times*, "we do know . . . that Mr Brown and Alistair Darling . . . have defined the character of the worldwide rescue effort, with other wealthy nations playing catch-up".[23]

IV

In the last few years, a consensus for higher bank capital ratios has been established. It is shared at the highest political level, in international financial circles and among most of the respected academics working in this field. In 2013, Anat Admati and Martin Hellwig brought out a new book, *The Bankers' New Clothes: What's Wrong with Banking and What to Do About It*, which advocated substantial increases in capital ratios over and above the figures mandated under Basel III. It was praised by Nobel laureate Roger Myerson, who described it as being "worthy of such global attention as Keynes' *General Theory*".[24] But is it necessarily true that banks with more capital are safer and stronger, and hence more resilient in coping with cyclical shocks? Lehman Brothers, which was incidentally not a *commercial* bank subject to supervision by the Federal Reserve, had a capital cushion that comfortably exceeded the regulatory minimum just before it collapsed into bankruptcy. (For the distinction between commercial and investment banks, see p. 32 above in Chapter 1.) Unless regulators are so intrusive as to undermine the autonomy of bank management altogether, there is always a risk that banks acquire assets of such low quality that high capital buffers fail to protect depositors.

Unhappily, as Figures 7.1 and 7.2 demonstrate, the reaction of most banks to the regulatory frenzy since 2009 has been to run scared. They have restricted claims on the private sector and expanded low-risk holdings of cash reserves and government securities. (Under the Basel III rules, cash and government securities require no capital backing as they are deemed to be "risk-free".) The new difficulties in raising finance from the banking industry that companies face may hamper growth and innovation, as even the IMF and the OECD sometimes acknowledge on the quiet. Since bank credit lines are a key source of working capital for some businesses – notably those which trade products, commodities and securities – the restriction on credit has acted like a supply constraint on the economy. For all the talk about the looseness of the Fed's monetary policy in the QE era, the inconvenient truth is that overall broad money growth in the US remained rather subdued even into 2014 and 2015.

By enforcing extra bank capital requirements in the middle of an economic downturn (that is, in late 2008 and 2009), central banks and the main regulatory agencies aggravated the *cyclical* weakness in demand. For a few quarters the resulting depression in asset prices made some banks even less safe, illustrating the warning by Irving Fisher in his 1933 paper on 'The debt-deflation theory of great depressions'. As Fisher noted, a paradox might be at work. Borrowers repay bank debt, but in the process they destroy money balances and undermine the value of stocks and shares, and houses and land. That increases the real burden of the remaining debt. In his words, "the mass effort to get out of debt sinks us more deeply into debt."[25]

Sure enough, it is now (September 2016) some years since the worst of the crisis, asset prices have recovered, and American banks have started once more to expand their lending. However, the economy is not firing on all cylinders. Banks today are not providing the same full range of loan facilities as before 2008, while the cost to non-banks of hedging risk (through arranging options and derivatives with banks) is higher than before. Arguably, the increase in capital–asset ratios in the financial sector constitutes a *structural* impediment to the supply side of the American economy.

Bank capital ratios that are too high have damaged the American economy on both a cyclical and a structural basis. The solution? Every bank shareholder has a strong interest in ensuring that managements do not take on too much risk relative to the capital entrusted to them. It cannot be emphasized too strongly that the stable macroeconomic performance of the Great Moderation (in the 20 or so years to 2007) occurred while banks operated with much lower capital–asset ratios than now prevail. The solution is to scale back untimely and excessive bank capital requirements, and restore market discipline on banks and other financial businesses. Let banks spend more time managing risks and less time managing regulators and politicians.

NOTES

* This chapter is based on Steve Hanke's 'Basel's capital curse', *Globe Asia*, January 2013 issue, with extensive changes by the author and Tim Congdon to reflect developments since early 2013.

1. Although mooted at the G20 meetings in late 2008, agreement between the key parties about Basel III was reached only in September 2010. But even that agreement has been followed by constant revision and modification. The Wikipedia entry on Basel III is sufficient to understand these developments, although the websites of the BIS and many national central banks are relevant.

2. Steve H. Hanke '"Stronger" banks, weaker economies', *Globe Asia*, August 2011.

3. A "systemically important bank" is a bank large enough to cause a financial crisis. Such banks are of two kinds, "domestic systemically important banks" and "global systemically important banks". Lists of such organizations are published by the Basel Committee under the aegis of the BIS, bearing in mind such criteria as size and interconnectedness with other businesses, but a precise definition has not been established.

4. Jim Brunsden 'Lenders step up their fight against global capital reform' *Financial Times*, 2 September 2016.

5. Steve Hanke 'Monetary policies misunderstood', *Globe Asia*, May 2016.

6. See Chapter 2 above for this pattern in the UK, and Chapter 4 for the EU.

7. QE also affected bond yields and indeed asset prices in general, but these developments were by-products of the effect on the quantity of money. See pp. 197–8 in Chapter 8 below in Chapter 2 above for further discussion.

8. Banks and bankers have long been unpopular in the USA. For a protest against the populist attack on the banks that has followed the Great Financial Crisis, see Richard Bove *Guardians of Prosperity: why America needs Big Banks* (New York: Penguin, 2013), particularly pp. 66–99.

9. Several good accounts of the Northern Rock crisis were published soon afterwards, such as Alex Brummer *The Crunch* (London: Random House, 2008) and Brian Walters *The Fall of Northern Rock* (Petersfield: Harriman House, 2008). See Tim Congdon *Central Banking in a Free Society* (London: Institute of Economic Affairs, 2009),

particularly pp. 117–44, for an attempt to place the crisis in the context of the long-run development of banking institutions.

10. Dan Conaghan *The Bank: Inside the Bank of England* (London: Biteback Publishing, 2012), p. 131.

11. The phrase "building society" is the British term for a financial intermediary that concentrates on housing loans, to be extended to depositors on a non-profit basis.

12. Ivan Fallon *Black Horse Ride* (London: Robson Press, 2015), p. 193.

13. Fallon *Black Horse Ride*, pp. 367–8.

14. The underlying principles for central bank action go back to Walter Bagehot's 1873 *Lombard Street*. (Walter Bagehot *Lombard Street*, vol. IX, in Norman St John-Stevas [ed.] *The Collected Works of Walter Bagehot* [London: The Economist, 1978, originally published in 1873].) But the Bank of England had published articles in its name on the last-resort role in the 20 years before the Northern Rock crisis, with none of them intimating that funding strains in the banking system would justify nationalization without compensation. See, for example, Xavier Freixas and others 'Lender of last resort: a review of the literature', *Financial Stability Review* (London: Bank of England), November 1999 issue.

15. On 18 November 1993 Eddie George, the then governor of the Bank of England, gave a lecture at the London School of Economics on the principles of last-resort lending. He said, "any support we will provide will be terms that are as penal as we can make them, without precipitating the collapse we are trying to avoid." *Bank of England Quarterly Bulletin* (London: Bank of England), February 1994 issue, p. 65.

16. Commission Decision of 5 December 2007, in State aid case no. NN 70/2007 – United Kingdom – Northern Rock, OJ C43, 16.2.2008, p. 1. See European Commission website.

17. Alistair Darling *Back from the Brink* (London: Atlantic Books, 2011), pp. 61–4.

18. Darling *Back from the Brink*, pp. 139–42.

19. Indeed, in Brown's words, "I wrote it on a piece of paper, in the thick black felt-tip pens I've used since a childhood sporting accident affected my eyesight. I underlined it twice." Gordon Brown *Beyond the Crash* (London and New York: Simon & Schuster, 2010), p. xviii.

20. Darling *Back from the Brink*, p. 69, for Brown's antipathy towards King.

21. Fallon *Black Horse Ride*, pp. 326–7 and pp. 360–61.

22. See the report in the *Financial Times* on Barclays' annual general meeting on 23 April 2009.

23. Paul Krugman 'Gordon does good', 12 October 2008 column in *The New York Times*.

24. Anat Admati and Martin Hellwig *The Bankers' New Clothes: What's Wrong with Banking and What to Do About It* (Princeton, NJ: Princeton University Press, 2013). Myerson's praise appeared in 'Rethinking the principles of bank regulation: a review of Admati and Hellwig's *The Bankers' New Clothes*', *Journal of Economic Literature*, vol. 52, no. 1 (March 2014), pp. 197–210.

25. Irving Fisher 'The debt deflation theory of great depressions' *Econometrica*, vol. 1 (1933), pp. 337–57. The quotation is from p. 344.

PART III

How Should the Great Recession be Viewed in Monetary Thought and History?

Introduction to Part III

Tim Congdon

The final part of the book is concerned with the range of intellectual responses to the Great Recession, and the parallels between that response and the response to the Great Depression. Inevitably, John Maynard Keynes and Milton Friedman are cited on numerous occasions. In the "tentative sketch" of the typical business cycle in their 1963 paper on 'Money and the business cycle' Friedman and Schwartz placed the linkages between money and asset prices at the centre of the story.[1] Since wealth is always the capitalization of an income stream, the determination of asset prices cannot be separated – either practically or analytically – from the determination of prices of goods and services. The determination of national wealth is inextricably linked to the determination of national income.

This was not a new theme in the early 1960s. Monetary economists had long understood that – if an economy's full equilibrium were to described – non-interest-bearing (or at any low-return) money balances had somehow to co-exist with higher-yielding bonds. Indeed, strictly speaking, theory and practice required that investors had to integrate every asset into their forward planning. They would buy and sell bonds, equities, houses, land and so on until relative prices had been established that would equalize expected total risk-adjusted returns on all these asset classes. Friedman objected to the widespread tendency after Keynes's *General Theory* to understand portfolio balance as definable with only two asset categories, money and bonds. In a 1964 paper with David Meiselman he contrasted a "credit" view of how economies function with a "monetary" view. In the credit view, monetary policy "impinges on a narrow and well-defined range of capital assets and a correspondingly narrow range of associated expenditures"; in the monetary view, it "impinges on a much broader range of capital assets and correspondingly broader range of associated expenditures".[2]

Chapter 8 by Philip Booth discusses the relationship between money and monetary policy on the one hand, and asset prices on the other. It is based on a paper originally submitted to a journal for actuaries (who take many of the major asset allocation decisions in big long-term savings institutions). Booth ranges widely over a number of different approaches, even bringing in New Keynesianism and the Austrian School.

In Chapter 9 on 'How would Keynes have analysed the Great Recession of 2008 and 2009?' Keynes's biographer, Robert Skidelsky, quotes extensively from his writings at the time of the Great Depression. *A Treatise on Money*, published in late 1930, has pride of place.[3] A conspicuous feature of the material from *A Treatise on Money* is the abundance of Keynes's references to money, even to particular types of bank deposit and categories of money holder. The prominence of money in Keynes's theoretical apparatus is accompanied by comments on contemporary events that would be unintelligible unless he believed that money affected expenditure and output, and that it did so largely through financial markets and effects on asset prices.

If they had not been warned that their remarks would be widely regarded as heretical, naive readers of the *Treatise* might think that Keynes had more than a trace of quantity-theory thinking in his vision of the economy's workings. They might even be so outlandish as to suggest that Keynes's writings were a major influence on Milton Friedman. But such readers would in fact be neither naive nor outlandish. One of Friedman's teachers, when he started his postgraduate course at Chicago in 1932, was Lloyd Mints. Mints gave a lecture course numbered 'Economics 330' which was organized around *A Treatise on Money*. The first words on macroeconomics that Friedman wrote in his still extant notes were "Econ 330 Keynes". He then added that Mints' judgement was that "General framework of Keynes likely to endure much longer than details".[4]

In the deflationary turmoil of 1930 and 1931 Keynes advocated what he termed "monetary policy *à outrance*", which consisted in central bank asset purchases to drive down the long-term rate of interest. Monetary policy *à outrance* and quantitative easing are surely similar, perhaps even identical, although the meaning of both phrases has been debated. (I have proposed that Keynes was in fact the inventor of QE. See note 7 to Chapter 2 above.[5]) According to Skidelsky, Keynes would have approved of central bank asset purchases in late 2008 and 2009, but criticized the suspension of QE in the UK in 2010. Skidelsky also says that Keynes would have deplored the fiscal austerity pursued in many countries, notably in the Eurozone, from 2010.

Thanks largely to his widely syndicated column in the *New York Times*, Paul Krugman of Princeton University is widely accepted as the world's most influential Keynesian. Three months after Friedman's death on 16 November 2006, Krugman published a critique of Friedman's work, under the title 'Who was Milton Friedman?', in *The New York Times Review of Books*. Krugman's remarks on *A Monetary History* were sharply hostile. While conceding that *A Monetary History* was "a vast work of extraordinary scholarship", the verdict on Friedman and Schwartz's account of the Great Depression was that they may have begun by seeming "a bit slippery", but had "eventually" descended into intellectual dishonesty. Krugman's attack turned on the discrepancy in the 1929–33 period between the 10 per cent increase in the monetary base and the 40 per cent fall in the quantity of money, broadly defined.[6] (This discrepancy was discussed in the Introduction, on p. 12.) The point was – according to Krugman – that the increase in the monetary base showed that the Fed had tried to combat deflation. It followed that Friedman's attempt to attribute the Great Depression to Fed bungling was groundless.

In Chapter 10 David Laidler – who helped Schwartz with data collection as a graduate student – recalls the theory of the money base multiplier. He reviews once more the changes that were seen during and after the Great Depression in the American public's preferences between cash and deposits, and in banks' desired cash/deposit ratio after the shock of thousands of bank failures. He offers a robust defence of Friedman and Schwartz against Krugman. In his words, "If these shifts are interpreted as the outcome of voluntary choices made by the relevant agents in the face of growing uncertainty about the banking system's viability", then the conclusion follows that the shifts "could and should have been offset by much larger increases in the stock of high-powered money than in fact occurred".[7] Laidler's reply to Krugman is nuanced and far from dogmatic, and he admits that policy-makers in the USA's Great Depression were frustrated that banks with ample cash reserves did not more actively seek to grow their assets.[8]

It is interesting to note as background to the Krugman–Laidler exchange that – in his ruminations on monetary policy *à outrance* – Keynes realized that central bank action might have to be on an enormous scale to counter a very severe downturn. In July 1931 he wrote a memorandum for the UK's Economic Advisory Council while on an ocean liner returning from the USA. Keynes said the Federal Reserve's "open-market purchases may have to take place on an inconveniently large scale before they are effective".[9] But he did believe that such purchases should be undertaken. Further, on sufficient scale and given enough time, he thought expansionary open market operations would work.

Indeed, a reasonable deduction from the Laidler and Skidelsky papers in the current volume is that in the early 1930s Keynes was a strong supporter of stimulatory monetary policy. In this respect Friedman was closer to Keynes than the Keynesians of the 1960s, and Laidler and Skidelsky today are closer to him than Krugman. Perhaps Krugman should spend more time reading what Keynes actually wrote. However, it has to be conceded to Krugman that during the 1930s Keynes's policy predilections did become more fiscalist and hence more "Keynesian", in the sense that Krugman understands this somewhat vexed term.[10] In the six years that separated *A Treatise on Money* from *The General Theory* Keynes did alter his emphasis, with less focus on monetary management and more on fiscal policy. Whether he was right to do so is another area of persisting controversy.

NOTES

1. The 1963 Friedman and Schwartz paper is discussed above in Chapter 1 on p. 7 and below in Chapter 10 on p. 237.
2. Milton Friedman and David Meiselman 'The relative stability of monetary velocity and the investment multiplier in the United States, 1897–1958' in *Stabilization Policies* (Englewood Cliffs, NJ: Prentice Hall for the Commission on Money and Credit).
3. The author's preface to *A Treatise on Money* was dated 14 September 1930. Johnson and Moggridge (eds) *Collected Writings of John Maynard Keynes*, vol. V: *A Treatise on Money* (London and Basingstoke: Macmillan for the Royal Economic Society, 1971, originally published in 1930), p. xix.
4. Robert Leeson 'From Keynes to Friedman via Mints', pp. 483–525, in Robert Leeson (ed.) *Keynes, Chicago and Friedman* (London: Pickering & Chatto, 2003), vol. 2. The quotation is from p. 485.
5. Tim Congdon 'Who invented QE?', *Economic Affairs* journal (London: Institute of Economic Affairs), vol. 32, no. 3, October 2012.
6. Paul Krugman 'Who was Milton Friedman?', *The New York Review of Books*, 15 February 2007 issue. Krugman's article was countered by a research paper from the National Bureau of Economic Research from Ed Nelson and Anna Schwartz, 'The impact of Milton Friedman on modern monetary economics: setting the record straight on Paul Krugman's "Who was Milton Friedman?"' NBER working paper 13546 (Cambridge: National Bureau of Economic Research, October 2007).
7. See pp. 239–40 below.
8. As Laidler observes in his chapter for the current volume, some people deem a situation in which banks are reluctant to lend despite having excess cash reserves as "a liquidity trap" or even "the liquidity trap". But this was not in fact Keynes's conception of the liquidity trap in *The General Theory*. The elusiveness of the liquidity trap idea was discussed in Roger Sandilands 'Hawtreyan "credit deadlock" or Keynesian "liquidity trap"? Lessons for Japan from the Great Depression', pp. 329–65, in Robert Leeson (ed.) *Scholarship and Stability: Essays in Honour of David Laidler's Contribution to Macroeconomics* (London: Palgrave Macmillan, 2010). A further debating point with Krugman is the meaning that he attaches to the phrase when he uses it, as he tends to use "liquidity trap" indiscriminately for any condition in which monetary policy seems not to be working as planned. I protested against the rather careless choice of words in Krugman's writing in essay 4, 'Keynes, Bernanke and Krugman, and the pathologies of capitalism', pp. 57–103, in Tim Congdon *Money in a Free Society* (New York: Encounter Books, 2011).
9. Johnson and Moggridge (eds) *Collected Writings of John Maynard Keynes*, vol. XX: *Activities 1929–31*, p. 565.
10. Arguably, "Keynesianism" is just as ambiguous as "monetarism". For example, the label "New Keynesianism" has been attached to a set of ideas which most old-style, fiscalist Keynesians regard as objectionable. See pp. 12–14 of my 2007 book on *Keynes, the Keynesians and Monetarism* (Cheltenham, UK and Northampton, MA, USA: Edward Elgar Publishing, 2007).

8. Monetary policy, asset prices and financial institutions*

Philip Booth

Asset price instability was a marked and unsettling feature of the Great Recession, and was a nagging worry for policy-makers in the periods of the greatest turmoil. Several alternative economic theories help to explain the interaction between "monetary policy" and securities markets. Admittedly, the concept of "monetary policy" is awkward, as it could be understood as the determination of either an interest rate or the quantity of money. The subject needs to be pinned down and clarified, not least because both policy-makers and financial practitioners (in investment and actuarial advice, for example) sometimes accept without question a debatable view of how financial markets work. This relies implicitly on equilibrium theories and the assumption that markets are efficient (or, for short, the "efficient markets hypothesis" or EMH). It is difficult to reconcile these theories, when stated in an unqualified form, with the violent asset price movements seen before, during and after the Great Recession.

Ideas from modern finance theory have been extended into pension scheme funding and investment policy, and in the use of market values in pension fund and insurance company accounting. Indeed, regulatory capital requirements for both life and non-life insurance companies under the newly introduced Solvency II arrangements mandate the use of market values of investments, with very limited discretion. The same spirit is at work in regulation for the banking industry, where so-called "fair value accounting" – such as the IFRS9 standards for the valuation of financial instruments – can have important implications for the calculation of solvency.[1]

Numerous qualifications limit the applicability of the EMH in practice. But discussions of the interactions between monetary policy and financial markets provide part of the information stream to investors in financial markets, and so have an obvious relevance to asset price determination. Enthusiasts for the EMH could argue that financial markets respond rapidly to disequilibrium conditions. Specifically, after a monetary disturbance (that is, after a major change in a central bank interest rate or the quantity of money), financial markets are characterized by such low transaction costs and such rapid information flows that equilibrium can be quickly restored.

This is a plausible view. However, sceptics about market efficiency might object that monetary disturbances may take several quarters, or even years, to work their way fully through financial markets and the real economy. Milton Friedman proposed that monetary policy operated with "long and variable lags", to recall one of his most celebrated observations.[2] Asset prices can therefore remain, for extended periods, far from the "equilibrium values" implied by economic theory. In that sense, they can be viewed as "distorted by monetary policy" until the transmission processes are complete. Like the Great Depression of the early 1930s, the Great Recession was accompanied by big movements in asset prices. The movements were indeed so large that various transaction costs, imperfections and frictions must be invoked if the real world is to be interpreted with any degree of seriousness.

The first section of the chapter looks at prima facie evidence for a relationship between monetary policy, in the sense of a change in interest rates, and investment markets. The next section discusses the monetarist transmission mechanism which directly links investment markets with monetary policy, where "monetary policy" now means a change in the quantity of money. Notable work has been undertaken in this area by Gordon Pepper, who is a professional actuary as well as an economist. The chapter then examines New Keynesian and New Classical approaches to monetary policy, where the meaning of these terms will become clear as the discussion proceeds. Finally, in this review of monetary theories, so-called "Austrian" ideas are discussed. (From its roots in nineteenth-century Vienna, the Austrian School of economics has been known for its suspicion of government intervention in the economy. It remains vigorous and influential.) All these schools of thought have something to say about the linkages between monetary policy and financial decision-making, and further between asset price determination, investment in structures and capital equipment, and activity in the real economy. Moreover, all have been widely cited in the debates on the causes of the Great Recession.

I

Financial market literature generally accepts an empirical relationship between monetary policy variables and investment values. In a comprehensive survey of the evidence, Conover et al. demonstrated a link between central bank interest rate changes and asset prices.[3] In their work, periods

Table 8.1   Statistical properties of the relationship between interest rates and asset prices

Country	β	t-statistic	Sample size
Belgium	−0.0082	−2.1	443
Germany	−0.0087	−2.03	462
Sweden	−0.0107	−2.31	451
UK	−0.0174	−3.57	431

of expansionary (contractionary) monetary policy were defined as those when interest rates were falling (rising). They estimated the following equation across a number of different countries for the years 1956 to 1995:

$$S_t = \alpha + \beta D_t^I + \varepsilon_t$$

S_t is the monthly equity return measured in local currency terms and D_t^I is a dummy variable equal to one if the last interest rate change was an increase and zero if it was a decrease. The results show significant and substantial relationships between the monetary policy stance and asset prices. Examples of values for the regression coefficients and t-statistics are given in Table 8.1, which also has the sample sizes. All four values for the regression coefficient shown in the table are significantly different from zero at the 5 per cent level. That for the UK is also significantly different from zero at the 1 per cent level.

The average investment return differences between periods of expansionary and contractionary monetary policy were substantial when compounded annually. In the USA, for example, the results suggested an average annual return difference of 14 per cent. All but one of the 16 countries studied (the exception being Austria) produced a negative value for the regression coefficient. Twelve out of the 15 countries with a negative value for the regression coefficient delivered values that were significant at the 5 per cent level. The results for real returns were similar to those for nominal returns. This work corroborated other contributions by Jensen and by Conover's co-authors.[4]

The results were important in their own right but – as the authors readily conceded – they provided little understanding of either cause and effect or the role of monetary policy relative to other variables. The move to inflation-targeting regimes by a number of countries in the last 25 years may have changed the relationships. The point here is that, if the central bank acts in a clear and transparent way, market interest rates ought to adjust in anticipation of central bank interest rate moves. By implication, the explanatory power of central bank interest rates in statistical models could be reduced. Nevertheless, the papers from Jensen, Conover and others represented preliminary evidence that changes in the interest rate under direct central bank control can impact powerfully on asset prices.

The relevance of central bank action for house prices is contentious, not least because of the common allegation that dysfunctional features of the US housing finance market were the root cause of the Great Recession. Schwartz and Greenwood in a 2009 volume *Verdict on the Crash: Causes and Policy Implications*, edited by the author, both suggested that loose monetary policy was an important contributor to the asset price bubble in the three years to 2007, which set the scene for the subsequent crash.[5] But this is disputed by central bankers on both sides of the Atlantic. In a 2010 speech to the American Economic Association, Ben Bernanke argued that direct linkages between monetary accommodation and the US house price boom preceding the crash were weak.[6] In the same year the Bank of England's chief economist, Charles Bean, claimed in a jointly authored paper that monetary policy only explained part of the growth in house prices before the crash, and that it explained a smaller part in the USA, widely deemed to be the source of the crisis, than in the UK.[7] Nevertheless, whatever the relative contribution of monetary policy and real factors to fluctuations in asset prices, all analysts agree that here is an important area for potential investigation.

II

Monetarism rests on "the quantity theory of money" and indeed the terms are sometimes regarded as interchangeable. The theory is often represented by the identity first explored in detail by Irving Fisher at the start of the twentieth century. The identity is $MV = PT$, where M is the quantity of money, V is its velocity of circulation, P is the price level and T is the volume of transactions. The identity provides a focus for analysis, but is far more elusive and ambiguous than recognized in many elementary treatments. In Fisher's own work, T included transactions in assets as well as transactions in goods and services, and he was well aware that the total value of all transactions is a high multiple of national income. However, the modern tendency is to view the velocity of circulation as nominal national income divided by the quantity of money. At any rate, monetarists argue that, over the long run and in normal circumstances, changes in the velocity of money are small compared with changes in either the quantity of money or national income. Further, such changes in velocity as do occur are readily interpreted by analysing the characteristics of agents' money demand function. All being well, the aggregate money demand function (that is, the demand functions of individual agents aggregated at the whole-economy level) is stable.

An exogenous increase in the quantity of money ought therefore to lead to an increase in *PT*, where *PT* can be equated with nominal national income. But what does that imply for the prices of assets, which can after all be viewed as the capitalization of certain income streams (profits, rent, returns to entrepreneurship) that form part of total national income? Do asset prices also respond to changes in the quantity of money? Do asset price changes precede or follow those in national income? And what part did they play in the Great Recession?

1.   Some Key Monetarist Propositions, according to Friedman

Milton Friedman's 1968 presidential address to the American Economic Association and his 1970 Wincott Lecture in the UK, on *The Counter Revolution in Monetary Theory*, were important turning points in the intellectual debate between monetarists and their opponents.[8] The Wincott Lecture was highly empirical and clearly related to his earlier work (with Anna Schwartz) on the repetitive features of American business cycles.[9] Given the irresistible factual basis for the claims being made, all economists – whatever their doctrinal affiliations – were obliged to debate the *extent and timing* of the various forces identified by Friedman and Schwartz, rather than *whether* these forces existed at all.

The Wincott Lecture highlighted seven common patterns in the relationship between money growth and the economy, in the course of successive business cycles. Readers are referred to the original sources to appreciate the subtlety of the analysis. For current purposes, the last two of Friedman's patterns are of immediate relevance. First, the initial effect of a change in the quantity of money is not on income, but on the prices of existing financial and physical assets. To answer the question above, changes in the rate of money growth affect the prices of assets before they affect wages and the prices of goods and services. More generally, financial markets are more sensitive to monetary policy events than labour or goods markets.

Secondly, a change in monetary growth affects interest rates in one direction at first, but in the opposite direction later on. The initial effect of an acceleration in money growth is to lower interest rates, whereas the ultimate effect is to raise interest rates due to the effect of faster monetary expansion on actual and expected inflation.[10] Friedman's observation is consistent with the earlier discussion in this chapter, to the effect that reductions in the central-bank-administered money market rate boost asset prices. But, eventually, bond yields have to be high enough to offer investors a positive real return, as noted by Irving Fisher in the distinction between nominal and real interest rates. Higher money growth boosts inflation, while the incorporation of that effect into expectations hurts the bond market. Expectations matter vitally to the relationships between money and macroeconomic outcomes.

2.   Money and Assets in the Transmission Mechanism, Past and Present

Current exponents of monetarism believe that insufficient explicit attention is given to the role of money and the way in which changes in monetary policy are transmitted through the financial and economic system.[11] Some standard central bank models – notably the New Keynesian and New Classical models discussed below – neglect almost entirely the bearing of money on asset pricing, and the interactions between financial markets on the one hand and labour and product markets on the other. It is evident from Friedman's analysis that monetarists believe a simple, mechanical relationship between the quantity of money and the price level of goods and services to be only the start of the analysis. In their view the linkages between money and the economy are complex, and vary within and across business cycles.

For much of the last 25 years monetary policy has been taken to be the setting of the short-term money market rate, with no mention whatsoever of any money aggregate. (The particular short-term interest rate in question varies between economies, but it is usually the rate of interest at which the central bank lends to the banking system or a rate closely related to it.) Changes in the central bank rate impact on the rate of money growth, because – for example – the rate of increase in bank credit to the private sector is interest-rate-sensitive. (As explained in the Introduction, new money balances are created when banks expand their loans to the private sector.) But these impacts are sidelined in contemporary discussions of "monetary policy", just as the quantity of money itself is sidelined. (Or, perhaps one should say has been sidelined until recently.) In the extreme, modern finance theories – with their assumptions of market clearing and rational expectations – dismiss altogether the possibility that changes in money balances can matter to anything.[12] Nonetheless, common sense argues for the existence of mechanisms that relate the quantity of money to macroeconomic outcomes, while investment markets are likely to feature in these mechanisms. Why, otherwise, are money balances and financial markets found in all modern economies?

A key observation was made by Irving Fisher in his 1911 *The Purchasing Power of Money* and his 1913 *Elementary Principles of Economics*. This was that an increase in the quantity of money – which may be caused by a reduction in central bank interest rates and the consequent boost to bank credit – does not alter agents' desired ratio of money balances to their "goods". The word "goods" can be thought of at this stage as their expenditure and income. In other words, the equilibrium value of the velocity of circulation is set by forces that are independent from the quantity of money, while change in the quantity of money can upset velocity only temporarily. In the long run, when equilibrium is restored after a disturbance or set of disturbances to the quantity of money, changes in the quantity of money and changes in income and expenditure should be equi-proportional.

Fisher had much to say about the "transition periods" during which agents restore equilibrium after a shock to the quantity of money. At one point he listed six different categories of transaction that enable agents – by changes in their holdings of cash and deposits – to return to their desired money-holding position.[13] But the crux of the matter had in fact been seen by Wicksell over a decade earlier. In Fisher's words in *Elementary Principles of Economics*, if "some mysterious Santa Claus suddenly doubles the amount [of money] in the possession of each individual", economic agents have excess money balances. They try to get rid of their excess money by increasing their purchases in shops and elsewhere, but "we must not forget that the only way that the individual can get rid of his money is by handing it over to somebody else. Society is not rid of it."[14]

In short, if for whatever reason the quantity of money or its rate of growth suddenly increases, transactions between agents can be assumed not to alter the quantity of money. Equilibrium can be recovered only by changes in the prices or quantities of the products and services being bought and sold. The ideas here must be highlighted as absolutely central to monetary economics. However, they are not intuitive and are often ignored in university teaching. The mechanism by which agents bring back equilibrium (at a higher price level) after an increase in the quantity of money has been called "the Wicksell process", after its original expositor. But it passes under other labels. For example, the "real balance effect" in Patinkin's 1956 *Money, Interest and Prices* comes to much the same thing as the Wicksell process. In addition, because the famous early-twentieth-century Cambridge economist, Arthur Pigou, pointed out the impact of excess or deficient money balances on the economy in a classic 1947 article, another valid term is "the Pigou effect".[15]

It should be noted that, despite his seminal elucidations of the quantity identity ($MV = PT$), Fisher said little about financial markets and asset prices in his account of the "transition periods". Indeed, only two of his six categories of transaction were important in affecting the overall value of transactions, and hence the price level. He called these "money against goods", where he meant money in the sense of legal-tender cash, and "deposits against goods". He did not use an alternative form of words, "money against goods *and assets*" or "deposits against goods *and assets*". In fact, neither *The Purchasing Power of Money* nor *Elementary Principles of Economics* had a focused and well-organized discussion of the relationship between money and asset prices.[16]

One of the objectives of Tim Congdon's 2005 study on *Money and Asset Prices in Boom and Bust* was to say that the Wicksell process (or real balance effect, or Pigou effect, or whatever) applied in financial markets as well as in labour and product markets. Financial markets could therefore be an important conduit through which changes in the quantity of money are transmitted to the wider economy. Congdon noted that money is held by different types of agent, specifically (following a classification adopted by the UK's Central Statistical Office in the 1950s) by households, companies and non-bank financial institutions. Any change in the overall quantity of money must be split between these three sectors. Using money data prepared in the UK since 1963, Congdon found a recurrent pattern. Households tended to keep their money balances close to the equilibrium level at all times. The growth of household money was therefore relatively stable from period to period. Two points followed. First, when the rate of money growth accelerated or decelerated sharply, the rate of change in household money holdings was invariably less than that of money in the aggregate. Second, the rates of change in money held by companies and financial institutions were higher, and indeed sometimes much higher, than the rates of change in aggregate money.

In an examination of the UK data over the 1963–2003 period, Congdon found no fewer than 12 quarters when the annualized growth rate of non-household money was above 30 per cent. (In other words, non-household money increased *by over 6.8 per cent in only three months*.) Recall Fisher's contention that an increase in the quantity of money does not alter agents' desired ratio of money to "goods", where "goods" can now be understood as embracing assets as well as consumer goods and services. Consider the position of non-bank financial institutions, particularly the long-term savings institutions (unit trust groups, pension funds, life insurance companies), for which a vital management decision was – and remains – that relating to the balance between low-return money holdings and higher-return non-money assets. If their money balances rise by, say, 10 per cent a quarter for several quarters on the trot, and if they keep the ratio of money to total assets constant, plainly their total assets (of bonds, equities and real estate) must also rise in value by 10 per cent a quarter (that is, at an annual rate of over 46 per cent).

In reality long-term savings institutions were only one group of holders of bonds, equities and real estate in the 1963–2003 period, and the ratio of their money holdings to total assets did fluctuate. So the relationships between, on the one hand, the rates of change in aggregate money and non-household money, and on the other the rates of change of asset prices were not direct and mechanical.

Nevertheless, the long-term savings institutions were the dominant UK holders of financial assets in the late twentieth century. Further, Congdon demonstrated from official data a remarkable long-run stability in the ratio of liquid assets (mostly money) to total assets, at pension funds and life companies combined. This ratio was much the same in 2000 as it has been in 1973, even though both money holdings and total assets had increased 50 times in the 27-year period.[17] Note that many institutions require fund managers to keep liquid assets in line with industry benchmarks. Even when fund inflows are so strong as to cause surging money balances, fund managers have little discretion. They are not allowed to let money holdings rise above some quite low ratio to total assets. The truth is that key strategic decisions are taken by rule of thumb, not in accordance with economic theory or rational expectations. Not surprisingly, with only two exceptions, the 12 quarters of 30-per-cent-plus annualized growth rates of non-household money were characterized by extreme asset price buoyancy.[18]

Congdon's work highlighted the role of non-bank financial institutions in the transmission mechanism.[19] Other potential channels of monetary policy affecting asset prices can be identified. For example, in a 1992 paper Bernanke and Blinder suggested that transmission channels through the banking system to asset markets can be important.[20] A tightening of monetary policy could lead to a shortage of liquid funds within banks, and this shortage of liquid funds, in the short term, cannot be rectified by reducing bank lending. Instead the shortage will be overcome by the banks selling securities. In practice, commercial banks rarely hold paper with a redemption date of more than five years from the present, and their own transactions in securities therefore affect the prices of only a small part of the investment universe.

3.   Money Balances and Asset Prices: the Work of Gordon Pepper

In a 45-year City of London career that blended actuarial advice with stockbroking and economics, Gordon Pepper studied relationships between money aggregates and investment markets. In particular, he used money supply measures extensively in his analysis of the behaviour of bond markets. The ideas have been published in three books, *Money, Credit and Asset Prices* (1994), *Inside Thatcher's Monetarist Revolution* (1998) and, with Michael Oliver, *The Liquidity Theory of Asset Prices* (2006).[21] Earlier work included two Institute of Actuaries' Sessional Meeting papers, in 1970 and 1973, with the 1970 paper dealing mainly with the institutional background.[22]

The 1973 paper, by Pepper and Robert Thomas, considered the issues from the perspective of practical investors, who have to take a view on how and when other market participants form expectations about inflation and yield movements. A more formal theory of the transmission mechanism is consistent with the authors' observations. Pepper and Thomas argued that above-normal increases in the money supply led to excess demand for financial assets, initially pushing down yields on gilt-edged bonds (that is, British government bonds) and later with a bit of a lag also increasing equity values. In a theme attributed earlier in this paper to Friedman, they envisaged the decrease in gilt yields being reversed in the medium term as expectations of inflation rose.

Pepper's theories concerning the influence of monetary policy on financial markets were refined in later work. The findings of Oliver and Pepper's 2006 *The Liquidity Theory of Asset Prices* can be summarized as follows:

> The supply of money can be in excess of the demand for money, or less than the demand for money, for prolonged periods. If money is in excess, some of the excess will be spent on existing assets. Conversely, assets will be sold if money is deficient. Purchases of assets for liquidity reasons can, as a result, exceed sales, or vice versa, for several months.

On this basis the authors recommended that monetary aggregates should be monitored and interpreted as background to investment decisions.[23] There is no contradiction between Pepper's analyses and those of the Austrian School (discussed below) or mainstream monetarism, although he approached the subject from a practitioner's perspective rather than from that of a theoretical economist. The analysis of Pepper and Thomas also came with caveats. For example, their 1973 paper contained an anticipation of Goodhart's Law. They suggested that their views might become invalid if the Bank of England attempted to control the money supply, which it began to do three years after their paper was written.[24]

III

As has already been noted, many modern academic models of monetary policy include only a "bit part" for asset markets and prices. These include the New Keynesian and New Classical schools which have been synthesized into models that are frequently used within central banks.

1. New Keynesianism

It is important to realize that many economists regard New Keynesianism as only tenuously related to Keynes's own work in *A Treatise on Money* and *The General Theory*. In *A Treatise on Money* Keynes wrote extensively on the nexus between the quantity of money and asset prices, as discussed below by Skidelsky in Chapter 9 in the current volume. At times *The General Theory of Employment, Interest and Money* explicitly repudiated the quantity theory of money, but the repudiations were justified by an assumed pathology of money-holding behaviour. More precisely, Keynes claimed that "the specu-lative demand for money" might in some circumstances become dominant, rupturing the usual proportionate relationship between money and national income.[25] Certainly *The General Theory* was critical of naive formulations of the quantity theory. But the book was still very much about money, as ought indeed to be obvious from the book's very title.

By contrast, the New Keynesianism found in contemporary profes-sional journals and explored in central bank research departments does not mention money at all. The basic New Keynesian approach has three equations:

- a Phillips-curve-related relationship in which the change in inflation is a function of the output gap (where the "output gap" is the differ-ence between actual and trend output);
- a Taylor rule (a "central bank reaction function", which shows how the central bank sets its rate of interest in response to levels of inflation and the output gap, named after John Taylor of Stanford University who proposed the idea in a 1993 paper); and
- a so-called "dynamic IS curve" (which is related to the IS curve in the IS–LM model of macroeconomic equilibrium taught in standard textbooks and shows how output responds to the interest rate set by the central bank).

It is evident that the three equations give the central bank a framework for setting interest rates (by applying the Taylor rule), and so determining both output (via the dynamic IS curve) and inflation (through the output gap relationship). But it is also evident that the three equations contain not a single reference to the quantity of money, financial markets and the banking system. Any asset price channel from monetary policy to macro-economic outcomes is at best implicit. During the Great Recession output fell so far and fast in some countries that the Taylor rule indicated a need for significantly negative interest rates. But, as Pigou had realized in his 1947 article, interest rates cannot go negative to any great extent.[26]

The New Keynesian approach can be viewed as a neat and succinct tool for guiding central banks in the setting of a short-term interest rate. In the context of the 1990s and the opening years of the twenty-first century, when many policy-makers saw monetary policy as exclusively about such interest-rate determination, New Keynesianism had its attractions. Its concerns were particularly about the behaviour of labour and product markets, with the authors of a definitive article remarking that, "we wish to make clear that we adopt the Keynesian approach of stressing nominal price rigidities, but at the same time base our analysis on frameworks that incorporate the recent methodological advances in macroeconomic modelling (hence the term 'New')".[27] Those recent advances included an important role for wage and price expectations in the Phillips curve relationship. But the New Keynesians were not, and are not, interested in banking or financial markets. Unlike Keynes himself, they have said next to nothing about the role of money and its relationship with financial markets. They focus on a different, although of course important, aspect of Keynes's work, that of nominal rigidities in the real economy.

2. The New Classical School

Like New Keynesianism, the New Classical School has little to say about the impact of monetary policy on asset prices. It more or less ignores the connections between often turbulent financial markets, and the more sedate labour and product markets, that are found in the real world. Its thinking emphasizes the speed and efficiency with which changes of policy can be transmitted through the economy, and contends that such changes can alter the behaviour of demand, output and the price level only if they are unanticipated. A good statement of the New Classical position is to be found in a 2002 article by Marvin Goodfriend and readers are referred to it if they want a more detailed exposition.[28] The equations in the model are concerned with the optimal path (over a sequence of many periods) of consumption by a so-called "representative agent", with the labour supply determined by the household's time constraint, real wages and the preference for work and leisure, and equilibrium output given by production technology. The "rate of interest" at work in the analyses is explicitly a real rate which equilibrates household consumption plans and companies' investment plans.

It is real factors and not changes in monetary policy that are at the root of such movements in asset prices as can be identified in these exercises. Such models of the economy, and of the role of interest rates in them, exclude – virtually by assumption – the possibility that monetary policy can cause substantial disequilibria in financial markets and asset prices.

3. Syntheses of New Keynesian and New Classical Models, and Practical Policy-making in Central Banks

The New Keynesian and New Classical Schools can be "synthesized" into models that form the basis of much current backroom research within central banks. Since both schools play down the roles of the quantity of money and the financial sector, so also do the syntheses. Econometric models have been developed by central bank research teams from New Keynesian and New Classical inputs, but they either have only occasional references to money or neglect it altogether. The focus is on the transmission mechanism from the central bank interest rate to expenditure decisions. The commercial banking system and its monetary liabilities (which are most of the quantity of money) are excluded from the story. Given the prominence of the banking system in the instabilities of the Great Recession, surely something has gone wrong. Central bank research departments have devoted much effort in the last 20 years to the so-called "credit channel" of banking system influence on the economy, but that channel works from the assets side of the balance sheet (that is, the loans and securities), not from the liabilities side (that is, from money).[29] The credit channel sometimes figures in New Keynesian models.

The credibility of New Keynesian and New Classical thinking, and of syntheses that reflected ideas in both schools, was badly dented in the Great Recession. The central bank rate was cut to almost zero in the USA, the Eurozone, the UK and elsewhere, and in this respect most advanced nations joined Japan, which in 2008 had had a central bank rate of under 1 per cent for more than a decade. With central banks unable to push interest rates down any further, they turned to "quantitative easing" to stimulate economic activity. Quantitative easing can be variously defined, but in the most familiar version it involves direct control of the quantity of money.[30] (The central bank borrows from the commercial banks, by adding sums to their cash reserves, and uses the loan proceeds to purchase assets from non-banks. The sellers of the assets see their bank deposits increase.) The change in approach – from defining monetary policy exclusively in terms of an interest rate to seeing it as a more eclectic mix that included the quantity of money – revealed that existing models were inadequate. Moreover, not only could monetary policy be conducted by means of outright money creation, but also some central bank statements frankly opined that the impact of money creation on financial markets and asset prices was important.[31]

At the start of the Great Recession most central banks' conventional economic models were not well suited to appraising the effects of QE on assets markets and the wider economy. However, Bank of England economists did publish work that examined the effect of QE on asset markets.

Two papers, in 2010 and 2011, by Joyce and others, recognized various possible channels by which an increase in the quantity of money could affect asset markets. The 2010 paper tried to separate the so-called "portfolio rebalancing effects" (that is, the effects of money expansion on spending, where these effects work through asset prices) from other effects. The margins of error surrounding the estimates were large. The authors were nevertheless able to conclude that a significant factor in the fall in conventional gilt yields – perhaps of as much as 100 basis points – during the key period was due to the portfolio rebalancing stimulated by QE. The 2011 paper suggested that QE's effects on output and inflation until the time of writing were roughly equivalent to cuts in base rates of 1.5 per cent to 3 per cent (that is, of 150 to 300 basis points), if with considerable uncertainty surrounding this.[32]

Further Bank of England papers, including a January 2012 paper by Jonathan Bridges and Ryland Thomas, supported the claim that QE had had powerful positive effects on asset prices and the economy.[33] To quote from the abstract to the Bridges and Thomas paper,

> Our central case estimate is that QE boosted the broad money supply by £122 billion or 8 per cent. We apply our estimates of the impact of QE on the money supply to a set of "monetarist" econometric models that articulate the extent to which asset prices and spending need to adjust to make the demand for money consistent with the increased broad money supply associated with QE. Our preferred, central case estimate is that an 8 per cent increase in money holdings may have pushed down [bond] yields by an average of around 150 basis points in 2010 and increased asset values by approximately 20 per cent. This in turn would have had a peak impact on output of 2 per cent by the start of 2011, with an impact on inflation of 1 percentage point around a year later. These estimates are necessarily uncertain.

(Thomas is the author of Chapter 3 in the current volume.)

IV

Austrian business cycle theories, and Austrian School views on banking and money, are not widely taught in standard economics courses at universities. However, Austrian ideas are interesting in the present context because, in sharp contrast to rational expectations thinking and the EMH, they envisage mistakes by both policy-makers and market practitioners. Indeed, they do so with a perhaps surprising explicitness. Much writing in the Austrian tradition is pooh-poohed by modern mathematically sophisticated economists, on the grounds that the writing is cavalier about statistical verification and too informal to be taken seriously.

But the Nobel Prize citation for the doyen of the Austrian School in the late twentieth century, Friedrich Hayek, noted that, "his theory of business cycles and his conception of the effects of monetary and credit policies attracted attention and evoked animated discussion" in the 1930s. Tribute was paid to him for penetrating "more deeply into the business cycle mechanism than was usual at that time". The Nobel committee further acknowledged that "this more profound analysis" may have helped Hayek to be "one of the few economists who gave warning of the possibility of a major economic crisis before the great crash came in the autumn of 1929". (By contrast, Irving Fisher failed altogether to anticipate the American stock market crash of 1929. He lost nearly all of a large personal fortune in the Great Depression.) Despite the scorn sometimes directed at Hayek, he was in 2009 the second most frequently cited Nobel Laureate (after Kenneth Arrow) in the Nobel lectures of other Nobel Laureates.[34]

1. Austrian Monetary Theory in Outline

An authoritative statement of Austrian monetary theory was given in von Mises's *The Theory of Money and Credit*. (The first edition was published in 1912. It was updated by the author until 1952, with the first English translation appearing in 1934.[35]) One of its most distinctive ideas was that an undue expansion of credit, due to the central bank's actions in holding interest rates below the appropriate level, would cause businesses to borrow and invest in capital-intensive production processes. In von Mises's words, "if the rate of interest on loans is artificially reduced below the natural rate as established by the free play of the forces operating in the market, then entrepreneurs are enabled and obliged to enter upon longer processes of production."[36] (Modern disciples of Austrian thinking might note that artificially low interest rates can lead to excessive household borrowing and over-investment in long-lived assets such as residential dwellings and consumer durables. The housing boom in Ireland before 2008 exemplified the pattern. A subsequent bust was a major component in that country's Great Recession experience.)

So, in Austrian thinking, monetary policy can be misguided. Central bank action may distort a price – the rate of interest – which would otherwise coordinate savings and investment in a socially optimal manner. If interest rates are held below the equilibrium level by the central bank, credit and money will expand too quickly, and consumers and businesses will spend too much on consumer durables and investment projects. Here we have an explanation for the common association between "monetary booms" and "property booms".

Austrian views on the business cycle seem to share some common features with, for example, Friedman's monetarist position. But there are at least two important differences between monetarists and Austrians. First, unlike the Austrians, the monetarists are not greatly interested in the balance between the production of consumer goods and investment goods or in the so-called "roundabout-ness" of investment in capital goods. Second, Austrians are fatalistic that a recession *must* follow a monetary boom. This is because the investment projects that have been started in the boom (particularly those in capital-intensive production methods) result in surplus capacity that will never be utilized properly. The misallocation of resources has to be reversed and this reversal is necessary for, indeed almost tantamount to, the adjustment process in a recession. For Austrians the contraction after the boom is inevitable and cathartic. By contrast, both Keynesians and monetarists (in the Friedman tradition) may believe that recession can and should be avoided by well-designed public-policy responses.

Many financial market participants and economics academics, especially those steeped in modern financial economics, are uncomfortable with the lack of mathematical formalism in the Austrian approach. In response, proponents of Austrian theories would argue that the language of mathematics is too precise to articulate the tendencies and subtleties that economic processes involve. Austrians are relaxed when they make statements about "tendencies", including, for example, the tendency for stock market prices to gain ground if savings rise or if monetary policy is loose. But they are reluctant to spell out exactly how a tendency will manifest itself in practice. So much depends on the interdependent actions of millions of people, investing in aggregate trillions of pounds (or dollars or euros or whatever), and reacting subjectively to very particular and local information. The Austrian School's epistemological anxieties discourage them from collecting data and conducting rigorous statistical tests. Proponents of the approach prefer to limit themselves to "pattern predictions", perhaps appealing to data to help understanding, but repudiating elaborate models.

2. Austrian Theory and Efficient Markets

Actuaries and financial economists may demur from Austrian reasoning on the grounds that it violates the EMH and rational expectations. If market actors can see that a money-stoked boom is causing a rise in asset prices, and if past experience shows that the boom must eventually come to a halt and reverse, why do fund managers not let their cash balances rise relative to asset totals and refuse to invest in the rising stock market? The Austrian response to this is that market participants are not perfectly informed. They are responding to particular information sets that they believe are relevant to their situation.

Indeed, they may be deceived by apparent improvements in the economy's supply-side performance (or "by real factors") into thinking that "this time it'll be different".[37] Low real interest rates, rising company profitability, reduced risk premiums because of the perceived rise in the value of collateral that is backing lending and other considerations make it difficult for private sector actors (entrepreneurs, company managers and fund managers) to distinguish between the real and monetary factors that affect stock market valuations. The difficulty of distinguishing between the real and monetary causes of asset price movements was emphasized in an account of the late 1980s' Swedish property bubble in a 2003 paper by Dillen and Sellin.[38] Possible justifications for higher real estate prices included expectations of permanently high inflation, tax relief on interest payments, higher trend output growth and credit market deregulation, as well as loose monetary policy.

V

This chapter has shown that different theoretical interpretations of a capitalist economy's monetary dynamics generate conflicting views on the relationship between policy and outcomes. The discussion leads naturally to the question, "should monetary policy be used to try to control asset market movements?"

On the whole, adherents to monetarist and New Classical views would argue that an environment of low and stable inflation is conducive to avoiding financial bubbles, and that price stability (or low inflation) should be the central bank's target. As it happens, two major stock-market booms (those of 1923–29 and 1994–2000) occurred when consumer price inflation was low. The recent financial crash also occurred during an environment of modest consumer price inflation. A 2004 paper by Bordo and Wheelock concluded that, while there is no consistent relationship between *inflation* and stock market booms, such booms "have typically occurred when *money and credit growth* were above average".[39] Bordo and Wheelock also contended that asset price booms are associated with strong real growth and advances in productivity.

In practice, even if some link between monetary policy and asset prices is accepted, it can be difficult to distinguish between real, monetary and speculative elements in an asset price bubble. The New Classical models in particular see little room for the analysis of asset prices in the determination of monetary policy. If a bubble is caused by real factors, using monetary policy to "burst" it can have significant dangers for the real economy, leading to unnecessary recession and deflation.[40] A 2003 paper by Goodhart and Hofmann emphasized the potentially catastrophic effects of a mistimed official decision to "burst" an "asset bubble", referring to the examples of both the Great Depression of the early 1930s and the prolonged macroeconomic malaise in Japan over the last 20 years. In general, mainstream central bankers are sceptical about the "bubble pricking" approach.

According to both the monetarist and Austrian approaches, high asset prices can be a "signal" of loose monetary policy. (In other words, they provide information to monetary policy-makers in the same way that currency movements might be understood to do so, if they were to believe the international monetarist position that exchange rate movements reflect the relative supply–demand conditions of different currencies.) Advocates of asset price targeting might recall a 1973 paper by Alchian and Klein, which argued that asset prices are the price of future consumption.[41] When monetary policy is loose, asset prices may rise as part of the transmission mechanism. Asset prices and the price of future consumption move before any impact is registered in consumer prices. Incorporating asset prices in the price indices monitored by central banks might therefore have the incidental advantage of leading the central bank to react to inflationary pressures earlier as well as taking a more comprehensive view of inflation pressures. In general, official statistical agencies have avoided the inclusion of asset prices in current price measures, apart from the cost of housing.

Other authors – such as Wadhwani and Cecchetti in influential papers written before the Great Recession – would go further, recommending that monetary policy should take explicit account of developments in asset markets, even if those developments are not obviously attributable to tight or loose monetary policy.[42] This is often described as "leaning into the wind". The argument is made in the framework of a model that synthesizes New Keynesian and New Classical concepts. Wadhwani suggests that, if inflation is forecast by an output gap model (that relies on modelling the difference between actual and potential output, as identified from markers about labour and product markets), policy-makers ignore the role that prices set in asset markets (financial markets, markets in housing and other real estate) play in the economy. According to Wadhwani, asset bubbles raise consumption and investment, and, crucially, they can arise exogenously (from changes in confidence or expected productivity growth, and regardless of monetary policy). The Taylor rule – whereby interest rates are set by inflation relative to a target and output relative to potential – should be adjusted if asset prices are at extreme values. The counter-argument is that the central bank cannot distinguish between investment market fluctuations caused by confidence shifts or changes in productivity growth from those caused by other forces. Official attempts to neutralize the results of herding and speculative behaviour in financial markets could complicate policy, leading to more mistakes.

VI

Hardly anyone with meaningful experience of financial markets denies that monetary policy affects asset prices. As this chapter has shown, a variety of approaches have emerged in the economics literature, with some schools of thought – such as New Keynesianism and the New Classical School – belittling the role of money. It is chastening that New Keynesianism and the New Classical School, and even more syntheses of their ideas, were deemed "state of the art" by central bank research teams in the run-up to the crisis.

Nevertheless, an understanding of monetary transmission mechanisms, including a realization that asset market bubbles can be induced by monetary policy, can be important when taking asset allocation decisions in large financial institutions. These institutions sometimes use formal models for capital-setting purposes, with regulators requiring the use of market values of assets and liabilities in their determination of the appropriate capital level. Should practitioners acknowledge more formally that monetary policy might affect asset values? Some of the theories discussed above suggest that a predictable and systematic component to asset price changes may result from monetary policy decisions. Further, monetary policy is not just one economic factor amongst many, but a highly discretionary and obtrusive instrument operated by a single economic agent, namely the central bank. If a period of loose monetary policy has inflated asset prices, the capital held by a financial institution could be overestimated. A remarkable feature of the post-Great Recession period was the unanimity with which regulators said that bank capital had been too low before 2008, whereas in fact all banks in the major jurisdictions were compliant with capital adequacy rules when the crisis hit.

This chapter has had one consistent theme. Problems in assessing the values on both sides of the balance sheet, and particularly in assessing solvency, affect every financial institution. Pension funds and insurance companies are vulnerable, as well as the banks. That is so, even though banks were very much in the eye of the storm at the worst moments in the crisis of 2008 and 2009. The sometimes erratic transmission mechanism of monetary policy may drive asset values away from those that reflect fundamental economic forces. Appraisals of the amount of capital needed may then be set too high or too low. Certainly, the occasional delinquencies and pathologies of financial markets – including the possibility of delinquent and pathological decisions by central banks and regulators – are among the risks that face all financial institutions.

Of course, the potential distortion of asset valuations by monetary policy is just one of many uncertainties against which financial institutions hold capital. Nevertheless, possible instability in monetary policy-making raises an important issue. To what extent is it reasonable to use judgement when presenting financial information and taking decisions based on it? There has been a move towards supposedly "objective" approaches to asset and liability valuation, based on market values, in recent years. It is possible that we have a false sense of security in such mechanisms.

NOTES

*   This chapter uses material from Philip Booth 'Monetary policy, asset prices and financial institutions', *Annals of Actuarial Science*, vol. 8, no. 1 (2014), pp. 9–41, reproduced with permission.
1.   Because banks are highly leveraged organizations, with capital-to-asset ratios commonly of 4, 5 or 6 per cent, changes in the value of total assets of a mere 1 or 2 per cent matter to them enormously. The IFRS9 proposals emanated from the International Accounting Standards Board on 24 July 2014 and are meant to be implemented by 1 January 2018.
2.   The phrase developed in an exchange with John Culbertson of the University of Wisconsin. See Milton Friedman 'The lag in effect of monetary policy', pp. 237–60, in Milton Friedman *The Optimum Quantity of Money* (London and Basingstoke: Macmillan Press, 1969), originally published in *The Journal of Political Economy* in 1961. The phrase appears on p. 260 of the 1969 book.
3.   M.C. Conover, G.R. Jensen and R.R. Johnson 'Monetary environments and international stock returns', *Journal of Banking and Finance*, vol. 23, no. 9 (1999), pp. 1357–81.
4.   See G.R. Jensen and R.R. Johnson 'Discount rate changes and security returns in the US, 1962–1991', *Journal of Banking and Finance*, vol. 19 (1995), pp. 79–95.
5.   See Philip Booth *Verdict on the Crash* (London: Institute of Economic Affairs, 2009). See Anna Schwartz 'Origins of the financial market crisis of 2008', pp. 45–50, and John Greenwood 'The successes and failures of UK monetary policy, 2000–08', pp. 37–43, in the 2009 IEA volume.
6.   See Ben Bernanke (2010), 'Monetary policy and the housing bubble', speech to the Annual Meeting of the American Economic Association, Atlanta, Georgia, available at http://www.federalreserve.gov/newsevents/speech/bernanke20100103a.htm, accessed on 30 July 2012.
7.   See Charles Bean, M. Paustian, A. Penalver and T. Taylor (2010), 'Monetary policy after the fall', speech at Federal Reserve Bank of Kansas City Annual Conference, Jackson Hole Wyoming, US, available at http://www.bankofengland.co.uk/publications/speeches/2010/speech444.pdf, accessed on 30 July 2012.
8.   See Milton Friedman 'The role of monetary policy', *American Economic Review*, vol. 58, no. 1 (1968), pp. 1–17, and Milton Friedman *The Counter-Revolution in Monetary Theory*, Institute of Economic Affairs, Occasional Paper 33 (London: Institute of Economic Affairs, 1970). The monetarist episode in policy-making in the English-speaking world, in the late 1970s and early 1980s, is controversial. For an

excellent discussion from different perspectives, see Thomas Mayer and Patrick Minford 'Monetarism – a retrospective', *World Economics*, vol. 5, no. 2 (2004), pp. 147–85, and Tim Congdon 'Monetarism – a rejoinder', *World Economics*, vol. 5, no. 3 (2004), pp. 179–97.

9. The 1963 Friedman and Schwartz paper on business cycles is discussed above, on p. 7 in the Introduction to this volume, and again below, on p. 23, in David Laidler's Chapter 10.

10. As regards the initial effect, Friedman seems to have been thinking about "the rate of interest" in the sense of the yield on bonds, in line with Keynes's liquidity preference theory in his 1936 *General Theory of Employment, Interest and Money*.

11. Contemporary monetarists are often taken to include, for example, Ben McCallum of Carnegie Mellon University's Tepper School of Business, Ed Nelson at the University of Sydney and Tim Congdon of the Institute of International Monetary Research at the University of Buckingham. But the views of different monetarists vary widely on many topics. The notion of "monetarism" is highly elastic.

12. [*The following note is by the editor*: For Eugene Fama's role in this way of thinking, see note 16 to Chapter 2 above, on pp. 73–4. The rejection of money's importance is sometimes associated with the view that the most significant money aggregate is the monetary base, that is, legal-tender "cash". Michael Woodford of Princeton University has then noted that cash has a diminishing role in modern payments, raising questions about its future role in monetary policy. See Woodford 'Monetary policy in a world without money', pp. 181–212, in Alec Chrystal and Paul Mizen *Recent Developments in Monetary Policy*, vol. II (Cheltenham, UK and Northampton, MA, USA: Edward Elgar Publishing, 2009), originally published in 2000.]

13. William J. Barber (ed.) *The Works of Irving Fisher*, vol. 4, *The Purchasing Power of Money* (London: Pickering & Chatto, 1997, originally published by Macmillan, New York, 1911), p. 47.

14. Barber (ed.) *The Works of Irving Fisher*, vol. 5, *Elementary Principles of Economics* (London: Pickering & Chatto, 1997, originally published by Macmillan, New York, 1912), p. 244. For Wicksell on the same point, see pp. 39–40, in Richard Kahn (trans.) *Interest and Prices* (London: Macmillan, 1936, originally published in German (1898) as Knut Wicksell *Geldzins und Güterpreise*). The Wicksell passage was quoted in note E, pp. 581–2, of Don Patinkin *Money, Interest and Prices* (New York: Harper & Row, 2nd edition, 1965).

15. Arthur Pigou 'Economic progress in a stable environment', *Economica*, vol. 14 (1947), pp. 180–88.

16. [*The following note is by the editor*: The nearest approach to such a discussion is on pp. 185–90 on the adjustability of the prices of different classes of goods *and assets*. At the end of p. 185 Fisher did indeed say that "goods" is "a collective term comprising all wealth, property and services". He pointed out the fixed terms of many financial contracts and the distributional consequences of changes in the value of money. In his much admired work *Economic Theory in Retrospect*, Mark Blaug distinguished between two kinds of effect from a change in the quantity of money on the economy, the direct effect (operating in commodity markets, with no help from a change in "the rate of interest") and the indirect effect (operating via financial markets, where – for example – excess money balances would lower "the rate of interest" [in the sense of the bond yield] and hence stimulate expenditure). He identifies Henry Thornton in his 1802 *Nature and Effects of the Paper Credit of Great Britain* as the first economist to describe the indirect effect. (Mark Blaug *Economic Theory in Retrospect* (Cambridge: Cambridge University Press, 4th edition, 1985), p. 161.) Maybe so, but Thornton's remarks did not turn on Wicksell's point about the invariance of the aggregate quantity of money as agents tried to recover equilibrium and did not amount to a fully-fledged monetary theory of asset price determination.]

17. Tim Congdon *Money and Asset Prices in Boom and Bust* (London: Institute of Economic Affairs, 2005), pp. 36–7.

18. Congdon *Money and Asset Prices*, p. 58. One of the two exceptions was the third quarter of 1987, which was affected by the first devaluation of the pound since 1949.
19. See also essays 15 and 16, pp. 330–73, in Tim Congdon *Money in a Free Society* (New York: Encounter Books, 2011).
20. See particularly section IV of Ben Bernanke and Alan Blinder 'The Federal funds rate and the channels of monetary transmission' *American Economic Review*, vol. 82, no. 4 (1992), pp. 901–21.
21. Gordon Pepper *Money, Credit and Asset Prices* (London: Macmillan, 1994); Pepper *Inside Thatcher's Monetarist Revolution* (London: Macmillan, in association with the Institute of Economic Affairs, 1998): and Oliver and Pepper *The Liquidity Theory of Asset Prices* (Chichester: Wiley, 2006).
22. Gordon Pepper 'The money supply, economic management and the gilt-edged market', *Journal of the Institute of Actuaries*, vol. 96, no. 1 (1970), pp. 1–46, and Gordon Pepper and Robert Thomas 'Cyclical changes in the level of the equity and gilt-edged markets', *Journal of the Institute of Actuaries*, vol. 99 (1973), pp. 195–248.
23. The quotation is from Oliver and Pepper, *The Liquidity Theory of Asset Prices*, p. 19.
24. Goodhart's Law – that a macroeconomic relationship breaks down when policy-makers try to exploit it in reaching policy goals – was put forward in 1975 to explain events of the early 1970s, though became more widely discussed in the early 1980s. There is an excellent discussion of Goodhart's Law in Alec Chrystal and Paul Mizen 'Goodhart's Law: its origins, meaning and implications for monetary policy', 2001 paper for Bank of England *festschrift* in honour of Charles Goodhart.
25. The speculative demand for money might be seen as the demand to hold money that arises from investors' wish to time acquisitions of non-money assets to best advantage.
26. To quote, "Since money can be held without appreciable cost it is impossible for the money interest rate to be less than nothing." (See p. 184 in the *Economica* article cited above.) In the last year or two some central banks have started charging banks for holding cash reserves with them and, in that sense, they have imposed "negative interest rates". But Pigou is right as regards cash and deposits held by non-banks.
27. Richard Clarida, Jordi Galí and Mark Gertler 'The science of monetary policy: a New Keynesian perspective', *Journal of Economic Literature*, vol. XXXVII (December 1999), pp. 1661–707. The quotation is from p. 1663.
28. Marvin Goodfriend 'Monetary policy in the New Neoclassical synthesis: a primer', *International Finance*, vol. 5, no. 2 (2002), pp. 165–91.
29. The standard reference is to Ben Bernanke and Mark Gertler 'Inside the black box: the credit channel of monetary policy transmission', *Journal of Economic Perspectives* (American Economic Association: Nashville, TN), Fall 1995 issue, vol. 9, no. 4, pp. 27–48. See the discussion in note 20 on p. 74.
30. The UK's QE exercise was discussed on pp. 238–9 of Tim Congdon *Money in a Free Society* (New York: Encounter Books, 2011). Essay 4 in *Money in a Free Society* provided a typology of central bank open market operations.
31. For a few years after the announcement of QE operations on 5 March 2009, the Bank of England website contained an interview between the Governor, Mervyn King, and the BBC journalist, Stephanie Flanders, in which King made clear that the intention of quantitative easing was to increase the quantity of money on a broad definition (that is, the quantity of bank deposits, in effect).
32. M. Joyce, A. Lasaosa, I. Stevens and M. Tong (2010), 'The financial market impact of quantitative easing', Working Paper No. 393, Bank of England, London and M. Joyce, M. Tong and R. Woods 'The United Kingdom's quantitative easing policy: design, operation and impact', *Bank of England Quarterly Bulletin*, vol. 51 (2011), pp. 200–12.
33. Jonathan Bridges and Ryland Thomas 'The impact of QE on the UK economy – some supportive monetarist arithmetic', Working Paper No. 442 (2012), Bank of England, London.
34. D. Skarbek 'F.A. Hayek's influence on Nobel prize winners', *Review of Austrian Economics*, vol. 22, no. 1 (2009), pp. 109–12.

35. Ludwig von Mises *The Theory of Money and Credit* (New York: Foundation for Economic Education, 1971, reprinted by permission of Jonathan Cape Ltd, London). The fifth edition of the book was subsequently reprinted in 1981 by the Indianapolis-based Liberty Fund.

36. Mises *Theory of Money and Credit*, 1971, pp. 360–61. The notion of the "natural rate of interest" is difficult, but is connected with the marginal productivity of capital. See pp. 208–15 in Chapter 9 for further discussion.

37. This is the title of the best-selling book, Carmen Reinhart and Kenneth Rogoff *This Time is Different: Eight Centuries of Financial Folly* (Princeton, NJ: Princeton University Press, 2011).

38. Hans Dillen and Peter Sellin 'Financial bubbles and monetary policy', pp. 119–44, in *Economic Review* (Stockholm: Riksbank), 2003, no. 3.

39. Michael Bordo and David Wheelock 'Monetary policy and asset prices: a look back at past US stock market booms', pp. 19–44, in *Federal Reserve Bank of St. Louis Review*, November/December, vol. 86, no. 6 (2004). See p. 19 particularly.

40. Goodfriend (2002) 'Monetary policy', see above, note 28. See, particularly, pp. 185–7.

41. Armen Alchian and Benjamin Klein 'On a correct measure of inflation', *Journal of Money, Credit and Banking*, vol. 5, no. 1, part 1 (1971), pp. 173–91.

42. Stephen Cecchetti, Hans Genberg and Sushil Wadhwani 'Asset prices in a flexible inflation targeting framework', NBER working paper no. 8970 (Cambridge, MA: National Bureau of Economic Research, May 2002) and Sushil Wadhwani 'Should monetary policy respond to asset price bubbles? Revisiting the debate', *National Institute Economic Review* (London: National Institute, 2008), no. 206, pp. 25–34.

9. How would Keynes have analysed the Great Recession of 2008 and 2009?

Robert Skidelsky

In recent years some monetary economists have voiced scepticism about aspects of the Keynesian revolution, particularly the importance of the 1936 *General Theory* relative to Keynes's entire corpus.[1] These sceptics have performed a valuable service by encouraging more whole-hearted Keynesians (including the author of this chapter) to look carefully at Keynes's earlier work, notably the 1930 *A Treatise on Money*. Arguably, the *Treatise* is in many ways a better guide than the *General Theory* to how Keynes would have thought about the Great Recession. The sceptics, notably David Laidler, have tried to position Keynes in the larger debates about monetary theory and policy in the inter-war period, so that the undoubted originality of some of Keynes's thinking can be set in the proper context. In particular, when writing the *Treatise* in the late 1920s Keynes was aware of Knut Wicksell's ideas about the "natural rate of interest", and the possible macroeconomic significance of differences between it and the "market rate of interest". But this strand of thought was sidetracked in the *General Theory*, where Keynes developed more rigorously his own liquidity-preference theory of the rate of interest.[2]

Britain's economic performance in the first five years from the collapse of late 2008 and early 2009 had similarities to that in the early 1930s, which saw an initially rather cautious recovery from the global downturn in the three years from 1929. In both the early 1930s and the early 2010s, parts of the UK economy were booming, but much of it was struggling. If he had been born in, say, 1963 instead of 1883, what would Keynes have made of the recent Great Recession and its sequel? A reasonable approach to the counterfactual is to recall what Keynes said about the Great Depression and its aftermath.

All depressions and their consequences are unique in detail, but the pattern of speculative boom, collapse and fitful recovery is common. To paraphrase Reinhart and Rogoff, "This time is not different." Distinctions need to be drawn between:

- the conceptual apparatus Keynes brought to the analysis of business cycles in *A Treatise on Money* (TM), including his discussion of policy responses;
- Keynes's "real time" explanations of, and remedies for, the slump of the early 1930s as it developed, based on the analysis in the TM; and
- the conceptual apparatus of the *General Theory* (GT), which was developed to explain a situation of persisting unemployment ("unemployment equilibrium"), and to suggest policies to restore and maintain full employment.

These discussions take up three of the following sections. They are essential background to Keynes's likely procedure in analysing the Great Recession and prescribing policies to deal with it, which are covered in the fourth section. Only the third section represents the "Keynesian model", as most economists understand the matter. But the ideas and proposals in the first and second sections need to be incorporated in our account if we are to develop a full counterfactual story.

I

The main topic of TM was the genesis and life history of the "credit cycle". This phrase, which is now almost an archaism, can be seen as synonymous with the "trade cycle" or "business cycle". Keynes used it repeatedly in the TM, in a policy environment still innocent of the notion of "macroeconomic policy" and even the word "macroeconomics".[3] The TM's Fundamental Equations of Value were versions of the quantity theory of money. In the hands of Wicksell and others, the quantity theory of money was evolving towards a theory of the workings of an economy where money is created entirely by bank credit and which is, in that sense, a "pure credit" economy. (For most of its history since the development of coinage by the Ionian Greeks in the sixth century BC, money has been either a commodity or linked to a commodity base.) In a pure credit economy banks create new money in response to the demand for loans, subject to such constraints as may be imposed by the central bank. Keynes's account in the TM set out from what he termed "identities or statical [*sic*] equations relating the turnover of monetary instruments to the turnover of things traded for money".[4] In the TM (unlike the GT), "investment" could differ from "savings", and much ink was spilt both on pinning down the meaning of the terms, and discussing the complications of the economy's response to differences between the two notions as thus defined. In equilibrium, the TM's concept of "savings" was equal to its concept of "investment". But there was nothing to guarantee equilibrium. Ahead of the event (or *ex ante*), the plans of savers and investors – who were distinct and separate agents – would not necessarily mesh.

In the TM Keynes's cycle was characterized by fluctuations in investment – driven by uncertain expectations of profit – around a stable rate of saving. In the upswing investment "runs ahead" of saving, while in the downswing it "runs behind". Another way of putting the matter was to appeal to Wicksell's language. The cycle could be characterized by movements in the "market" rate of interest around its "natural rate" (which in the GT was to become the marginal efficiency of capital) or fluctuations in the "natural" rate when these were not offset by appropriate changes in the "market" rate. (Changes in the market rate of interest reflected developments in the banking system, whereas changes in the natural rate might be due to new technologies.) In an economy insulated against external shocks, booms and slumps were viewed in the TM as "simply the expression of the results of an oscillation of the terms of credit about their equilibrium position".[5] We shall see later that Keynes used these ideas to explain the global depression of 1929–32, and the recovery from it.

In the TM Keynes was concerned to link his analysis of what he termed "changes in the investment factors" and "due to industrial factors" to the banking system and the quantity of money. Bank deposits were understood to be the dominant form of money in a modern economy, and they were divided into income, business, and savings deposits. Cutting across this, some deposits supported transactions in the "industrial circulation", whereas others were committed to the "financial circulation". By the industrial circulation Keynes meant "the business of maintaining the normal process of current output, distribution, and exchange and paying the factors of production their incomes"; by the financial circulation he understood "the business of holding and exchanging existing titles to wealth . . . , [including] speculation and the process of conveying current savings and profits into the hands of entrepreneurs".[6]

The industrial circulation absorbed the income deposits and parts of the business deposits (labelled "Business Deposits A"), and money in the financial circulation comprised the savings deposits and the remainder of business deposits ("Business Deposits B"). It was the variability of the two "circulations", and particularly the shifts between Business Deposits A and B, which intruded on the business cycle. Money flowed from the financial circulation to the industrial circulation in a boom, and the other way round in a downturn. The central bank had to be concerned to keep the proportions of the two circulations constant. Keynes was under no illusions. Credit cycles might take many forms, but "the behaviour of the banking system can always intervene to mitigate or aggravate their severity".[7] Perhaps the "effective" bank rate might be manipulated to keep savings and investment "at an approximate equality", but only with successful currency management might the credit cycle "not occur at all".[8]

Books III and IV took up 13 chapters and covered over 200 pages of the first volume (on *The Pure Theory of Money*) of the TM. They were Keynes's most detailed and consecutive exposition of the credit cycle, with the economy clearly being out of equilibrium most of the time. The different causal ingredients (from "the monetary side" as opposed to "the investment side", as he put it) were brought together in often complex statements about hypothetical sequences of events. The discussion could not have been easy for contemporaries to follow and it remains difficult for twenty-first-century readers. At any rate, towards the end of Chapter 19 Keynes offered a synoptic account of the "normal course of a credit cycle". It does not start in the banking system. To quote,

> Something happens – of a non-monetary character – to increase the attractions of investment. It may be a new invention, or the development of a new country, or a war, or a return of "business confidence" as the result of many small influences tending the same way. Or the thing may start – which is more likely if it is a monetary cause which is playing the chief part – with a stock exchange boom, beginning with speculation in natural resources or *de facto* monopolies, but eventually affecting by sympathy the price of new capital goods.
>
> The rise in the natural rate of interest is not held back by increased saving; and the expanding volume of investment is not restrained by an adequate rise in the market rate of interest.

Now banking and money come very much into the story.

> This acquiescence of the banking system in the increased volume of investment may involve it in allowing some increase in the total quantity of money; but at first the necessary increase is not likely to be great and may be taken up, almost unnoticed, out of the general slack of the system, or may be supplied by a falling off in the requirements of the financial circulation without any change in the total volume of money.
>
> At this stage the output and price of capital goods begin to rise. Employment improves and the wholesale index rises. The increased expenditure of the newly employed then raises the price of consumption goods and allows the producers of such goods to reap a windfall profit. By this time practically all categories of goods will have risen in price and all classes of entrepreneurs will be enjoying a profit.
>
> At first the volume of employment of the factors of production will increase without much change in their rate of remuneration. But after a large proportion of the unemployed factors have been absorbed into employment, the

entrepreneurs bidding against one another under the stimulus of high profits will begin to offer higher rates of remuneration.

It is striking how – unlike many modern economists – Keynes freely blends discussion of factor and product markets with the monetary analysis. To continue,

> All the while, therefore, the requirements of the industrial circulation will be increasing . . ..A point will come, therefore, when the banking system is no longer able to supply the necessary volume of money consistently with its principles and traditions [e.g. reserve ratios] . . .
>
> It is astonishing, however – what with changes in the financial circulation, in the velocities of circulation, and in the reserve proportions of the central bank – how large a change in the earnings bill can be looked after by the banking system without an apparent breach in its principles and traditions.
>
> It may be, therefore, that the turning-point will come, not from the reluctance or the inability of the banking system to finance the increased earnings bill, but from a faltering of financial sentiment, due to some financiers, from prescience or from their experience of previous crises, seeing a little further ahead than the business world or the banking world. If so, the growth of "bear" sentiment [liquidity preference in the GT] will . . . increase the requirements of the financial circulation. It may be, therefore, the tendency of the financial circulation to increase [for speculative purposes], on the top of the increase in the industrial circulation, which will break the back of the banking system and cause it at long last to impose a rate of interest, which is not only fully equal to the natural rate but, very likely in the changed circumstances, well above it.

Keynes realized that, in practice, cyclical fluctuations might have more than one cause and warned that the collapse might come

> in the end as the result of the piling up of several weighty causes – the evaporation of the attractions of new investment, the faltering of financial sentiment, the reaction in the price level of consumption goods, and the growing inability of the banking system to keep pace with the increasing requirements, first of the industrial circulation and later of the financial circulation also.[9]

For Keynes, analysis was always the prelude to prescription. His aim was to prevent, or at least mitigate, the "credit" cycle. The duty of the central bank was to supply the appropriate quantity of money for each phase of the cycle, meaning to offset both boom and slump tendencies. In his words, now from the second volume (*The Applied Theory of Money*) of TM, "To maintain that the supplies in a reservoir can be maintained at any required level by pouring enough water into it is not inconsistent with admitting that the level of the reservoir depends on many other factors besides how much water is poured in."[10] The claim in TM was that by its influence on the price and volume of credit the central bank could control the rate of investment, and hence influence demand, output and employment.[11] Three instruments were available to the central bank for this purpose. It could vary the terms of its "advances" (loans) to its member banks; it could alter the amount of its own investments; and it could adjust member banks' reserve requirements. Keynes concentrated on the first two. (He did not consider at all changes to banks' capital requirements, which [as discussed in the chapters to the second part of this book] was the principal initial policy response to the Great Recession in late 2008. When Keynes was writing, the size of their capital buffers was regarded as a matter to be determined mainly by banks' own boards of directors. The ownership and control rights of the shareholders were respected.) Keynes was confident that, by varying its "bank rate", the central bank could control the short-term rate of interest. But the effect of the short rate on the long rate was uncertain.

In Keynes's judgement, the long-term rate – the yield on long-dated bonds rather than the rate in the money markets – was the important one in determining fixed investment. If movements in bank rate failed to shift bond yields, the central bank could still bring those yields to any figure it wanted by buying or selling the right kind and amount of securities. This second method was a further development of what Keynes called "the British system".[12] The second volume of TM proposed that,

> The new post-war element of "management" consists in the habitual employ-ment of an "open-market" policy by which the Bank of England buys and sells investments with a view to keeping the reserve resources of the member banks at the level which it desires. This method . . . seems to me to be the ideal one. . . . [I]t enables the Bank of England to maintain an absolute control over the creation of credit by the member banks . . . It is no exaggeration to say that the individual member banks have no power to influence the aggregate volume of bank money . . .[13]

Plainly, Keynes attached great significance to "the aggregate volume of bank money" or, in modern parlance, the quantity of money broadly defined. If somehow errors in monetary management had led to highly depressed economic conditions, the central bank should be prepared to embark on open-market operations *à outrance*. The "extraordinary methods" he contemplated were

> in fact, no more than an intensification of the normal procedure of open-market operations. I do not know of any case in which the method of open-market operations has been carried out *à outrance*. Central banks have always been too nervous hitherto – partly, perhaps, under the influence of crude versions of the quantity theory – of taking measures which would have the effect of causing the total volume of bank money to depart widely from its normal volume, whether in excess or in defect. But this attitude of mind neglects, I think, the part which

the "bullishness" or "bearishness" of the public plays in the demand for bank money; it forgets the financial circulation in its concern for the industrial circulation, and overlooks the statistical fact that the former may be quite as large as the latter and much more capable of sharp variation.

I suggest, therefore, that bolder measures are sometimes advisable, and that they are quite free from serious danger whenever there has developed on the part of the capitalist public an obstinate "bullishness" or "bearishness" towards securities. On such occasions the central bank should carry its open-market operations to the point of satisfying to saturation the desire of the public to hold savings deposits, or of exhausting the supply of such deposits in the contrary case.

The industrial and financial circulations, which are barely mentioned in modern macroeconomics, remained at the centre of the stage in the cyclical drama envisaged by Keynes in 1930.

> The risk of bringing to bear too rapidly and severely on the industrial circulation, when it is the financial circulation which is being aimed at, is greater I think in the case of a contraction of credit than in the case of an expansion. But, on the other hand, it is less likely to be necessary to resort to extreme measures to check a boom than to check a slump. Booms, I suspect, are almost always due to tardy or inadequate action by the banking system such as should be avoidable; there is much more foundation for the view that it is slumps which may sometimes get out of hand and defy all normal methods of control. It will be, therefore, on the problem of checking a slump that we shall now concentrate our attention.

Keynes now offered his thoughts on the specifics of anti-deflationary monetary action.

> My remedy in the event of the obstinate persistence of a slump would consist, therefore, in the purchase of securities by the central bank until the long-term market rate of interest has been brought down to the limiting point . . . .It should not be beyond the power of a central bank (international complications apart) to bring down the long-term market rate of interest to any figure at which it is itself prepared to buy long-term securities. For the bearishness of the capitalist public is never very obstinate, and when the rate of interest on savings deposits is next door to nothing the saturation point can fairly soon be reached. If the central bank supplies the member banks with more funds than they can lend at short term, in the first place the short-term rate of interest will decline towards zero, and in the second place the member banks will soon begin, if only to maintain their profits, to second the efforts of the central bank by themselves buying securities. This means that the price of bonds will rise . . . .If the effect of such measures is to raise the price of "equities" (e.g. ordinary shares) more than the price of bonds, no harm *in a time of slump* will result from this; for investment can be stimulated by its being unusually easy to raise resources by the sale of ordinary shares as well as by high bond prices. Moreover, a very excessive price for equities is not likely to occur at a time of depression and business losses.[14]

Keynes thus envisaged two transmission channels from money to activity, the bank lending channel via the fall in short-term rates, and what would now be called the "portfolio rebalancing channel", reflecting the direct effect of the Bank's bond purchase programme on the prices of "securities".

II

Keynes used the apparatus in TM both to analyse the causes of the slide in asset prices and economic activity that began in 1929 and 1930, and to suggest policies to counter the worst of the effects. But it is important as a preliminary, before seeing how Keynes applied his theories, to dismiss a tiresome argument about whether Hayek or Keynes was more successful at foreseeing the collapse of 1929. The truth is that both Hayek and Keynes foresaw a collapse of the boom, but from different analytic positions. Hayek thought that the slump originated in the credit expansion started by the Fed in 1927. This unleashed an orgy of over-investment – "mal-investment", in his terminology – which could not be checked by the dear money subsequently imposed in 1928. The Fed's discount rate went up from 3.5 per cent in January 1928 to 5 per cent in July. On 15 August 1928 Keynes wrote to an American correspondent, "I cannot help feeling that the risk just now is all on the side of a business depression . . . If too long an attempt is made to check the speculative position by dear money, it may well be that the dear money, by checking new investments, will bring about a general business depression".[15] Keynes was to insist repeatedly that no Hayekian "over-investment" had taken place in the 1920s. Rather that decade had featured "under-investment" in new capital equipment relative to corporate savings.

Keynes's "real time" analysis of the causes of the slump started in the TM itself, in early 1930.[16] It was repeated in more or less identical form in lectures, speeches and letters over the coming three years, and in the GT in 1936. It is important in understanding the contemporary discussion to realize that the global downturn emanated from the USA, and was much worse in the USA than in the UK. According to recognized authorities, the USA's real gross national product fell by 28 per cent between 1929 and 1932, whereas the UK's went down by less than 6 per cent.[17] (The UK's problems were almost entirely caused by the external environment. Domestic demand dropped only 1.5 per cent between 1929 and 1932 and consumption actually *rose* in the three years, despite a significant fall in net foreign income. As noted elsewhere in this volume the USA's quantity of money, broadly defined and according to the Friedman and Schwartz data, collapsed by over 38 per cent between October 1929 and April 1933.[18] In the same period the UK's M3 money measure – as estimated by Capie and Webber – *increased*, from £2549.0 billion to £2740.3 billion, or by 7.5 per cent.[19] Thousands of banks in the USA could not repay depositors with cash and "closed their doors". Not a single bank in the UK – or indeed the British Empire – went under in the 1929–32 period.)

The most succinct explanation of the US collapse comes from a lecture in Chicago which Keynes delivered in June 1931. The leading characteristic of the 1920s boom, he said, was "an extraordinary willingness to borrow for purposes of real new investment at very high rates of interest". The resulting prosperity, based on "building, the electrification of the world, and the associated enterprises of roads and motor cars", diffused prosperity globally. The part played by inflation in maintaining expenditure was "surprisingly small". The slump since mid-1929 was due to "extraordinary imbecility", not over-investment producing an inevitable reaction. Business conditions required interest rates to fall, but instead the Federal Reserve Board had pushed up interest rates to check speculation on Wall Street. Very dear money in the USA had global contractionary effects by pushing up interest rates in other gold standard countries. Also capital flows were attracted to the USA, to the detriment of foreign bond issuance in other countries. Once the decline started it gained cumulative force. This was "the whole of the explanation of the slump".[20] In the GT Keynes again rebutted Hayek's emphases on mal-investment that had recurred in the polemical exchanges they had had since Hayek had taken up a position at the London School of Economics in January 1931. To quote,

> It would be absurd to assert of the United States in 1929 the existence of over-investment in the strict sense. The true state of affairs was of a different character. New investment during the previous five years had been, indeed, on so enormous a scale in the aggregate that the prospective yield of further additions was, coolly considered, falling rapidly . . . In fact, the rate of interest was high enough to deter new investment except in those particular directions which were under the influence of speculative excitement and, therefore, in special danger of being overexploited; and a rate of interest, high enough to overcome the speculative excitement, would have checked, at the same time, every kind of reasonable new investment. Thus an increase in the rate of interest, as a remedy for the state of affairs arising out of a prolonged period of abnormally heavy new investment, belongs to the species of remedy which cures the disease by killing the patient.[21]

Pride of place in Keynes's explanation of Britain's milder problems went back to the egregious policy mistake of the Bank of England in overvaluing the pound by returning to the gold standard in 1925. This had created an adjustment problem which was too difficult to overcome. In Keynes's words, contributing in 1932 to the *Lloyd's Bank Monthly Review*,

> On the one hand, it was obviously impracticable to enforce by high Bank Rate or contraction of credit a deflation sufficiently drastic to bring about a reduction in internal costs appropriate to the parity adopted. On the other hand, the maintenance of a low Bank rate would have ... led to a rapid loss of gold and a much earlier collapse of the gold standard ... the policy actually adopted was to preserve a middle-course – with money dear enough to make London an attractive centre for foreign short-term funds but not dear enough to force an adjustment of internal costs.[22]

Keynes had already developed these ideas to some extent in testimony to the Macmillan Committee in March 1930, remarking that,

> The way prices are forced down is this. You put the bank rate at a level at which savings are in excess of investments. Business men make losses, prices fall, and then at long last the business man forces down the remuneration of the factors of production. But if you jam the machine halfway through so you have a chronic condition in which business men make losses, you also have a chronic condition of unemployment, a chronic condition of waste.[23]

Keynes's analysis of the slump pivoted on the growing divergence between the opinions of lenders and borrowers, that is, between the market and natural rates of interest. In his earliest account, in the TM, written early in 1930 when the downturn was gaining force, Keynes emphasized the role of what he called "artificial" borrowers in preventing the market rate of interest from falling in line with a presumed decline in the natural rate. Among such borrowers he included "distressed" borrowers, chiefly governments, which borrowed not for investment in productive enterprise but to repay their debts, "banking" borrowers (sometimes governments and sometimes banks) which borrowed to build up liquid reserves following the general return to the gold standard, and "speculative" borrowers, such as the rich individuals who emerged in 1928 and 1929 to participate in the feverish, final "bull" phase in US equities.[24] In all these cases, the lender called the shots and could prevent a drop in the rate of interest.

At this stage Keynes referred mostly to the collapsing confidence of borrowers. In other words, it was the collapse in non-banks' marginal efficiency of capital rather than a general reluctance to lend (on the part of both banks and non-banks) which was undermining demand. Thus in December 1930 he opined that, "the fall of prices has been disastrous to those who have borrowed, and anyone who has postponed new enterprise has gained by his delay".[25] This was consistent with the typical causal sequence as he saw it. First, a collapse in the *expected* rate of profit led to a fall in investment. Then demand weakness would cause a reduction in prices and the *actual* rate of profit, leading to another fall in investment. Like Irving Fisher, Keynes realized that, once expectations of deflation had become widespread, they became self-feeding and might initiate a vicious downward spiral.

The banking system – a feature of the capitalist economy which is both fractionally reserved and highly leveraged, and in these respects is inherently fragile – might aggravate the downward instability. Once profit expectations had been hit, and once the natural rate of interest (in this sense) had declined, the banks were in trouble. In December 1930 Keynes warned that, "It is obvious that the present trend of events cannot go much further without something breaking. If nothing is done, it will be amongst the world's banks that the really critical breakages will occur."[26] On cue came the global banking crisis of summer 1931. Keynes wrote from the USA in June 1931 that the American banks "have purchased great quantities of second-grade bonds which have depreciated in value", while "their advances to farmers and against real estate are inadequately secured". So nervous were depositors that safe boxes (to look after the cash withdrawn from banks) were no longer obtainable. Again in his words, "At any moment bank runs are liable to break out almost anywhere in the country. All this tends towards a mania for liquidity." "Barmy" opposition from New York banks was inhibiting the Fed from expansionary open-market operations on a sufficient scale.[27] Keynes's analysis here was identical to – and indeed anticipated by over 30 years – Milton Friedman's and Anna Schwartz's retrospective analysis of the Fed's failure in the 1963 *A Monetary History of the United States*.

In one of his magazine articles on 'The consequences to the banks of the collapse of money values', Keynes – unusually – discussed banks' capital position as distinct from their cash reserves.[28] Given the importance of the regulatory upheaval in late 2008 and its role in the Great Recession, the article might have received more comment in the Keynes renaissance of recent years. Written in August 1931, but published in *Vanity Fair* in January 1932, the article illustrated Keynes's deep understanding of banking practices. After discussing banks' tendency to lend amounts less than the collateral by a "margin" for safety, it observed,

> A year ago it was the failure of agriculture, mining, manufactures, and transport to make normal profits, and the unemployment and waste of productive resources ensuing on this, which was the leading feature of the economic situation. Today, in many parts of the world, it is the serious embarrassment of the banks which is the cause of our gravest concern. *Never* before has there been such a world-wide collapse over almost the whole field of the money values of real assets as we have experienced in the last two years. And, finally, during the

last few months – so recently that the bankers themselves have, as yet, scarcely appreciated it – it has come to exceed in very many cases the amount of the conventional "margins". In the language of the market the "margins" have "run off". Much of the world banking system is technically insolvent, and much less willing than they would normally be to finance any project which might involve a lock up of their resources.

In a typical sally Keynes continued, "Banks and bankers are by nature blind". Quite simply, and again as in 2008 and 2009, they had not seen what was coming. Keynes's derision was nicely put.

> Some of them have even welcomed the fall of prices towards what, in their inno-
> cence, they have deemed the just and "natural" and inevitable level of pre-war,
> that is to say, to the level of prices to which their minds became accustomed
> in their formative years. In the United States some of them employ so-called
> "economists" who tell us even today that our troubles are due to the fact that
> the prices of some commodities and some services have not yet fallen enough,
> regardless of what should be the obvious fact that their cure, if it could be real-
> ised, would be a menace to the solvency of their institution. A "sound" banker,
> alas! is not one who foresees danger and avoids it, but one who, when he is
> ruined, is ruined in a conventional and orthodox way along with his fellows, so
> that no one can really blame him.[29]

Early in the Great Depression Keynes did not doubt that "natural forces" would bring about *some* recovery. In 1930 he could write, "A partial recovery, therefore, is to be anticipated merely through the elapse of time and without the application of purposeful remedies." In principle, a new point of equilibrium could be reached by an all-round reduction in money-wages accompanied by a fall in the market rate of interest. But the first was politically impossible, while the fall in the long-term rate of interest was likely to be "a long and a tedious process". The drive for cheaper money needed to be "accelerated by deliberate policy. For the slump itself produces a new queue of 'distress' borrowers who have to raise money on the best terms available to meet their losses, particularly governments of countries whose international equilibrium has been upset by the fall in the price of their exports."[30]

In these circumstances, "purposeful" action was needed to raise the price level. To be precise, quoting now from TM,

> The Bank of England and the Federal Reserve Board might put pressure on
> their member banks to do what would be to the private advantage of these
> banks if they were all to act together, namely, to reduce the rate of interest which
> they allow to depositors to a very low figure, say ½ per cent. At the same time
> these two central institutions should pursue bank-rate policy and open-market
> operations *à outrance*, having first agreed amongst themselves that they will take

steps to prevent difficulties due to international gold movements from interfer-
ing with this. That is to say, they should combine to maintain a very low level
of the short-term rate of interest, and buy long-dated securities either against
an expansion of central bank money or against the sale of short-dated securities until the short-term market is saturated. It happens that this is an occasion
when, if I am right, one of the conditions limiting open-market operations *à
outrance* does not exist; for it is not an occasion – at least not yet – when bonds
are standing at a price above reasonable expectations as to their long-term
normal, so that they can still be purchased without the prospect of a loss ...
Not until deliberate and vigorous action has been taken along such lines as these
and has failed, need we, in the light of the argument of this treatise [TM], admit
that the banking system can *not*, on this occasion, control the rate of investment
and, therefore, the level of prices.[31]

In Chicago in June 1931, Keynes insisted that the main task facing public
policy was to lift the level of investment. He offered two main policy suggestions for doing this. First was a set of "new construction programmes
under the direct auspices of government"; second was a concerted attempt,
by means of "banking policy", to bring down the long-term rate of interest. But by the start of 1932 the banking system in the USA and many
other countries (although not the UK) appeared to be frozen, as losses on
old loans damaged solvency and the ability to extend new credits. Keynes
was losing his faith in the ability of "banking policy", and monetary policy
in the round, to lift the world economy out of slump. "It may still be the
case", he said in February 1932,

> that the lender, with his confidence shattered by his experience, will continue to
> ask for new enterprise rates of interest which the borrower cannot be expected
> to earn ... If this proves to be the case there will be no means of escape from
> prolonged and perhaps interminable depression except by direct state interven-
> tion to promote and subsidise new investment.[32]

In spring 1933 Keynes wrote a pamphlet, *The Means to Prosperity*, based
on four articles in *The Times*. By now he had almost given up on monetary
policy. In his words, there was "no means of raising world prices except by
an increase of loan-expenditure throughout the world".[33] In the US edition
of *The Means to Prosperity* he introduced material on the multiplier which
he had developed in *The New Statesman and Nation* of 1 April. This was
the first time that Keynes used multiplier analysis to support the case for
public works. His words may have been for an American readership, but he
referred to the British situation. To quote,

> it is a complete mistake to believe that there is a dilemma between schemes
> for increasing employment and schemes for balancing the budget – that we
> must go slowly and cautiously with the former for fear of injuring the latter.

Quite the contrary. There is no possibility of balancing the budget except by increasing the national income, which is much the same thing as increasing employment.

Half a page later he resumed,

Substantially the same argument also applies to a relief of taxation by suspending the Sinking Fund and by returning to the practice of financing by loans those services which can properly be so financed, such as the cost of new roads charged on the Road Fund and that part of the cost of the dole which can be averaged out against the better days for which we must hope. For the increased spending power of the taxpayer will have precisely the same favourable repercussions as increased spending power due to loan-expenditure; and in some ways this method of increasing expenditure is healthier and better spread throughout the community. If the Chancellor of the Exchequer will reduce taxation by £50 million through suspending the Sinking Fund and borrowing in those cases where formerly we thought it reasonable to borrow, the half of what he remits will in fact return to him from the saving on the dole and the higher yield of a given level of taxation – though . . . it will not necessarily return to him in the same budget.[34]

He mocked the critics of expansionary fiscal policy, as it would nowadays be called. The trouble was that many participants in the policy debate tacitly assumed a fully employed economy. Keynes asked, "Why should [his] method of approach appear to so many people to be novel and odd and paradoxical?" He conjectured,

I can only find the answer in the fact that all our ideas about economics, instilled into us by education and atmosphere and tradition are, whether we are conscious of it or not, soaked with theoretical pre-suppositions which are only properly applicable to a society which is in equilibrium, with all its productive resources already employed . . . Obviously if the productive resources of the nation were already fully occupied, none of the advantages could be expected which, in present circumstances, I predict from an increase of loan-expenditure. For in that case increased loan-expenditure would merely exhaust itself in raising prices and wages and diverting resources from other jobs.[35]

The discussion in this section can now be summarized. Keynes's "real time" analyses in the Great Depression had the following four noteworthy features. First, at all times he rejected the "liquidationist" policy being urged by conservative bankers and far too many economists. While he accepted that, theoretically, a new equilibrium could be attained by reducing costs in line with prices, he thought the attempt to do this would destroy the capitalist system. Capitalism could be crippled by the downward spiral of "debt deflation" highlighted by Irving Fisher. In Keynes's words,

> If we reach a new equilibrium by lowering the level of salaries and wages, we increase proportionately the burden of monetary indebtedness. National debts, war debts, obligations between the creditor and debtor nations, farm debts, real estate mortgages – all this financial structure would be deranged ... A widespread bankruptcy, default, and repudiation of bonds would necessarily ensue. Banks would be in jeopardy ... And what would be the advantage of having caused so much ruin?[36]

Second, although Keynes, like Fisher, deployed powerful arguments against deflation, he could not explain why, left to itself, the economy should not run down almost indefinitely. This was because, according to the TM theory, during the downward spiral saving would always be running ahead of investment. A new equilibrium had to wait till the community was too poor to save. The lacuna in his understanding stemmed partly from the incompleteness of his theoretical rethinking. At this stage he lacked vital bits of what was to become Keynesian theory, such as the consumption function, the multiplier, and the theory of effective demand.

Third, his progress towards the revolutionary concepts and ideas in the GT was hampered by the dysfunctional definitions of saving, income and profits in the TM. In the GT the $S = I$ equality holds for all states of equilibrium; in TM it prevailed only for full employment equilibrium. Keynes realized that savings decline during the downturn. He talked of them being "spilt on the ground" in financing "business losses". He also talked of government "dissaving", as deficits automatically expanded. In short, he understood perfectly well that savings declined with income, and that "excess saving" was an artefact of his definitions and, specifically, of excluding profit and loss from income. (As Dennis Robertson noticed, "the savings which are so deplorably abundant in a slump consist largely of entrepreneurs' incomes which are not being spent, for the simple reason that they have not been earned."[37]) But Keynes wanted to explain what happens in the passage from one state of equilibrium to another. He would have spared himself much misunderstanding had he distinguished between what people want to save *ex ante* and what they succeed in saving *ex post*. But this would have led him to focus on what happened to income and output, rather than on what happened to prices, and that shift in focus came only with the GT.

Fourth, and crucially, as the Great Depression deepened in 1932 and 1933, his policy emphasis switched from monetary policy, even monetary policy *à outrance*, to reflationary fiscal action.

III

For all his insight, brilliance and influence, Keynes was not a rigorous technical economist. Much of his work was loosely stated and open to more than one interpretation, and its ambiguity has led to disagreement and trouble. Members of his profession squabble not just about the meaning of his theories, but even about the type of method he employed. Some say that the GT is largely about disequilibria, with Keynes concerned to explore the processes by which equilibrium is restored.[38] Others claim that the GT's theory of national income determination is an equilibrium statement. At any rate, a contrast in approach between the TM and the GT is undeniable. The GT is much more structured and consecutive than the TM. The argument arrives at theoretical propositions, which can be converted into equations, even if Keynes himself did not do that. Unlike the TM, the GT offered no extended treatment of the phases of the business cycle, and it says little about banking institutions and avoids the phrase "the natural rate of interest".

By 1936, when the GT was published, all the upheaval which produced the Great Depression had already happened. There were no disequilibrium phenomena – disequilibrium prices, windfall profits and losses, excess savings, and the like – which time could be expected to rectify. All the adjustments had been made through changes in income and output, and the US and UK economies had settled down to a condition of chronically low employment or – in Keynes's language – to an "unemployment equilibrium". The risk that this condition might be semi-permanent – and that the semi-permanence of high involuntary unemployment invalidated the notion that capitalist economies had innate stabilizing properties that would ensure cyclical recovery – was implicit in his "real time" analyses of the Great Depression. Crucially for the wider public debate, the semi-permanence of high involuntary unemployment invalidated the notion that capitalist economies had innate stabilizing properties that would ensure cyclical recovery.

In the GT Keynes cut through the maze to focus on a single question: what determines the level of output at any time? The answer he gave was "effective demand", understood as the point (implicitly in a diagram, which did not in fact appear in the GT) where the aggregate demand function intersects with the aggregate supply function, and spending does give rise to decisions to produce and employ.[39] In the GT Keynes showed that effective demand could be – and long remain – at a level too low for full use of the community's resources. Demonstration of the result hinged on blockages to the "natural" recovery of investment. The description of this parlous condition started from an assumption of an earlier shrinkage in investment, and with that the community's income, output and employment had also fallen. There were no "surplus" savings, because saving had fallen in line with income. Real wages remained above the level necessary for full employment, because they depended on the state of aggregate demand, not on labour market money-wage bargains. The rate of interest was fixed above the natural rate (or the marginal efficiency of capital) by liquidity preference. There was no escape from low employment via the export channel, because the analysis applied to an economy that was "closed" to trade and capital flows. (This made sense if Keynes was writing about an economy, such as the USA's, that was big relative to the world economy as a whole. Alternatively, he could be viewed as theorizing about the world as a whole suffering from a deficiency of aggregate demand.)

How could the economy escape from this unsatisfactory state of chronic underemployment? The move to a higher equilibrium depended on an increase in the marginal efficiency of capital, but there was nothing in the existing situation to warrant it. In both the TM and the GT Keynes emphasized the dependence of long-term expectations on short-term expectations.[40] The depression could cast a long shadow, persisting several years from the initial adverse shock. The lifting of the clouds had to be engineered by the government.

The tendency of the TM was to use disequilibrium analysis, whereas the GT makes statements about equilibrium. Nevertheless, the substantive differences between the two can be exaggerated. First, no more than in the TM, did Keynes in the GT envisage his "unemployment equilibrium" as static and rigid. Chapter 22 of the GT is about the trade cycle. There would always be a bounce – perhaps only a dead cat bounce – from the lowest point in the cycle. Capital equipment would have to be replaced, while working capital would need replenishment. There might even be bursts of speculative excitement. The theme he wanted to argue was that no sustainable recovery was possible unless the "inducement to invest" reached its pre-recession level. This would not happen spontaneously. A push from the government, in the form of extra spending or lower taxation, was needed.

Secondly, the "unemployment equilibrium" of the GT is much closer to the low-wage equilibrium of the TM than the term suggests. The phrase "unemployment equilibrium" implies no wage adjustment has occurred, whereas the TM account envisaged a return to equilibrium via wage adjustment. But Keynes also said that in the low-wage equilibrium of TM, many workers would be employed outside the industrial system as "gardeners and chauffeurs".[41] His thinking was that, as industries with high value added per person retrench because of weak demand, the economy would decant workers into the bottom end of the service sector. "Unemployment equilibrium" could be viewed as an institutional artefact created by the availability of unemployment benefits. The notion of "underemployment equilibrium" sums up better Keynes's idea of what an *inferior* equilibrium would look like, combining insights from both the TM and GT.

But in one vital respect the GT goes beyond the TM. The TM's agenda is still very much monetary. In the GT, by contrast, monetary expansion yields to public investment as the route to recovery. Monetary policy must help and accommodate public investment policy. It must do that, because on its own, it cannot push the economy all the way back to full employment.

The GT envisaged a situation in which confidence was so low that repeated injections of money into the banking system failed to bring down the long-term rate of interest to the required level. He conjectured a possible deep depression, in which bond yields were so low that investors feared eventual yield rises and capital losses. If the authorities engineered increases in their money balances, the non-bank public would let the ratio of money to non-money assets (and to national income and expenditure) rise without limit. This was Keynes's famous "liquidity trap". A long-term interest rate of 2 per cent "leaves more to fear than to hope, and offers at the same time, a running yield which is only sufficient to offset a very small measure of fear [of illiquidity]". In this case, liquidity preference may become "virtually absolute", in the sense that almost everybody would commit any extra wealth to cash rather than to bonds (or indeed to equities and real estate). In the mid-1930s there had been no examples of the pure liquidity trap, as Keynes understood that notion, although he thought that the USA had come close to it in 1932.[42]

Ultimately, the rate of interest, like the marginal efficiency of capital, was "a psychological phenomenon". An expansionary monetary policy (of big asset purchases) which appeared to the investing public as being "experimental in character or easily liable to change" might cause liquidity preference to strengthen, which would counteract the stimulatory effect. On the other hand, the same policy might succeed if it "appealed to public opinion as being reasonable and practicable and in the public interest, and promoted by an authority unlikely to be superseded".[43] However, the uncertainty attaching to the outcome of monetary operations led Keynes in the GT to be:

> sceptical of the success of a merely monetary policy directed towards influencing the rate of interest. I expect to see the State, which is in a position to calculate the marginal efficiency of capital-goods on long views and on the basis of the general social advantage, taking an ever greater responsibility for directly organising investment; since it seems likely that the fluctuations in the market estimation of the marginal efficiency of different types of capital, calculated on the principles I have described above, will be too great to be offset by any practicable changes in the rate of interest.[44]

In the GT portfolio choice was confined to two assets only, money and bonds, unlike the TM which offered a choice between money, bonds and "securities", where securities of course included equities. The basic reason for the omission of securities was that Keynes wanted to direct attention to the difficulty facing the monetary authority in forcing down the long-term rate of interest when risk aversion in the investment community was particularly strong. However, his scepticism about monetary policy in a depression had a long-term effect on thinking about economic policy-making, particularly in Britain. It affected both academic tuition and actual policy decisions for at least a generation after his death. The Keynesians were known to be supporters of "cheap money" (that is, very low interest rates) well into the inflationary 1960s and 1970s, even if by then exchange controls and lending restrictions were required to make very low interest rates possible.

IV

In the light of what Keynes wrote about the Great Depression, how would he have analysed the contraction which started in 2008? And what prescriptions would he have made? Five points are now developed. They are surmises, but they seem justified by consistent themes in all of his work in the late 1920s and 1930s.

First, as in 1930 and later, he would not have attributed the 2008 downturn to cheap money and over-investment. He would have had no truck with the Austrian School's diagnosis and recommendations. Keynes regarded the speculative aspects of the pre-recession situation as a secondary phenomenon, masking a basic situation of under-investment in fixed capital relative to corporate saving. (This turned out to be Greenspan's retrospective view as well.[45]) He would have regarded the triggering cause of the crisis as the stiffening of the Federal Reserve's monetary stance from 2005 onwards, as it tried to control the housing boom. He would have considered that the Fed made exactly the same mistake in the 2000s as it had in the 1920s. To recall his words, "If too long an attempt is made to check the speculative position by dear money, it may well be that the dear money, by checking new investments, will bring about a general business depression". The Fed should have sought to limit credit to the housing sector, without choking off credit to the rest of the economy.

Second, Keynes would have approved of the concerted central bank rescue operations of 2009, which followed closely his prescription of "open market operations *à outrance*", and would have attributed to them a decisive role in stopping the slide down into another Great

Depression. He might well have considered the bank bail-outs excessive. In the British bank run which immediately preceded the outbreak of war in 1914, he advised a Treasury guarantee for commercial banks' illiquid assets only. (This paralleled a similar proposal for the establishment of a "bad bank" [to absorb banks' bad assets, which could not be sold and so were illiquid] in 2009 and 2010. The bad bank idea was implemented only in Ireland.)

Third, Keynes would have deplored the UK's premature suspension of QE in 2010 before the recovery was secure. (Admittedly, inflation was at the time running well above target and the UK did return to QE at a later date.) Keynes would probably have attributed the Eurozone relapse of 2012 and 2013 to the ECB's withdrawal of the so-called "non-standard measures" and been critical of the Bundesbank thinking from which the decision to withdraw them was derived. (Eurozone output fell by 4.5 per cent in 2009, in the Great Recession as such. But it slipped again by 0.9 per cent in 2012 and 0.3 per cent in 2013, after only a weak recovery in 2010 and 2011. For more on the debate on the non-standard measures, see Chapter 4 above, pp. 114–20.) He would have attributed the greater success of the Fed's QE policy at least partly to its purchase of a wider range of assets, especially mortgage-backed securities. (The USA – unlike the Eurozone – suffered no output declines, on an annual basis, after 2009. Output rose by 2.2 per cent in 2012 and 1.5 per cent in 2013.)

Fourth, Keynes would have rejected policies of fiscal austerity which were widely enacted after the 2009 fiscal stimulus agreed at the G20 meetings in late 2008. (See Table 9.1.) He would have done so for exactly the same reason he gave in 1933. In his words,

> it is a complete mistake to believe that there is a dilemma between schemes for increasing employment and schemes for balancing the budget – that we must go slowly and cautiously with the former for fear of injuring the latter. Quite the contrary. There is no possibility of balancing the budget except by increasing the national income, which is much the same thing as increasing employment.

He would have approved the pursuit of a balanced budget on current account, *if* accompanied by an enlarged programme of capital spending. He would have been prepared, if necessary, to finance the government deficit from the central bank. In his view, a combination of better-targeted QE and loan-financed public investment would have made the slump shorter and shallower.

Fifth, Keynes would not have believed the present recovery securely based, despite the improvement in asset prices. He would have pointed to the lack of recovery of investment, the speculative basis of the revival, and

Table 9.1 Fiscal policy in the Great Recession and after

The table shows change in general government structural (that is, cyclically adjusted) balance, according to the International Monetary Fund. This change is usually accepted as a definition of the direction of fiscal policy, although some authorities prefer the level of the balance. A decrease in the balance – meaning an increase in the deficit – is "expansionary", in Keynesian terms. It is evident that fiscal policy was "expansionary" in 2009 everywhere in the advanced world, in line with commitments made at the November 2008 G20 Washington summit. It is also evident that after 2010 fiscal policy was generally "contractionary" in the Keynesian sense. Indeed, over the decade to 2015 – in which the Great Recession was the major cyclical event – governments took action to reduce their structural budget deficits. This pattern is particularly obvious in Germany, as might be expected.

	2006	2007	2008	2009	2010	2011	2012	2013	2014	2015	Change in fiscal policy in decade to 2015
Advanced economies	0.5	-0.1	-1.4	-1.9	-0.6	0.9	1.2	1.2	0.5	0.2	0.6
USA	0.7	-0.8	-1.9	-1.7	-1.9	1.4	1.9	2.2	0.5	0.4	0.8
Euro area	0.3	-0.1	-1.0	-1.3	0.1	0.8	1.7	0.8	0.2	0.2	1.7
– Germany	0.4	0.9	0.1	-0.1	-1.3	0.9	1.3	0.4	0.3	0.0	2.8
Japan	1.1	1.4	-1.3	-3.9	-0.4	-0.5	0.6	-0.3	2.5	0.9	-0.1
UK	0.2	-0.5	-1.1	-3.1	1.5	1.5	0.0	1.8	-0.7	0.8	0.4
Canada	0.1	0.0	-1.1	-1.4	-1.6	0.7	0.8	0.4	0.9	-0.7	-1.9
Other advanced economies	0.2	0.5	-1.4	-1.5	0.1	0.3	0.2	0.1	0.0	-0.1	-1.6

Note: * "Other advanced economies" are advanced economies excluding G7 and the Eurozone.

Source: IMF database, as at April 2016.

the continued deficiency of aggregate demand. In other words, he would expect another downturn.

Is there room for final, more wide-ranging reflections? The first decade of the new millennium resembled the 1920s in that, about the middle of both decades, supply-side performance was challenged by a fall in the TM's "natural rate of interest". In other words, the marginal returns on new capital equipment seemed to deteriorate, after bursts of heavy investment in new technology. Western economies now await the next burst of innovation to revive the "animal spirits" of entrepreneurs after the latest bout of "creative destruction". But can we rely on investment to restore full employment?

In his essay, 'Economic possibilities for our grandchildren' (1930), Keynes predicted a secular decline in the rate of capital accumulation, leading to growing "technological unemployment".[46] He was more explicit in the GT, where the 'Concluding notes' proposed such a looming abundance of capital that its "marginal efficiency" would fall to "a very low figure". The result would be the "euthanasia of the rentier", where the rentier could be regarded as "the functionless investor".[47] In the 1940s, hypotheses about "secular stagnation" became common in the USA, based on the decline in population growth and the "closing of the frontier".[48] These were dispelled by the strong investment performance and economic growth of developed countries in the 1950s and 1960s. But this occurred after the Second World War, which had created a huge pent-up demand for new equipment, transport infrastructure, and household appliances, as well as the requirements of a "military-industrial complex" which fed the needs of the Cold War.

It may be that some tendency for the natural rate of interest to decline had started in the developed countries by the late 1960s. Productivity growth has undoubtedly slowed down since then. Some crucial changes in the political economy of capitalism after about 1980 can be viewed as a response to this, specifically the upsurge of neo-liberal ideology, the growing inequality of wealth and incomes, and the increased importance of financial services, and an apparent rise in structural unemployment. The Old Normal of the early post-war decades now seems confined to "moments of excitement", as in the dot.com revolution of the 1990s. Invention may continue, but it will require smaller inputs of capital and labour than in the past. The New Normal will be of slower growth, as too many companies and households struggle to escape the burden of debts incurred in a past era of more buoyant expectations.

Keynes's policy response to the Depression of the 1930s was to restore investment activity to "normal". But what if, for us today, the New Normal is marked by a permanent decline in the demand for new capital? It is entirely possible that, in the aftermath of the collapse of 2008, Keynes would have had a different set of recovery priorities. This is suggested by two quotations which show the way his mind was working at the end of his life. The first is from a memorandum, 'The long-term problem of full employment', dated 25 May 1943:

> We are more likely to succeed in maintaining employment if we do not make this our sole, or even our first, aim. Perhaps employment, like happiness, will come most readily when it is not sought for its own sake. The real problem is to use our productive powers to secure the greatest human welfare. Let us start then with the human welfare, and consider what is most needed to increase it. The needs will change from time to time; they may shift, for example, from capital goods to consumers' goods and to services. Let us think in terms of organising and directing our productive resources, so as to meet these changing needs; and we shall be less likely to waste them.[49]

The second is from a letter to T.S. Eliot:

> the full employment policy by means of investment is only one particular application of an intellectual theorem. You can produce the result just as well by consuming more or working less. Personally I regard the investment policy as first aid. In the US, it almost certainly will not do the trick. Less work is the ultimate solution (a 35 hour week in the US, would do the trick now). How you mix up the three ingredients of a cure is a matter of taste and experience, i.e. of morals and knowledge.[50]

How to "mix up these three ingredients of a cure" – investment, consumption, increased leisure – remains the most important problem facing economic policy in the Western world in the post-recession years.

NOTES

1. The sceptics include David Laidler and Tim Congdon. See Laidler *Fabricating the Keynesian Revolution* (Cambridge: Cambridge University Press, 1999) and Congdon 'What was Keynes' best book?', pp. 46–54, essay 2, in Tim Congdon *Keynes, the Keynesians and Monetarism* (Cheltenham, UK and Northampton, MA, USA: Edward Elgar Publishing, 2007).
2. In a celebrated 1981 paper Axel Leijonhufvud called Wicksell's influence on both Keynes and other monetary theorists "the Wicksell connection". (Axel Leijonhufvud 'The Wicksell connection: variations on a theme', pp. 131–202, chapter 7 in Leijonhufvud *Information and Coordination* [New York and Oxford: Oxford University Press, 1981].)
3. This remained the underlying concern of the *General Theory*, where the first chapter of the final Book VI set out 'Notes on the trade cycle'. See pp. 313–32 in Elizabeth Johnson and Donald Moggridge (eds) *The Collected Writings of John Maynard Keynes*, vol. VII (London and Basingstoke: Macmillan for the Royal Economics Society, 1973, originally published 1936). The word "macroeconomics" was first used by Ragnar Frisch in his

1933 *Propagation Problems and Impulse Problems in Dynamic Economics* (London: Allen & Unwin).

4. CW, V, p. 120.
5. Ibid., p. 165.
6. Ibid., p. 217.
7. Ibid., p. 250.
8. Ibid., p. 262.
9. Ibid., pp. 271–3. The passage can be compared with a letter from Keynes to Ralph Hawtrey, 28 November 1930, which recounted the "normal order of events in the cycle", with, first, "a decline of fixed investment relative to saving", second, a fall in prices less than necessary for adjustment, third, "a fall in output, as a result of falling prices and accumulating stocks on the minds of entrepreneurs", fourth, a fall in prices greater than needed for adjustment as a result of a "declining level of output". But, as soon as output stops falling, "there will be some kick-up in prices". (Skidelsky *John Maynard Keynes*, vol. 2 [London: Macmillan, 1992], p. 446.)
10. CW, VI, p. 304.
11. CW, V, pp. 164–5. To quote, "insofar as the banking system is a free agent acting with design, it can, by coming in as a balancing factor, control the final outcome."
12. CW, VI, p. 206.
13. Ibid., pp. 206–7.
14. Ibid., pp. 331–3. The most important "limiting point" mentioned by Keynes was the fall in the bond rate towards zero. Continuation of the asset purchasing programme would then push the price of assets to a figure above what the central bank considered their long-term norm, which would mean the deliberate acceptance of losses. But the central bank should be prepared to do this in the public interest.
15. See Skidelsky *Keynes*, vol. 2, p. 341.
16. TM was published on 24 October 1930.
17. Robert Gordon (ed.) *The American Business Cycle: Continuity and Change* (Chicago and London: University of Chicago Press, 1986), p. 794, and Charles Feinstein *Statistical Tables of National Income, Expenditure and Output of the UK 1855–1965* (Cambridge: Cambridge University Press, 1976), p. T22.
18. See above, note 4 on p. 17, in the Introduction to this volume.
19. Forrest Capie and Alan Webber *A Monetary History of the United Kingdom 1870–1982*, vol. 1, *Data, Sources, Methods* (London: Allen & Unwin, 1985), pp. 86–7.
20. Keynes gave three lectures in Chicago in June 1931. See CW, XIII, pp. 343–67.
21. CW, VII, p. 322.
22. CW, XXI, pp. 68–9.
23. CW, XIX, p. 611.
24. CW, VI, pp. 339–42.
25. CW, IX, p. 126.
26. Ibid., p. 156.
27. Skidelsky *Keynes*, vol. 2, pp. 390–91.
28. For clarity, and despite the risk of repetition, equity capital is a liability of the banks to their shareholders, whereas cash reserves are assets to meet payment instructions and deposit withdrawals.
29. Keynes 'The consequences to the banks of the collapse of money values', CW, IX, pp. 150–58. The quotations are from p. 151 and p. 156.
30. CW, VI, p. 344.
31. Ibid., pp. 346–7.
32. Halley-Stewart Lecture, 4 February 1932, CW, XXI, pp. 59–60.
33. CW, IX, p. 255.
34. In a footnote (to CW, IX, p. 248), Keynes added, "I strongly support, therefore, the suggestion which has been made that the next budget should be divided into two parts, one of which shall include those items of expenditure which it would be proper to treat as loan-expenditure in present circumstances."

35. CW, IX, pp. 347–9.
36. CW, XIII, p. 361. The passage might be compared with Irving Fisher's exposition of "debt deflation". Fisher had noted a potential "fallacy of composition", because the repayment of debt might exacerbate deflation and a drop in asset prices, which would increase the debt burden in real terms. In his words, "the more the debtors pay, the more they owe." (See also p. 199 in the previous chapter.) Fisher claimed to have devised his "debt deflation" theory in 1931 and, as he coined the actual term, it is "his" theory. All the same, Keynes was using exactly the same argument against deflation. Two differences between Fisher's and Keynes's positions might be highlighted. First, Fisher's explanatory chain starts with over-indebtedness produced by cheap money and inflated business expectations that are doomed to disappointment. The Keynes sequence starts with dear money and the fall in the natural rate (or MEC). For Keynes "speculation" in fixed assets is a secondary cause of collapse; for Fisher it is primary. Secondly, Fisher's remedy seems to rely on an old-fashioned quantity theory of money. (In other words, expand the quantity of money and the price level will rise proportionately.) He does not specify a transmission mechanism. Keynes, who also wanted to restore prices to their pre-recession level, thought this could only be done by increasing investment, a by-product of which would be a rise in prices. See Irving Fisher 'The debt deflation theory of the Great Depression', *Econometrica*, vol. 1 (1933), pp. 337–57, and also *The Economist*, 2 February 2010.
37. Dennis Robertson 'Mr Keynes's theory of money', *Economic Journal*, September 1931, p. 402 and p. 407, quoted in Skidelsky *Keynes*, vol. 2, p. 453.
38. Victoria Chick takes this line at several points in her *Macroeconomics after Keynes* (Cambridge, MA: MIT Press, 1983).
39. CW, VII, p. 25 and p. 55.
40. For a passage in the TM, see CW, VI, p. 323; for Keynes's treatment in the GT, look at Chapter 12 *passim.*
41. Keynes's involvement in the Macmillan Committee is covered in Chapter 2 of CW, XX, pp. 38–311. The reference is to a passage on p. 127.
42. CW, VII, p. 262 and pp. 272–8.
43. Ibid., p. 273.
44. Ibid., p. 164.
45. See Alan Greenspan *The Age of Turbulence* (New York: Penguin Books, 2008), p. 387 and p. 472.
46. CW, IX, 'Economic possibilities for our grandchildren', pp. 321–32.
47. CW, VII, pp. 375–6.
48. See Alvin Hansen *Fiscal Policy and Business Cycles* (New York: W.W. Norton & Sons, 1941).
49. CW, XXVII, p. 324.
50. JMK to T.S. Eliot, 5 April 1945, CW, XXVII, p. 384.

10. Why Friedman and Schwartz's interpretation of the Great Depression still matters: reassessing the thesis of their 1963 *Monetary History**

David Laidler

On 28 November 2008, barely two months after the collapse of Lehman Brothers, Paul Krugman told his *New York Times* readers[1] that:

> A central theme of Keynes's *General Theory* was the impotence of monetary policy in depression-type conditions. But Milton Friedman and Anna Schwartz in their magisterial monetary history of the United States claimed that the Fed could have prevented the Great Depression. . . .
>
> [T]he Depression could have been prevented if the Fed had done more – if it had expanded the monetary base faster and done more to rescue banks in trouble.

He continued:

> So here we are, facing a new crisis reminiscent of the 1930s. And this time the Fed has been spectacularly aggressive about expanding the monetary base: And guess what – it doesn't seem to be working . . . I think the thesis of the *Monetary History* has just taken a hit.

Given that the monetarist model underlying the *Monetary History* and its thesis about the Depression held that monetary policy works with long and variable time lags, Krugman was surely a little quick off the mark with his comment. But he was certainly to the politico-economic point in several dimensions.[2]

By the time he was writing, a major financial crisis had been developing for more than a year, economic activity in many countries, not least in the USA itself, was contracting sharply, and the Fed had begun to react vigorously (along with the Treasury and Congress). Krugman was by no means

alone in noticing resemblances to the onset of the USA's Great Depression
in 1929. Nor was he the only one to surmise that the lessons economists
thought they had learned from this earlier disaster were available to be
deployed, so that their validity would be put to a new test, in the looming
"Great Recession". More than competing ideas about the proper conduct
of counter-cyclical economic policy were at stake. Profound and ideologi-
cally loaded questions about the capacity of the market economy to function smoothly without the benefit of constant attention from government,
and hence about the appropriate political framework that should underpin
macroeconomic policy, became newly topical in the closing months of
2008.

I

For two decades following the Second World War a consensus prevailed
about the vulnerability of capitalist economies to cyclical instability. The
Great Depression of the 1930s, and the Keynesian revolution in economic
thought that been prompted by it, were widely held to have established
certain obvious truths. To be explicit, the largely unregulated economies
of North America and Europe were judged to have come catastrophically
adrift in the early 1930s for reasons inherent in their very nature. Even
worse, the then available policy tools had proved powerless to stabilize it.
By implication, a rather pervasive role for the state in economic life was
necessary. Specific policy responses to this way of thinking, whose smooth
arrival was both delayed and heavily conditioned by the war, diverged
considerably among countries. In the Kennedy–Johnson era, the structure of the US economy was very different from, say, Sweden, or even the
UK. Viewed from today's vantage point, however, macroeconomic policy
almost everywhere in the 1960s did indeed seem to be conforming to essentially the same activist principles. These stressed the primacy of output and
employment goals over the objective of price stability, and elevated fiscal
policy above monetary tools.

As the decade wore on, such policies generated incipient inflationary
problems. A new economic doctrine – "monetarism" – that claimed to
have solutions to inflation began to emerge. Crucial to the argument of
the current chapter, this doctrine also suggested that "Keynesian" policy
orthodoxy was based upon pessimistic misconceptions about the self-
regulating capacity of the market economy. Further, according to the
monetarists, supporters of the dominant Keynesian policy approach had
misunderstood what the evidence generated in the 1930s implied about
capitalism's cyclical resilience. One of monetarism's defining texts, *A*

Monetary History of the United States 1867–1960 and more specifically its Chapter 7 on "The Great Contraction", proposed that the Depression had not resulted from an inherent flaw in the market economy.[3] Instead the slump in demand from 1930 was the consequence of inept monetary policy, which undermined the American economy's ability to deal with what began in the late summer of 1929 as a routine cyclical downturn. The Friedman and Schwartz thesis supported monetarism's more general insistence on "the inherent stability of the private sector".[4] In the early years of the debate with Keynesianism, monetarism's emphasis on such stability was an empirical hypothesis that had to be re-examined with every new cyclical episode. But in due course it was turned into an un-debatable axiom by the New Classical School, which for a time seemed to forge a macroeconomic orthodoxy that went beyond and succeeded monetarism. (See pp. 196–7 of Chapter 8 for more on the New Classical School.) The *Monetary History's* interpretation of the Depression thus played a pivotal role, albeit at one remove, in bringing about a shift in the intellectual climate that led to lighter financial regulation (in the USA and elsewhere) from the early 1980s.

There is rich irony here. Robert Lucas, often seen as the New Classical School's leading figure, long remained an admirer of the *Monetary History*, writing an appreciative essay in 1994.[5] But he would also note, in a controversial statement a decade later, that New Classical Economics itself evolved through the 1980s and 1990s along lines that left it unable to analyse episodes such as the Depression.[6] So Friedman and Schwartz's 1963 interpretation of the Depression could no longer provide intellectual support for what had become the mainstream macroeconomics that Lucas had done so much to create and promote. Lucas was a pioneer of so-called "dynamic stochastic general equilibrium" (DSGE) analysis that was said to have been built on secure microeconomic foundations. With the Lehman Brothers failure being followed by financial market turmoil from September 2008, the DSGE approach became too remote and theoretical for most policy practitioners. It was small wonder that so acute a political economist as Krugman would conclude that a debate about macroeconomic fundamentals lay ahead. Would the *Monetary History's* thesis about the Depression, with its focus on the quantity of money and the Fed's inadequacy, prove as compelling as the alternative Keynesian interpretation of this episode, with its finger-pointing at the weaknesses of capitalism?

At its publication in 1963, the *Monetary History's* importance was quickly and widely recognized. Within months it drew no fewer than six major review articles. As Michael Bordo (in 1989) and Frank Steindl (1995) would later stress, it had staying power too.[7] Three more review articles in the August 1994 *Journal of Monetary Economics* marked its thirtieth anniversary. Meanwhile its account of the causes of the Great Depression, which was only one episode in the century of monetary history it covered, received a major boost from the 1981 publication of *The Great Depression Revisited*, edited by Karl Brunner.[8] The Brunner collection was later followed by among others, seminal articles from Ben Bernanke (1983), and Christina and David Romer (1989), an extended treatment in book form in the 2003 first volume of Allan Meltzer's *A History of the Federal Reserve*, and Robert Hetzel's 2008 *The Monetary Policy of the Federal Reserve: A History.*[9] More recently, the fiftieth anniversary of the *Monetary History*'s publication was celebrated by a special session at the January 2013 meetings of the Allied Social Sciences Association (under American Economic Association auspices), where the papers presented did the book the honour of building upon, rather than simply reiterating, its themes.[10]

To be sure, subsequent monetarist work on the Depression differed in some details from the story that the *Monetary History* had told. For example, Anna Schwartz (1981), writing alone in the 1981 Brunner volume, was more definite in attributing the initial sharp downturn of 1929 and 1930 to monetary impulses than Friedman and Schwartz had been. Meltzer and, following him, Hetzel placed more emphasis than had Friedman and Schwartz on faulty economic analysis within the Fed. Specifically, they highlighted the Riefler–Burgess view of the monetary policy process, and neglect of the Fisher distinction between real and nominal interest rates, in explaining the intellectual sources of its policy errors. Moreover, under the influence of Charles Kindleberger's 1973 book *The World in Depression 1929–1939* and Barry Eichengreen's 1992 *Golden Fetters: The Gold Standard and the Great Depression*, later accounts have usually paid more attention to the Depression's international dimension. Surely, this is right, in that the cyclical upheaval of the Great Depression was far from being a uniquely American event.[11] But these modifications have left largely intact the basic thesis of the *Monetary History* about the US economy itself in the 1930s. To repeat, the *Monetary History* alleged that a collapse of the US money supply between 1929 and 1933, precipitated by inept Fed policy, was the principal immediate cause of the extraordinarily severe economic contraction that the country experienced in those years.

It is true that recently a younger generation of macro-theorists, writing in the New Classical tradition, have been inclined to take the *Monetary History*'s story less seriously. For example, in a contentious 2007 paper, Harold Cole and Lee Ohanian treated monetary impulses in a somewhat naive and even perfunctory fashion, even though their investigation of the 1930s was otherwise of extreme technical sophistication.[12] Here the main goal was to assess the explanatory power of real business cycle theory for those years. Cole and Ohanian's message was that the American economy's behaviour might be an equilibrium response to productivity shocks and other supply-side setbacks in the context of institutional rigidities, not least in the labour market. But the RBC approach to analysing the Depression, which Christiano, Motto and Rostagno extended in a 2004 article to incorporate the effects of an adverse money-demand shift, is very much a work in progress.[13] In short, the *Monetary History* is still respected and influential. If the Friedman and Schwartz emphasis on the quantity of money retains traction in an account of the Great Depression, is there not a possibility that a similar emphasis ought to have value in an interpretation of the Great Recession?

II

The *Monetary History* interpretation boils down to the assertion that the collapse on the US economy between 1929 and 1933 was a disaster that the Fed could have prevented. Meanwhile, as already noted, a monetarist view of the nature of economic fluctuations underlies it. This in turn may be summarized in three propositions. First, the main influence on the course of the business cycle is the rate of growth of the quantity of money in circulation. When this rate of growth slows down, it usually brings on a downturn, if with something of a lag; when it speeds up, the sequel is an upturn, again with a lag. Second, the amplitude of cyclical fluctuations in nominal national income's growth rate tends to vary with the magnitude of preceding changes in money growth, with variations in its real components on the whole preceding those in rates of change of prices.[14] Third, the transmission mechanism involved here (which was described in some detail, not in the *Monetary History* itself, but in a separate but contemporaneous paper on 'Money and business cycles') is not unidirectional.[15] Rather it has the potential to generate feed-backs from the course of economic activity to the subsequent behaviour of money growth, in a recursive process with considerable capacity to amplify business fluctuations. The *Monetary History* deployed this framework in a systematic account of the progress of the US economy between 1867 and 1960. The Great Contraction could be analysed as a particular application of the framework in extreme circumstances. In that sense it was not a unique event, a fact that the later publication of its Chapter 7 as a stand-alone volume has sometimes tended to obscure.[16]

A narrative discussion may help in understanding the causal processes at work. The US economy started to turn down in the late summer of

1929. The initial contraction was reinforced by the financial uncertainty that followed the stock market crash of October 1929. It was steep, but it turned into a collapse only later, in the second half of 1930. (Real gross national product in the second quarter (Q2) 1930 was 8 per cent lower than a year earlier, but a larger fall of almost 10 per cent then occurred in the two quarters to Q4 1930.[17]) In 1930 the quantity of money, which had dropped in late 1929, was stable for most of the year. But it started to fall in the autumn as the first of a series of banking crises took hold. The decline in the quantity of money accelerated in 1931. The destabilization of the monetary system gathered further momentum, reaching its climax in the full-scale banking panic in the opening months of 1933. According to Friedman and Schwartz, the cumulative collapse in the broadly defined quantity of money (which was of 38.2 per cent between October 1929 and April 1933) could have been avoided by prompt and determined actions on the part of the Fed in 1930 and later.[18] Such action could have consisted of both the extension of last-resort loan facilities to banks suffering runs and large-scale asset purchases. Indeed, top officials at the New York Fed repeatedly urged in late 1930 and 1931 that the Fed should expand its balance sheet and buy government securities, but were opposed by representatives from the regional Feds. Friedman and Schwartz documented the antagonism between the New York bankers, seen as being too close to Wall Street and stock market speculation, and banking interests elsewhere in the USA.[19]

In their interpretation of events the change in the quantity of money may have been the active driver of economic activity, but it was not treated as a variable directly controlled by the Fed. Rather it was linked to the variable that was (or could be) controlled, namely the monetary base (or "the stock of high-powered money"), by way of a "money multiplier". (Note that the monetary base includes the legal-tender currency used in many retail transactions, as well as the cash reserves that banks need for settlement between themselves.) The multiplier's value in turn was seen to be the outcome of choices made both within the banking system and among the non-bank public. Banks were concerned about the ratio of the reserves of high powered money to liabilities subject to withdrawal, that is, to their deposits; the non-bank public had to maintain a balance between legal-tender currency and bank deposits in their overall money holdings.

One formulation of this relationship may be written succinctly. Denote the quantity of money by M, currency held by the non-bank public as C, their bank deposits as D, high-powered or base, money as H, and banks' cash reserves as C. The monetary base is the sum of cash held by the non-bank public and banks' cash reserves. So $H = C + R$, while $M = C + D$. Let r be the ratio of banks' reserves to their deposits and c the ratio of non-banks' currency holdings to their deposits. Then a little rearrangement gives:

$$M = (1 + c)/(r + c).H$$

In the first instance this equation is simply an accounting identity. But if the ratios, c and r, are indeed the outcome of systematic and predictable choices made by the relevant agents, it becomes a behavioural relationship. Vitally, the relationship links the variable that matters for economic activity, the quantity of money, to the variable assumed to be under the Fed's control, the stock of high-powered money.[20] A crucial element in the *Monetary History*'s thesis about the Great Contraction was that these ratios, although far from constant, reflected considered choices within the private sector. They were not a mere will-o'-the-wisp; they would not see significant, erratic and inexplicable variations over short periods of time. According to Friedman, to quote his own words in a letter to Frank Steindl and recalled twice by the latter, the implication was clear. Throughout the Great Contraction, "The Federal Reserve could, at all times have controlled the stock of money."[21] It needed only to vary H, the stock of high-powered money, to offset the effects of changes in c and r.

In 1928 and 1929 in the run-up to the Depression, the Fed had kept the stock of high-powered money steady, but then allowed it to fall by 7 per cent in the twelve months following October 1929, the month of the stock market crash.[22] It is true that thereafter the stock of high-powered money slowly but steadily increased. In February 1933 it was almost 30 per cent up on its October 1930 figure.[23] But, according to the *Monetary History*, this gave only the appearance of actively expansionary policy. Because increases in the public's holdings of currency more than absorbed the increase in question, banks' cash reserves actually declined over the four years from October 1929. It needs to be remembered that the broadly defined quantity of money was the variable that mattered to macroeconomic outcomes. As already noted, it tumbled by more than 30 per cent from peak to trough. In terms of the money multiplier, the decline was overwhelmingly driven by increases in the currency-to-deposit (c) and reserve-to-deposit (r) ratios.

The shifts in the c and r ratios should be interpreted as the outcome of voluntary portfolio choices by the relevant agents in the face of growing uncertainty about the banking system's viability. To repeat, the ratios are not characterized by significant, erratic and inexplicable variations over short periods of time. Friedman and Schwartz's conclusion then follows. Changes in the ratios may have had a large effect on the quantity of money in the early 1930s, but that effect could and should have been offset by much larger increases in the stock of high powered money than in fact occurred. More specifically, from early 1930 the Fed should have purchased bonds and bills on a greater scale than seen in the historical record. Banks' cash reserves would then have grown vigorously rather than contracted, the banking panics that began late in that year would have been averted, and the troublesome further shifts in r and c engendered by the banking panics would never have happened.[24] Again, in 1931 expansionary open market operations should have been pursued and were indeed recommended by Fed insiders, but these insiders were a minority of those able to influence and take decisions. In mid-1932 such operations were undertaken for a few months, under Congressional pressure, and in Friedman and Schwartz's judgement they showed signs of working. Unfortunately, they were abandoned prematurely. Their opinion on these matters was shared by at least one contemporary commentator, namely Lauchlin Currie, the author of a 1934 article entitled 'The failure of monetary policy to prevent the Great Depression of 1929–32'.[25] Currie observed in another publication of that year:

> Much of the current belief in the powerlessness of the reserve banks appears to arise from a complete misreading of the monetary history of 1929–32. It is generally held that the reserve administration strove energetically to bring about more expansion throughout the Depression but that contraction continued despite its efforts. Actually the reserve administration's policy was one of almost complete passivity and quiescence.[26]

He would surely have concurred with Friedman and Schwartz's later and much quoted verdict: "The contraction [was] in fact a tragic testimonial to the importance of monetary forces".[27]

Evidently Krugman in his November 2008 *New York Times* column disagreed with the analysis above. His later journalism has reiterated a key contention that should not be dismissed out of hand and is shared with many others: it is that in the early 1930s the increases in the currency-to-deposit and reserve-to-deposit ratios were due to a piling-up of excess cash, with both banks and non-banks having infinitely elastic demands to hold liquidity. Perhaps any further policy-induced increases in the stock of high-powered money would have been passively absorbed, with no effect on the quantity of money. Support for this view was expressed by some notable contemporary observers. Paul Douglas for one argued that the 1932 experiment with open market operations had been futile: "The expectation was that the banks would be so choked with cash that they would have to increase their loans ... That did not happen, because in a period of depression businessmen are afraid to borrow and banks are afraid to lend".[28] To Keynes, this same episode presented the only credible evidence of a real-world "liquidity trap".[29]

III

The thesis which troubled Krugman in 2008 involves not only what actually did happen during the Great Contraction; it also relies on beliefs about a counterfactual, that is, about what would have happened had the Fed's policy been different. The plausibility of this counterfactual needs to be examined. Analysts need to consider a wider range of experience than that of 1929–33, or even 1929–39. Hugh Rockoff has noted that the *Monetary History*'s longer story rests on a "statistical underpinning" published in Phillip Cagan's 1965 study of *Determinants and Effects of Changes in the Stock of Money 1875–1960*.[30] The statistical material had been available to Friedman and Schwartz long before it saw print, as Friedman himself acknowledged when he wrote the foreword to Cagan's book.[31] The *Monetary History*'s account of the Great Contraction derives much of its empirical integrity from Cagan's work, particularly the finding that in a long-run perspective the behaviour of currency-to-deposit and reserve-to-deposit ratios in the 1930s was not unusual. To use Cagan's own words, "All sudden large increases in the currency-money ratio during peacetime have reflected banking panics, stemming from expectations that banks might suspend payments" and "The growing distress of banks in the three years preceding the 1933 holiday had the same effect [as had actual financial panics in earlier cycles] of drastically increasing the demand for currency".[32]

After the bank holiday of 1933 and the revaluation of gold that soon followed, the stock of high-powered money in the US began to grow rapidly. The non-bank public's currency-to-deposit ratio at first fell and then stabilized in the wake of the introduction of deposit insurance. But banks' reserve-to-deposit ratio continued to increase. Money growth nevertheless became systematically positive until early 1937. In the four years from April 1933 the compound annual rate of growth of broadly defined money was over 11 per cent, according to Friedman and Schwartz. The real economy enjoyed a significant recovery, with national output up by over 50 per cent in the same period. But full employment was not restored. In a well-known simile mentioned by Cagan, this apparent "failure of monetary expansion" has been compared "to the futile gesture of pushing on a limp string".[33] Alternatively put, the faster increase in bank deposits needed to bring about a full recovery was elusive, because of a lack of willing business borrowers among the banks' customers. Such an interpretation of post-1933 events invites speculation that a similar pattern was also at work earlier, in 1929–33, as Paul Douglas suggested. No doubt Krugman would offer similar conjectures about the behaviour of the financial system in the years since 2008.

Cagan took pains to address these issues along similar lines to those of Friedman and Schwartz. He argued that the correct metaphor for monetary policy's purported inability to achieve full employment was not the "futile gesture of pushing on a limp string; but . . . pushing on a taut coil spring, which compresses – but not indefinitely".[34] Cagan followed a then unpublished study of the topic by George Morrison, which appeared later as a chapter in Morrison's 1966 work, *Liquidity Preferences of Commercial Banks*.[35] To quote him, the rise in banks' cash-to-deposits ratio was due to deliberate, if lagged, choices driven by "continuing apprehension instilled by the 1933 panic".[36]

Cagan, again echoing Morrison, also drew explicit attention to the response of Federal Reserve member banks to the three-step doubling of cash reserve requirements in 1936 and 1937. The trebling of the reserve requirements was seen by the Fed as a pre-emptive measure, as it feared that the large build-up in usable reserves over the preceding three years had put its capacity to control monetary conditions at risk. A sudden and potentially inflationary increase in bank lending might occur at any time. If those usable reserves were in excess, if they had been sitting idly in banks which had no well-calculated desire to hold them, then re-designating them as required should have had no further consequences for the quantity of money or macroeconomic outcomes.

In fact, the quantity of money fell in 1937, and demand and output weakened abruptly. On the face of it, banks in the late 1930s maintained much higher reserve-to-deposit ratios than before the Great Depression for conscious precautionary reasons. The evidence from 1937 therefore supports the contention that at all times during these problematic years, including 1929–33, the Fed could have controlled the quantity of money. All that was necessary to increase the quantity of money was a sufficiently large boost to the monetary base. Nevertheless, the persistence of high unemployment needs to be squared with the monetarist view of a reliably self-stabilizing economic system that can recover, through downward wage and price flexibility, and consequent positive "real balance effects", from falls in the quantity of money.[37] That was not exactly how the New Deal recovery of the mid-1930s played out. It seems that the 1930s had unique features. As historical parallels are never perfect enough to carry the weight of replicative experiments, so a counterfactual hypothesis about a particular historical event can never be entirely compelling.[38]

IV

The Great Recession in the United States had much in common with the Great Depression. The years preceding both events saw asset market booms, in the stock market in the earlier case and the housing market in the later. Both booms were supported by innovations in financial markets. Investment trusts with geared equity portfolios were introduced in the USA from 1924 and delivered high returns while the stock market boom continued.[39] The first decade of the twenty-first century saw extensive securitization of mortgages and a proliferation of derivatives and derivative-based products, including credit default swaps. Both booms eventually prompted monetary tightening that brought them to abrupt ends and precipitated real downturns. The downturns from autumn 1929 and autumn 2008 were strikingly similar in both pattern and magnitude during their first year. This last similarity marked not only the United States, but other economies linked to it as well, as Barry Eichengreen and Kevin O'Rourke would quickly document.[40] Finally, the Fed's actions in both instances were initially hesitant, even inconsistent, thus creating much confusion.

Even so, the similarities end there. In late 2008 the Fed suddenly seemed to remember the famous confession and promise that Chairman Bernanke had made to Milton Friedman on his 90th birthday: namely, that it had indeed caused the Great Depression and would not do it again. The failure of Lehman Brothers in September 2008 was the first, but also the last, major institutional collapse it permitted; it was not the first of a sequence as the December 1930 closing of the Bank of United States had been. The Fed's subsequent collaboration with the Treasury in the rescue of AIG, an insurance company and a major seller of credit default swaps, was unprecedented. But among other things it helped to prevent a repeat performance in Europe of the kind of crisis associated with the 1931 failure of Credit-Anstalt, which occurred in the wake of the withdrawal of US lending to Europe. Moreover, the Fed also operated in close cooperation with the Treasury as the Federal Government became a major shareholder in large banks and mortgage providers, not to mention automobile producers. Further, having cut its policy interest rate essentially to zero in December 2008, the Fed followed up with extensive and highly innovative actions to boost bank liquidity, and by entering financial markets as a massive purchaser of assets.

Three programmes of "quantitative easing" were implemented, sometimes involving purchases of mortgage-backed securities from non-banks with a direct positive effect on the quantity of money. To the extent that the asset purchases were from non-banks, these programmes were different from the sort of open market operations recommended by Friedman and Schwartz in Chapter 7 of *A Monetary History*. Friedman and Schwartz had envisaged purchases of government securities from banks to boost their cash reserves and hence, via a relatively stable reserve-to-deposits ratio, the quantity of money. However, the Fed never justified its QE exercises by reference to a money aggregate, citing instead the impact on bond yields and credit spreads. As mentioned elsewhere in this volume, the Fed's preparedness from 2008 to buy a wide range of assets, including long-dated bonds issued by the private sector, would have pleased Keynes as it recalled his advocacy from 1930 onwards of open market operations *à outrance*. (See note 7 to Chapter 2 on pp. 71–2. Ralph Hawtrey, one of the most important of Keynes' interlocutors and the Treasury's "in-house economist" in the inter-war period, supported a similar stance on monetary policy in a slump.[41])

As a result of these measures, stimulatory monetary policy was pursued from late 2008. Further, contrary to Krugman's musings in the *New York Times*, it did matter enormously to the USA's macroeconomic fortunes. Not only was the *Monetary History*'s thesis about the role of money in the Great Depression remembered by policy-makers, but it also affected the actions they took. It is a simple fact that, in the wake of the Fed's aggressive response to events after the autumn of 2008, the quantity of money did not collapse. That is so, whether money is measured narrowly or broadly. Again, in contrast to the Great Depression, the price level did not fall heavily at any point. Moreover, the extremely sharp falls in output and employment in the first year of the Great Recession did not persist. By mid-2009 they petered out, demand and output stabilized, and then started to revive. The expansion of high-powered money was enormous, with this aggregate more than doubling in the year immediately following the collapse of Lehman Brothers. Money growth as measured by the M2 aggregate varied in the course of the Great Recession. Although it remained sluggish in the year from Q1 2009, it grew respectably in 2011, and bounded ahead in 2012 and 2013. The transactions-oriented MZM aggregate (of "money balances with zero time to maturity", that is, money immediately available for transactions) is widely tracked among monetary analysts. It grew strongly even in 2009. Some commentators, such as Peter Ireland, have plausibly suggested that this was connected with the Fed's policy of paying interest on reserves, which began in 2008 and had no precedent in the 1930s.[42] But controversy over the data persists. In his 2012 volume on *The Great Recession* Hetzel noted that money growth had been slow for much of 2008 and 2009, and this offered a straightforward and not implausible monetarist explanation of the hesitant initial recovery in consumer demand and investment in 2009 and 2010. (The recovery in output from mid-2009 owed much to the working-out of the inventory cycle, with real final sales in 2011 being no higher than in 2008.) In Hetzel's view the Fed could have been more vigorous and single-minded in trying to expand the quantity of money in 2009 and 2010.[43] (For more on US money growth in this period, see Chapters 1 and 7 above.)

Despite the traumatic events of late 2008 and early 2009, the currency-to-deposit ratio remained relatively stable. As far as the behaviour of small depositors was concerned, this must have owed something to deposit insurance. First introduced in 1934, it was extended and strengthened in 2009. Even so, the combination of a huge rise in banks' reserve-to-deposit ratio and sluggish money growth gave new credibility to the old "pushing on a limp string" argument about the ineffectiveness of monetary policy in depressed times. But in reality bank credit to the private sector was being restrained by tighter regulation and banks' consequent reluctance to take on new risk assets. (The point is emphasized in Chapters 5 and 7 above.)

In any case, anxieties on this score faded as money growth resumed. On the wider and more comprehensive M3 aggregate progress came later, with a satisfactory increase of above 3 per cent at an annual rate being recorded from 2012 onwards. Moderate but positive growth of the quantity of money was surely one of the reasons that aggregate demand then moved ahead with some consistency. Indeed, the resilience of the American economy in 2013 is important in the battle of ideas. Keynesian commentators, including Paul Krugman, expressed fears in late 2012 that a prospective big tightening of fiscal policy (or so-called "fiscal cliff") would cause a recession. These fears proved totally groundless. Perhaps more attention could have been paid to Milton Friedman's constant insistence, in the second half of his career, that monetary policy was almost always more reliable than fiscal policy.[44] The third QE programme, launched in September 2012, was followed by several quarters in which the annual growth rate of the M3 quantity of money was between 3.5 and 5 per cent. The rationale for this sort of policy was not new. Back in 1932 Hawtrey, in his *The Art of Central Banking*, had supported large-scale official asset purchases to revitalize economic activity. He remarked that, "There must ultimately be a limit to the amount of money that the sellers [of long term securities to the central bank] will hold idle."[45] Too many Fed officials in the early 1930s turned a deaf ear to such advice. In the Great Recession matters were very different. The *Monetary History*'s thesis that the Fed could have prevented the Great Depression if only it had tried hard enough seems to have emerged from recent experience much strengthened. Further, Friedman's long-term concern that the state should maintain stable growth of the quantity of money has again been vindicated, despite Krugman's doubts. At least Krugman did not oppose the stimulatory policies adopted by the Fed from 2008. Rather, he treated them as a futile and unimportant distraction, since in his view fiscal policy ought to be the centrepiece of attention.

V

Most economists have forgotten about Milton Friedman's dictum that "money matters" and will need more than evidence from one cyclical episode before they adopt it with any enthusiasm. The economic theory underlying the thesis of *A Monetary History* gave a strategic role to the rate of money growth in driving economic fluctuations and therefore in the conduct of monetary policy as well. Continuing interest in the *Monetary History* itself notwithstanding, this element in monetary policy analysis had fallen into neglect before the Great Recession and has generally remained so afterwards. Arguably, the Fed's rapid reduction of policy interest rates to their practical lower bound by December 2008 and the subsequent vigorous expansion of its balance sheet were ideal responses to the cyclical situation. They first prevented a collapse of money growth and then promoted its renewal. Indeed, action on these lines was exactly what an attentive reader of Friedman and Schwartz's 1963 classic might have hoped for ahead of another potential Great Depression. But the impact of the Fed's 2008–14 decisions on the quantity of money was almost nowhere discussed in the academic literature, while the link between its actions and money growth formed no part of the official promotion or defence of those actions.

As Jeffrey Hummel documented in a 2012 paper, much stress was laid by the Fed on the need to restore and/or maintain credit markets in working order, but very little, if any, on supporting the money supply.[46] As Hummel also emphasizes, the immediate inspiration in academic work for this stems not from the *Monetary History*. Instead the seminal influences were papers by chairman Bernanke himself, on both the Great Depression and the place of credit markets in the transmission of monetary impulses.[47]

Much more surprising, however, was the reaction to Fed policies of several prominent monetarists, who might have been expected to take their lead from the *Monetary History*. Rather than welcome those policies as doing essentially the right thing, leading monetarist commentators, notably Allan Meltzer (in 2009 and later) and for a while at the onset of the crisis Thomas Humphrey and the late Anna Schwartz herself, were among the Fed's most strident critics. Far from applauding the Fed for halting another Great Depression, they warned of impending inflation. Instead of seeing the rapid growth of the Fed's balance sheet as activism justified by deflation risks, they were anxious that excess demand and rising inflation were around the corner. They articulated these concerns, even while money growth (on the broad measures) remained extremely subdued and the real economy had barely returned to pre-recession output levels.

The rationale in monetary theory for all these warnings about an inflationary threat was unclear. A key element of monetarist doctrine is that the monetary aggregate critical to demand and output outcomes is an appropriate measure of the money supply (that is, of currency held by the public *plus some portion or even all bank deposits*). No one has seriously suggested that the monetary base *by itself* bears on asset prices, aggregate demand and so on. It is hard to believe that some monetarist critics of recent Fed policy, not least that institution's historian, Allan Meltzer, could forget this, but apparently they did, if only for a while.[48] Perhaps, as the US economy continues its recovery, pressures arising from the "coil spring" of banks' excess cash reserves will generate faster growth of the quantity of money, and then of nominal national income and the price level. But this proposition is distant from the original circumstances of the cash injection, which was justified by the need to stop a collapse of the money stock. The experience of 1937 and 1938 should be recalled. The Fed trebled cash reserves, which drove up bond yields and upset financial markets. It is plausible to argue that these measures precipitated another plunge in aggregate demand less than a decade after the 1929–33 Great Depression. The ghost of inflations past may always be around the corner, but worries about inflation present are misplaced until the economy is over-heating. In the USA in recent years, the dangers of premature monetary restraint have been more serious than any chances of an imminent upturn in inflation.

Many economists accept that money and banking play a crucial role in macroeconomic fluctuations. Nevertheless, the blunt reality is that neglect of the money supply in discourse about the Great Recession has been pervasive. Edward Nelson was surely right, in an unpublished 2013 note prepared while he was working at the Fed, to characterize this neglect as "an example of a dog that did not bark".[49] The author has discussed elsewhere the disappearance of references to money from policy analyses, arguing that the recent history of macroeconomics in the wake of the so-called "New Classical revolution" must take much of the blame. But the subject is too complex to cover in detail here.[50] Let it suffice to recall that by the late 1990s the dominant theory of monetary policy had come to focus on the central bank's control over interest rates rather than monetary or credit aggregates of any description. Further, the omission of quantity-of-money variables was supported by equilibrium macroeconomic models with accounts of the transmission mechanism that completely bypassed the institutional complications presented by banks and the wider financial system.

Given that central bank praxis nevertheless made the control of inflation the lodestar of monetary policy, and given also that it denied the existence of a long-run inflation–unemployment trade-off, the whole apparatus of thinking came to be called "monetarism without money". Curiously, it was deemed attractive by some of those who had previously stressed the importance of money in the face of the Keynesian orthodoxy of the 1960s. For example, Anna Schwartz's preface to a new 2008 edition of Chapter 7 of *A Monetary History*, again being published as a stand-alone book under the title, *The Great Contraction 1929–33*, gave the impression that she was reasonably comfortable with the newly orthodox emphasis on interest rates. Her later criticisms of the Fed's policy followed John Taylor, the author of the widely respected "Taylor rule" for the setting of central bank policy rates. She focused in particular on the alleged error of keeping interest rates too low for too long in the wake of the earlier "dot.com" bubble and bust.[51] She failed to comment on the rate of money growth. She did not notice that, on the broad measures, money growth in the years just before the 2008 crisis was rapid and perhaps signalled undue monetary ease.[52]

For his own part Ben Bernanke, as Fed chairman, answered such criticisms by arguing that interest rate settings were appropriate in the light of available evidence on inflation at the time. He never appealed to money growth data to justify Fed decisions on interest rates. When explaining the aim of "quantitative easing" to a sometimes sceptical public, he and his colleagues invariably emphasized the importance of putting downward pressure on long-term interest rates, not upward pressure on money growth. (See also p. 61 above for Bernanke and QE.) In this respect they overlooked the quantity-of-money arguments developed in the 1930s and 1940s by Hawtrey, Currie and Warburton, and revived by Friedman and Schwartz in *A Monetary History*.[53]

VI

Some of the Fed's right-wing critics, often with monetarist leanings, were worried about aspects of the Fed's behavior, less for their monetary policy implications than for their meaning for the Fed's role in the economy overall. How large and active should a state-sponsored institution, the central bank, be in an ostensibly free-market economy like the USA's? The critics saw the last-resort-lending decisions, in particular, as undermining market disciplines. Their bill of particulars included two charges. First, the Fed had exceeded its constitutional responsibilities by rescuing insolvent investment banks, mortgage lenders, insurance companies and the like instead of confining itself to the provision of liquidity to solvent commercial banks. Second, by cooperating with the Treasury in such activities, it had surrendered its policy-making independence.

There can be little doubt that the Fed did violate the textbook principles for lender-of-last-resort interventions which are usually attributed to Walter Bagehot and found in his 1873 classic, *Lombard Street*. According to these principles, such interventions should be limited to lending freely at a "high" interest rate to all solvent borrowers. In papers written shortly after the Great Recession, Thomas Humphrey documented the case thoroughly and accurately.[54] But, behind such specific rules, a more general core principle has been implicit in the theory of central banking since Henry Thornton's path-breaking 1802 *Paper Credit*.[55] Specifically, the central bank is the entity that issues liabilities used among monetary institutions to meet what Hyman Minsky in his 1954 doctoral thesis eloquently labelled their "survival constraints".[56] The central bank has an overriding obligation, indeed it is almost its defining contribution to public policy, to keep the banking system functioning. Bagehot devised his rules for a system much simpler than that of 2008. The Bank of England's primary task in the nineteenth century was the preservation of the gold convertibility of the currency. Stabilizing the financial sector came second, while even in the 1870s the principles of limited liability had not yet been universally adopted by commercial banks.[57] Bagehot's rules still resonate, but their applicability in modern conditions is not straightforward.

To begin with, in the late-nineteenth-century context a major purpose of Bagehot's "high" interest rate was to forestall convertibility problems. The intention was to generate a gold inflow when market uncertainty was provoking an outflow. Bagehot was well aware that in times of financial crisis an "internal drain", the tendency of domestic depositors to withdraw funds from the banks, had to be distinguished from an "external drain", an adverse balance of payments. He also knew that the two types of drain should be countered in different ways. An internal drain should prompt expansionary action, with enlargement of the central bank balance sheet, whereas an external drain had to be met by dear money, with contractionary effects. With the USA on a well-established flexible exchange rate regime in 2008, only the internal drain mattered. (This took the form of an implosion of the so-called "shadow banks", with their customers transferring funds from them to the Fed-regulated banking system.) No justification could be offered therefore for a high interest rate to protect the dollar internationally, while a very low rate was surely an appropriate response to the home-grown tensions in the American banking system. Further, the line between liquidity and solvency has a very different significance today from that which it had in Victorian Britain. Nowadays banks are limited liability companies, and shareholders have no obligation to remedy a shortfall in equity and losses to depositors. In Victorian Britain they did have such an obligation in many instances. In Bagehot's time recapitalization of a high proportion of banking system liabilities would in this sense be automatic, up to the point of shareholders' personal bankruptcy. The Bank of England in the 1860s and 1870s did not have to worry about these matters in the way the Federal Reserve would have to in 2008 and for the next few years. More generally, as Nelson remarked in a 2013 note:

> In a modern context, a broad conception of the financial institutions that require support in an emergency is consistent even from a viewpoint, such as Friedman's, that sees maintenance of commercial bank deposits as paramount. Because of counterparty relationships, contraction of a major part of the financial system is likely to have repercussions for commercial banks' balance sheet positions and thereby aggregates like M2.[58]

From a viewpoint such as Bernanke's – and Bagehot's as well – maintaining the counterparty relationships in working order was valuable in its own right. This argument provides a compelling case for the Fed accepting a wide range of responsibilities, perhaps trespassing outside the banking system as such, and interpreting those responsibilities liberally and expansively in pragmatic fashion.[59] Crucially as far as the right-wing critics are concerned, it is difficult to fault the Fed's broad interpretation of its functions and role after the Lehman collapse of September 2008. This interpretation resulted in it becoming, in cooperation with the Treasury, not just the lender of last resort, but also – in Perry Mehrling's felicitous phrase in a 2011 book – "the dealer of last resort" to American capital markets.[60] Indeed, by its extension of vast dollar swap arrangements to foreign central banks, the Fed was for a time a full-scale international lender of last resort. It in effect usurped a task that had once been envisaged for the International Monetary Fund.[61]

Ample historical precedents exist for close cooperation between the central bank and political authorities, including central government, in times of crisis. To refer to British experiences with which Bagehot was familiar, in 1797 the Bank of England required government help to secure parliamentary authority to suspend gold convertibility, while in 1847, 1857 and 1866 only the government could relax provisions in the 1844 Bank Charter Act, which needlessly hampered the Bank of England's ability to combat crisis conditions. Again in 1890 Lord Goschen, the Chancellor of the Exchequer, was an important player in the Bank's successful efforts to organize the rescue of Baring Brothers. In view of the current controversy about whether the Fed's regulatory ambit should be restricted to the commercial banking system, it is interesting that Barings was an *investment* bank, not a *commercial* bank. Indeed, despite the gap of over a century between the two events, the British authorities' assistance for Barings in 1890 might be regarded as well-judged and adroit compared with the American authorities' failure to assist another investment bank, Lehman Brothers, in September 2008. Further, it cannot be overlooked that the Fed participated in, indeed orchestrated, the negotiations that prevented the collapse of Long Term Capital Management in 1998. LTCM was a hedge fund, but at the time little criticism of the Fed's involvement came from either Congress or free-market academic economists.

VII

To conclude, the *Monetary History*'s stand on the importance of monetary policy in general, and of the quantity of money in particular, during the Great Contraction has emerged stronger rather than weaker from recent American experience. Krugman's late 2008 ruminations in the *New York Times* were wide of the mark, and his jibes against Friedman and Schwartz seem misplaced. Perhaps in 2007 and 2008 the Fed was slow and even inconsistent in coming to grips with the developing crisis. But the initial hesitation was followed by swift, vigorous and innovative actions when financial markets were paralysed after the Lehman collapse. Although private sector demand and national output fell sharply in the six quarters to mid-2009, the Fed funds rate was slashed to almost nil, the fall in money growth was eventually arrested and the price level did not collapse. In short, the 2007–10 cyclical upheaval began like that of its 1929–33 predecessor, but it followed a very different trajectory. Indeed, the pattern of events in the Great Recession, as policy decisions interplayed with financial variables and macroeconomic outcomes, validates Friedman and Schwartz's counterfactual speculations in the *Monetary History*.

Even so, one doubts that Paul Krugman will be converted to monetarism. The Fed's efforts after 2008 perhaps worked as the *Monetary History*'s thesis implied they would, but they did so in concert with considerable fiscal stimulus. Traditional Keynesianism, which lamented the absence of such stimulus in the early years of the Depression, can surely find support from this fact. (More problematic for them is the persistence of satisfactory growth in aggregate demand, in the USA and elsewhere, during the fiscal restraint of 2012–14. See Table 9.1 on p. 228 for more detail on the scale of the change in budget positions.) The relative significance of fiscal and monetary policies in the cyclical fluctuations of the inter-war period are much debated, with more than one observer attributing the 1937–38 downturn to fiscal tightening rather than the Fed's handling of monetary policy.[62] A similar difficulty afflicts analysis of the two branches of macroeconomic policy in the years since 2007. The actions of European governments to reduce budget deficits since 2010 have been accompanied by, at best, lacklustre demand conditions, with the return to recession in 2013 and 2014 being hardly an endorsement of their approach. Would even most dedicated monetarists deny a major role to fiscal retrenchment in causing the economies in the Eurozone's Atlantic and Mediterranean peripheries to underperform so markedly in this period? The current rematch between monetarist and Keynesian views of macroeconomic policy is not settled. Of course, big drops in the quantity of money contributed to the agonies of the Eurozone periphery economies, as described in more detail in Chapter 4. (See pp. 120–23 in Chapter 4 above.)

To sum up, the Great Recession came as a shock not just to the world's leading economies, but also to the economics profession. Practitioners of the dismal science had for some years been lulled into a mood of self-congratulation by the stable growth and low inflation seen in the two decades of the Great Moderation. The Great Moderation was accompanied by a cessation of hostilities in the monetarism–Keynesian debate. In retrospect, it is clear that this debate has long needed revival and clarification. Krugman deserves credit at least for realizing that Friedman and Schwartz's *Monetary History* had to be cited in the debate, even if his aim was to mock their work. Most economists continue to accord deep respect to the *Monetary History*. The issues that it raised are very much back on the agenda, testifying to the enduring importance of this great book.

NOTES

*   This chapter grew out of speaking notes prepared for a conference entitled *Retrospectives on the Great Depression*, held at Princeton University on 15–16 February 2013. It is a revised and abbreviated version of a paper originally circulated as Working Paper 2013–5, Economic Policy Research Institute, University of Western Ontario. The influence of conversations and correspondence with Michael Belongia, James Boughton, Michael Bordo, David Glasner, Bob Hetzel, Jeff Hummel, Douglas Irwin, Jim MacGee, Allan Meltzer, Edward Nelson, Russ Roberts, Roger Sandilands, Scott Sumner and Lawrence White on its subject matter is gratefully acknowledged, as are subsequent extremely helpful written comments from Peter Howitt, Douglas Irwin, Allan Meltzer, Edward Nelson and Roger Sandilands on earlier drafts. I am grateful to Tim Congdon for much help and advice in its adaptation for this volume. Nevertheless, the views expressed herein are entirely the author's responsibility.

1.   Paul Krugman 'Was the Great Depression a monetary phenomenon?', column in *New York Times*, 28 November 2008.

2.   By the end of 2008 Krugman had already been involved for over a year in a debate about

Milton Friedman's contributions to economics, including, but by no means confined to, the *Monetary History*, with Edward Nelson and Anna Schwartz. This debate was precipitated by Krugman's not always accurate obituary of Friedman in the 15 February 2007 issue of the *New York Review of Books*, and culminated in an exchange in the May 2008 issue of the *Journal of Monetary Economics*. (See Nelson and Schwartz 'The impact of Milton Friedman on modern monetary economics: setting the record straight on Paul Krugman's "Who was Milton Friedman?"' *Journal of Monetary Economics*, no. 55 [May 2008], pp. 835–56, and 'Rejoinder to Paul Krugman', *Journal of Monetary Economics*, no. 55 [May 2008], pp. 861–2.) Thus, Krugman's views as quoted here had not been formulated on the spur of the moment. As Doug Irwin has stressed to me, Krugman has subsequently attacked Friedman's work on occasions too numerous to cite in detail. A later comment (Krugman 8 August 2013, again in the *New York Times* column) bearing the title 'Milton Friedman, Unperson' concludes that, "Friedman has vanished from the policy scene – so much so that I suspect that a few decades from now, historians of economic thought will regard him as little more than a footnote". Readers of this essay may form their own judgement.

3. Also see the discussion in the Introduction, pp. 2–6.

4. Thomas Mayer *The Structure of Monetarism* (New York: Norton, 1978), p. 2.

5. Robert Lucas *Collected Papers on Monetary Theory* (Cambridge, MA, USA and London, UK: Harvard University Press, 2013), 'Review of Milton Friedman and Anna Schwartz *A Monetary History of the United States, 1867–1960*', pp. 361–74. This Lucas review is also mentioned in note 24 to the Introduction; see above, p. 18.

6. Robert Lucas (2004) 'Keynote address to the 2003 HOPE (History of Political Economy) conference: my Keynesian education', in Michel deVroey and Kevin Hoover (eds) *The IS–LM Model: Its Rise, Fall, and Strange Persistence*, Annual Supplement to History of Political Economy (Durham, NC: Duke University Press), vol. 36.

7. Michael Bordo 'The contribution of *A Monetary History of the United States, 1867–1960* to monetary history', in Bordo (ed.) *Money, History, and International Finance: Essays in Honor of Anna J. Schwartz* (Chicago, IL: University of Chicago Press, 1989), pp. 15–78, and Frank Steindl *Monetary Interpretations of the Great Depression* (Ann Arbor, MI: University of Michigan Press, 1995).

8. Karl Brunner (ed.) *The Great Depression Revisited* (Dordrecht, the Netherlands: Springer, 1981), vol. 2 in *Rochester Studies in Economics and Policy Issues*.

9. Ben Bernanke 'Non-monetary effects of the financial crisis in the propagation of the Great Depression', *American Economic Review*, vol. 73, no. 3 (June 1983), pp. 257–76; Christina Romer and David Romer 'Does monetary policy matter? A new test in the spirit of Friedman and Schwartz', chapter in Olivier J. Blanchard and Stanley Fischer (eds), *NBER Macroeconomics Annual 1989* (Cambridge, MA: The MIT Press for the National Bureau of Economic Research, 1989), vol. 4, pp. 121–84; Allan Meltzer *A History of the Federal Reserve* vol. 1: 1913–1951 (Chicago, IL: University of Chicago Press, 2002); and Robert Hetzel *The Monetary Policy of the Federal Reserve: A History* (Cambridge, UK: Cambridge University Press, 2008).

10. See Bordo and Hugh Rockoff 'Not just the Great Contraction: Friedman and Schwartz's *A Monetary History of the United States 1867 to 1960*', Romer and Romer 'The missing transmission mechanism in the monetary explanation of the Great Depression', and Kris Mitchener and Gary Richardson 'Shadowy banks and financial contagion during the Great Depression: a retrospective on Friedman and Schwartz', all in *American Economic Review* (May 2013), vol. 103, no. 3, pp. 61–5, pp. 66–72 and pp. 73–8 respectively. Some of the *Monetary History*'s durability and capacity to withstand close scrutiny surely stems from the fact that it was only one, albeit the most important, product of a research programme that had begun in the late 1940s, and did not really come to an end until the publication of Friedman and Schwartz's 1982 *Monetary Trends in the United States and the United Kingdom* (Chicago, IL, USA and London, UK: University of Chicago Press for the NBER). Centred on the NBER (in Cambridge, MA), but also involving Friedman's "Money Workshop" at Chicago, this

programme's output was meticulously checked and edited. It included two books – Philip Cagan *Determinants and Effects of Changes in the Stock of Money, 1875–1960* (New York: Columbia University Press for the NBER, 1965) and George Morrison *Liquidity Preferences of Commercial Banks* (Chicago, IL: University of Chicago Press, for the Economics Research Center of the University of Chicago, 1966) – to be discussed below. In addition, there was a flow of technical papers and journal articles, sometimes later incorporated in books, not to mention doctoral dissertations, which might initially be unpublished, and would later emerge in books and journals. In this highly collaborative enterprise, ideas and data sets moved freely among contributors, while publication dates gave little guidance to scholarly priorities.

11. Charles Kindleberger *The World in Depression 1929–1939* (Berkeley, CA: University of California Press, 1973), Barry Eichengreen *Golden Fetters: The Gold Standard and the Great Depression 1919–1939* (New York: Oxford University Press, 1992) and David Glasner 'Why Hawtrey and Cassel trump Friedman and Schwartz', *Uneasy Money* blog, 21 August 2013, argues that the *Monetary History's* relative neglect of the botched attempts to restore the international gold standard after the First World War, which set much of the scene for the Great Depression's international dimension in the 1930s, was an extremely serious flaw. But the book's focus was after all the USA. Since the USA had never given up the gold standard during or after the war, it might be argued that the USA's contribution to international monetary affairs in the 1920s must be interpreted in the light of its relative detachment from foreign influences. Glasner's 21 August 2013 blog covers the ground. See https//uneasymoney.com/2013/08/.

12. Harold Cole and Lee Ohanian (2007) 'A second look at the U.S. Great Depression from a neoclassical perspective', pp. 21–58, in Timothy Kehoe and Edward Prescott (eds) *Great Depressions of the Twentieth Century* (Minneapolis, MN: Federal Reserve Bank of Minneapolis, 2007).

13. Larry Christiano, Roberto Motto and Massimo Rostagno 'The Great Depression and the Friedman–Schwartz hypothesis' (Frankfurt: European Central Bank), ECB Working Paper no. 326.

14. Note that the *Monetary History's* analysis uses NBER chronology to date cyclical turning points rather than the behaviour of any single simple indicator such as nominal national income.

15. The paper was republished as Milton Friedman and Anna Schwartz 'Money and business cycles', in Milton Friedman (ed.) *The Optimum Quantity of Money*, pp. 189–235. See note 18 to the Introduction of this volume.

16. Friedman and Schwartz *The Great Contraction* (Princeton, NJ: Princeton University Press, 1965; 2nd edition with a new preface and introduction, 2008).

17. Robert J. Gordon *The American Business Cycle: Continuity and Change* (Chicago, IL, USA and London, UK: University of Chicago Press, 1986), p. 794.

18. Milton Friedman and Anna Schwartz *A Monetary History of the United States, 1867–1960* (Princeton, NJ: Princeton University Press, 1963), pp. 712–14, also mentioned in the Introduction above, see note 4 on p. 17.

19. Friedman and Schwartz *Monetary History*, pp. 362–80.

20. This is the version of the multiplier that this author always used when teaching this material. Cagan's 1965 book (see note 10 above) worked with a slightly different formulation, in which the critical ratio describing the non-bank public's behaviour is that of currency held to total money holding, rather than deposits. Other presentations are found in the literature, but in general nothing of substance hinges on the distinctions.

21. The quotation was in a 1986 letter to Frank Steindl, quoted twice in Steindl *Monetary Interpretations*, on p. 58 and in a note on p. 75.

22. Friedman and Schwartz *Monetary History*, p. 803.

23. Ibid., pp. 803–4.

24. Ibid., pp. 392–3.

25. Lauchlin Currie 'The failure of monetary policy to prevent the depression of 1929–32', *Journal of Political Economy*, no. 42 (April 1934), pp. 145–77.

26. Lauchlin Currie *The Supply and Control of Money in the United States* (Cambridge, MA: Harvard University Press), p. 147.
27. Friedman and Schwartz *Monetary History*, p. 300.
28. Paul Douglas *Collapse or Cycle* (Chicago, IL: American Library Association, 1933), p. 10.
29. Elizabeth Johnson and Donald Moggridge (eds) *The Collected Writings of John Maynard Keynes*, vol. VII, *The General Theory of Employment, Interest and Money* (London and Basingstoke: Macmillan for the Royal Economics Society, 1973, originally published 1936), pp. 207–8. This phrase, which was coined not by Keynes but by Dennis Robertson (in an essay 'Mr Keynes and the rate of interest' in his 1940 *Essays in Monetary Theory* [London: Staples Press]) is used indiscriminately nowadays to refer to a variety of phenomena that might prevent expansion of the monetary base, and/ or the supply of money itself, affecting aggregate demand. For discussions of these issues, which are by no means merely semantic, see Ingo Barens '"To use the words of Keynes . . .": Olivier J. Blanchard on Keynes and the "liquidity trap"', in Hagen Kramer and others (eds) *Macroeconomics and the History of Economic Thought: Festschrift in Honour of Harald Hagemann* (London: Routledge, 2012) and Roger Sandilands 'Hawtreyan "credit "deadlock" or Keynesian "liquidity trap"? Lessons for Japan from the Great Depression', in Robert Leeson (ed.) *David Laidler's Contributions to Economics* (Basingstoke: Palgrave Macmillan, 2010).
30. Hugh Rockoff 'On the origins of *A Monetary History*', pp. 81–113, in Ross Emmett (ed.) *The Elgar Companion to the Chicago School of Economics* (Cheltenham, UK and Northampton, MA, USA: Edward Elgar Publishing, 2010).
31. Friedman in Cagan *Determinants* 1965.
32. Cagan *Determinants*, p. 139 and p. 265.
33. Ibid., p. 287.
34. Ibid., p. 268.
35. Morrison *Liquidity Preferences of Commercial Banks*, mentioned above in note 10.
36. Cagan *Determinants*, p. 200.
37. For the meaning of the phrase "real balance effects", see Don Patinkin's entry 'Real balances', pp. 295–7, in John Eatwell, Murray Milgate and Peter Newman (eds) *The New Palgrave Dictionary of Money & Finance* (London and New York: Macmillan, 1992), vol. 3, pp. 295–7. The entry originally appeared in the 1987 edition of *The New Palgrave Dictionary of Economics*.
38. Tim Congdon (see, for example, Tim Congdon 'Monetary policy at the zero bound', *World Economics* vol. 11, no. 1, Jan.–Mar. 2010, pp. 11–46) has long contended that the redemption period and instrument composition of the securities in open market operations, as well as the size of these operations, matter for their monetary policy effectiveness. (His position is in line with Keynes's remarks in *The General Theory*. See *CW*, vol. VII, pp. 206–8.) Banks are highly geared and must, in principle, have assets with 100 per cent nominal value certainty. Again in principle, they therefore hold only short-dated, very safe securities, such as those issued by governments. When the banks' demand to hold cash reserves is infinitely elastic at a zero central bank rate, central bank purchases of short-dated securities have no effect on the quantity of money. (The ratio of cash to assets rises towards 100 per cent.) Congdon calls this state of affairs "a narrow liquidity trap" and it comes to much the same thing as Cagan's "limp string". By contrast, central bank purchases of long-dated securities from non-banks, when financed by the issue of new cash reserves to commercial banks, increase the quantity of money dollar for dollar, euro for euro or whatever. Indeed, the government could bypass the central bank and borrow directly from commercial banks, and then use the proceeds of the loans to buy back its outstanding long-dated debt from non-banks, directly adding to the quantity of money. Congdon has distinguished between "money market operations" (at the short end, involving the central bank and commercial banks) and "debt market operations" (at the long end usually, involving the state sector [perhaps just the government], commercial banks *and the non-bank public*). Congdon has told the author that

in a private correspondence in summer 2003 Friedman questioned the validity of this distinction, on the grounds that central banks conduct open market operations with all participants, and do not discriminate between banks and non-banks. As it happens, Friedman and Schwartz's discussion of the transmission mechanism in their 1963 'Money and business cycles' paper noted that the effect of central bank asset purchases depended on whether the counterparty was a bank or non-bank (see Friedman *The Optimum Quantity of Money* [London and Basingstoke: Macmillan, 1969], p.230), and in this sense Congdon's argument recalled analyses from both Friedman and Keynes. (This note reflects input from Tim Congdon.)

39. Ray Westerfield *Money, Credit and Banking* (New York: Ronald Press Company, 1938), p. 1091.

40. Barry Eichengreen and Kevin O'Rourke (2010) 'A tale of two depressions: What do the new data tell us?' (8 March 2010 update of 6 April 2009 original blog, 'A tale of two depressions'), http://www.voxeu.org/article.

41. See Ralph Hawtrey *Trade Depression and the Way Out* (London: Longman, Green & Co., 1931, 2nd edition, 1933). Hawtrey is described as the Treasury's "in-house economist" on p. 23 of George Peden *The Treasury and British Public Policy, 1906–1959* (Oxford: Oxford University Press, 2000). His title, Director of Financial Enquiries, did not capture his uniqueness and importance in the Treasury at the time, since he was the department's senior official on economic issues.

42. Peter Ireland 'The classical theory of inflation and its uses today', *Position Paper* presented at Shadow Open Market Committee meeting of 3 November 2014, in New York.

43. Hetzel, *Great Recession*, pp. 236–8.

44. Essay 8 'Friedman (1948), Friedman (1996) and the effectiveness of fiscal policy in the United States', pp. 188–99, in Tim Congdon *Money in a Free Society* (New York: Encounter Books, 2011) discussed Friedman's scepticism on fiscal policy in his late career.

45. Hawtrey *The Art of Central Banking* (London: Longman Group 1932, p. 17).

46. Jeffrey Hummel 'Ben Bernanke versus Milton Friedman: the Federal Reserve's emergence as the US economy's central planner', pp. 165–210, in David Beckworth (ed.) *Boom and Bust Banking: the Causes and Cures of the Great Recession* (Oakland, CA: The Independent Institute, 2012).

47. Ben Bernanke 'Non-monetary effects of the financial crisis in the propagation of the Great Depression', *American Economic Review*, no. 73 (June 1983), pp. 257–76, and Bernanke and Mark Gertler (1995) 'Inside the black box: the credit channel of monetary policy', *Journal of Economic Perspectives*, no. 9 (Fall 1995), pp. 27–48.

48. Thus, in a 2012 mimeo note on 'Lender of last resort' (Richmond, VA, USA: Federal Reserve Bank of Richmond) Humphrey did not repeat the warnings of imminent inflation that he gave in a 2010 *Cato Journal* article (Thomas Humphrey 'Lender of last resort: what it is, whence it came, and why the Fed isn't it', *Cato Journal*, no. 30 [spring/summer 2010], pp. 337–64). Meanwhile in a 2013 mimeo paper 'A slow recovery with less inflation', for the Brookings/Hoover Conference and published by the Hoover Institution, Meltzer paid considerable attention to money growth, as opposed to base growth. His qualms about the latter were explicitly linked to inflationary difficulties that this might cause in a less than immediate future.

49. Edward Nelson 'Friedman's monetary economics in practice' (Washington, DC: Federal Reserve Board, 2013), mimeo.

50. David Laidler 'Three revolutions in macroeconomics: their nature and influence', *European Journal of the History of Economic Thought*, vol. 22, no. 1 (2015), pp. 1–25.

51. Anna Schwartz 'Origins of the financial crisis of 2007', *Cato Journal* (Washington: Cato Institute), no. 29 (winter 2009), pp. 19–23, and John Taylor *Getting off Track* (Stanford, CA: Hoover Institute Press, 2011).

52. The USA provides to the IMF the data necessary for the calculation of a "broad money" aggregate for the IMF's *International Financial Statistics* database, and the resulting series is different from any aggregate now published by the Fed. (See Tim

Congdon 'Money matters: post-Great Recession re-appraisal', *Central Banking Journal* [London: Central Banking Publications], vol. xxvii, no. 1 [2016], pp. 24–30.) In the two years to end-2005 the IMF's US broad money expanded at moderate annual rates of 4 to 6 per cent; in the year to the first quarter of 2008 it increased by no less than 13.4 per cent. See also Congdon *Money in a Free Society*, p. 382.

53. Clark Warburton was the first economist at the Federal Deposit Insurance Corporation, newly created in 1934. Like Lauchlin Currie, he criticized the Federal Reserve for allowing the quantity of money to fall in the Great Depression. Also like Currie, he did so well before Milton Friedman's work in this area. See Clark Warburton 'The misplaced emphasis in contemporary business fluctuation theory', *Journal of Business*, vol. 19, no. 4 (1946), pp. 199–220. Warburton's work seems to have been an important influence on Friedman in the early 1950s. See Richard Selden 'Reflections on Friedman's macroeconomics', pp. 156–64, in Robert Cord and J. Daniel Hammond *Milton Friedman: Contributions to Economics and Public Policy* (Oxford: Oxford University Press, 2016), particularly p. 159.

54. Humphrey 'Lender of last resort', *Cato Journal*, 2010, as cited above in note 48.

55. Henry Thornton *An Enquiry into the Nature and Effects of the Paper Credit of Great Britain* (London, Allen and Unwin, 1939, reprint of original 1802 edition, with an introduction by Friedrich von Hayek).

56. Hyman Minsky *Induced Investment and Business Cycles*, unpublished PhD dissertation, Department of Economics, Harvard University, pp. 157–62. See the discussion of Minsky on Perry Mehrling's website (www.perrymehrling.com).

57. The evolution of the liability regimes of British banks in the nineteenth century is a complicated business. It will suffice to note here that in 1869 a majority of banks (89 out of 136) operated under unlimited liability arrangements. A general shift to limited liability took place in the 1880s and thereafter. For this and many other details, see Graeme Acheson and others 'Does limited liability matter? Evidence from nineteenth century British banking', *Review of Law and Economics*, vol. 6, no. 2 (2010), pp. 247–73.

58. Edward Nelson 'Friedman's monetary economics in practice' (Washington, DC: Federal Reserve Board, 2013), mimeo, p. 24.

59. It was Henry Thornton ('Paper Credit', 1802), not Bagehot (*Lombard Street*, 1873), who stressed support of the money supply, broadly defined, as a major goal of lender-of-last-resort activities. The "money market" that *Lombard Street* describes is the market for short-term credit, including inter-bank credit, not that for currency plus deposits. See David Laidler 'Two views of the lender of last resort – Thornton and Bagehot', *Cahiers d'économie Politique*, no. 45 (2003), pp. 61–78.

60. Perry Mehrling *The New Lombard Street: How the Fed Became the Dealer of Last Resort* (Princeton, NJ: Princeton University Press, 2011).

61. William Allen and Richhild Moessner 'Central bank cooperation and international liquidity in the financial crisis of 2008–09', *BIS working paper* no. 310 (May 2010).

62. See the central section on 'Fiscal deficits, excess reserves and the recession of 1937/8' in Sandilands 'Hawtreyan "credit deadlock" or Keynesian "liquidity trap"?', in Leeson (ed.) *David Laidler's Contributions to Economics*, cited above in note 29.

Index

Note: Entries preceded by "a" or "the" are indexed under the subject initial, for example, under G for "the Great Depression".